Ju

Jumpstart

The Economic Unification of Germany

Gerlinde Sinn
Hans-Werner Sinn

translated by
Juli Irving-Lessmann

The MIT Press
Cambridge, Massachusetts
London, England

First MIT Press paperback edition, 1994

© 1992 Massachusetts Institute of Technology

This work originally appeared in German under the title *Kaltstart: Volkswirtschaftliche Aspekte der deutschen Vereinigung* (© 1991 J.C.B. Mohr (Paul Siebeck)).

Set in Palatino by Asco Trade Typesetting Ltd., Hong Kong.
Printed and bound in the United States of America.

Library of Congress Cataloging-in-Publication Data

Sinn, Gerlinde.
  [Kaltstart. English]
  Jumpstart: the economic unification of Germany / Gerlinde Sinn,
  Hans-Werner Sinn; translated by Juli Irving-Lessmann.
     p.   cm.
  Includes bibliographical references and index.
  ISBN 0-262-19327-2 (HB), 0-262- 69172-8 (PB)
    1. Germany—Economic policy—1990– 2. Germany—Economic
  conditions—1990– 3. Germany—History—Unification, 1990.
  I. Sinn, Hans-Werner. II. Title.
  HC286.8.S5613   1993
  330.943087'9—dc20   92-30545
                                                              CIP

Esau ... said to Jacob, "I am exhausted; let me swallow some of that red broth." ... Jacob said, "Not till you sell me your rights as the first-born." Esau replied, "I am at death's door; what use is my birthright to me?" Jacob said, "Not till you swear!"; so he swore an oath and sold his birthright to Jacob. Then Jacob gave Esau bread and the lentil broth, and he ate and drank and went away without more ado. Thus Esau showed how little he valued his birthright.

Genesis 25: 27–34

Contents

Preface to the First English Edition

This book is a report on one of the most fascinating of all experiments in economics: the integration of a formerly communist economy into a market economy. The East German experiment is unique in that the integration occurred at a single stroke and in that there is a big brother to help. All the other countries of the former Eastern Bloc that are currently dismantling the communist system chose a more gradualist approach, and for them there are at best a few remote relatives who are willing to lend a hand. Nevertheless, the example of Germany may provide a number of lessons for those countries.

One of these lessons, and a major theme of this book, is that a transformation policy should not try to outwit fundamental economic laws. Every student of economics learns that distributional objectives can be achieved through the allocation of factor endowments, but that one should not try to reach them through the manipulation of factor prices. German economic policy has not respected this wisdom. Property rights worth mentioning have not been assigned to the East Germans, but unrealistically high wages have been promised—wages that, even under optimistic circumstances, cannot be earned in the foreseeable future. More and more people are beginning to realize that this unrealistic policy threatens to slow down the economic upswing in East Germany.

The new economic miracle that many expected in East Germany has not occurred. Despite West Germany's powerful battery, the jumpstart in the cold has not yet succeeded—and, what is more, there is some risk that the good battery will be run down. In this book we attempt to understand East Germany's starting problems and to discuss the options for policy improvements.

This is a revised translation of the second German edition of *Kaltstart*. It parallels the third edition, published by Beck–DTV in the autumn of 1992.

We are grateful to Juli Irving-Lessmann for excellent assistance. She translated most of the book and gave us useful advice. Without her help we would not have been able to prepare this edition now.

We are indebted to a great many people who lent us various kinds of support during the process of writing *Kaltstart*. Their names are mentioned in the prefaces to the previous German editions, which are translated below.

This edition benefited greatly from detailed comments by Paul Bethge of The MIT Press, John Black of the University of Exeter, and Edwin von Böventer of the University of Munich.

The manuscript was typed in a cumbersome iterative process by Valerie Morfill and Ingrid Wutte, whom we admire for their care and infinite patience. We would also like to mention Kai Konrad, Angela Lechner, Ronnie Schöb, Harris Schlesinger, Marcel Thum, and Alfons Weichenrieder, who generously offered various support in the course of preparing this edition.

We gratefully thank all those who contributed to this book, but take full responsibility for whatever errors may remain.

Munich, August 1992

Preface to the First German Edition

On November 9, 1989, a song was broadcast from the Brandenburg Gate: "Auf der Mauer, auf der Lauer sitzt 'ne eine kleine Wanze/ Seht euch mal die Wanze an, wie die Wanze tanzen kann/ Auf der Mauer ..." ("On the wall, on the lookout, sits a little bug/Look at the bug, how it can dance! On the wall ..."). The playing of this children's song symbolized the end of decades of repression, anxiety, and tension. Suddenly, amazingly, the wall that had separated the two Germanies had been breached. Feelings were mixed—jubilation and anger, hope and resentment intertwined. Jubilation at the breaking down of the barrier, anger at the oppressors and the hypocrites who had acclaimed the wall as a "mighty bulwark against capitalism" and the East German state as a stronghold of freedom and prosperity. Hope for a better future, resentment against the liars who had glossed over their blunders with false statistics and against the border guards who enjoyed exposing unsuspecting visitors to the latest chicanery emanating from the sick minds of the Politbüro.

One of us, then 13 years old, was present when the East German authorities suddenly started to build the wall on August 12, 1961. How exciting it had been to ride eastward through the Brandenburg Gate in the morning, and how shocking to find the way back barred by barbed wire and soldiers in the afternoon! Today all this is history. For months, thousands of "wall woodpeckers" made the area around the Brandenburg Gate ring with the monotonous sound of their hammers, turning the "mighty bulwark" into souvenir chunks of concrete—and now the wall is gone.

The German policy-makers were quick to take advantage of the opportunity that had so unexpectedly appeared. In a daring act of diplomacy, the Kohl-Genscher government succeeded in bringing off German unification only nine months after the first assault on the wall. When history opened the gate, the Germans made their way through—quickly and decisively.

Nationalistic euphoria has not been a feature of the German drive toward unification. The American historian Gordon Craig, who had served on a committee set up by Margaret Thatcher with the dubious aim of penetrating the German soul, had warned publicly against resurgent chauvinism and burgeoning megalomania. In the event, however, his fears proved to be groundless. The celebration of unification was a moderate affair, characterized by thoughtfulness and sobriety rather than by euphoria.

The emotional problem associated with unification—if indeed there is one—is that the wave of patriotism that could have triggered a vigorous policy of rebuilding was nowhere to be seen. Some people reacted skeptically to the poor Eastern relatives, responding to the appeal of outstretched hands by nervously protecting their wallets. Others, conveniently forgetting the fortunate circumstances of their own success, arrogantly and wrongly attributed the poverty of their Eastern relatives to differences in mentality rather than to differences in the systems. Most people, however, acted as if the whole thing was no business of theirs and deceived themselves into thinking that German unification would in no way disturb the even tenor of their ways.

There is absolutely no doubt that the people of the former German Democratic Republic will benefit from unification, given the inexorable dynamics of market forces and given their integration into the West German social system. Even the most serious policy errors will not prevent this. Nevertheless, the West Germans cannot rightly claim to have demonstrated their solidarity with their East German brothers and sisters by sacrificing their own interests. The tax increases agreed on are less than the West German productivity gains made in the year of unification; the "natural restitution" of property expropriated after 1949 will provide the former owners in the West with windfalls but will impede the upswing in the East; the Treuhand—the new resolution trust—is selling off state property at giveaway prices; the Bundesbank charged a high price for the stake required to enter the market economy; and instead of Berlin, a small city on the Rhine—Bonn—nearly became the national capital. All in all, West Germany is behaving like an official receiver who has been forced to agree to a social plan for the workers of a bankrupt firm but who would really prefer to leave them to their fate. Gordon Craig really need not have worried—there has not been any chauvinism, not even any patriotism.

The East Germans would like to have Western wages overnight. This is of course understandable, but it is not really practicable. The double-digit wage increases in the year of unification, and hourly wage rates approaching those in Japan by 1993, are hardly compatible with the continued existence of the East German economy. The very fact that such wage increases could be pushed through despite their disastrous impact on employment is an indication of how much is at stake in the struggle over distribution in Germany. Everybody is trying to grab as much as he can for himself, and "the devil take the hindmost" is the prevailing attitude. Energy that should be directed toward reconstruction is being dissipated in the struggle for individual starting places in the new system.

The distribution battle is still raging, and there are only weak signs of an upswing. Certainly there are optimists who bravely maintain that they can see the light at the end of the tunnel, but quite a different message is being conveyed by the economic data. It is incontrovertible that in all the history of the industrial nations there has never been a worse depression than the one in East Germany, and that the current level of investment is far below what had been expected. "Disaster" was the word used by both the former president of the Bundesbank, Karl-Otto Pöhl, and the former chairman of the Treuhandanstalt, Detlev Rohwedder, to describe the situation in East Germany—and not without reason.

It was always obvious that the East's economic engine would be unable to start up smoothly. Nobody is the least bit surprised when a cold engine stalls many times before the car finally moves off, especially when the weather is bad. And jumpstarts are never smooth starts. Nevertheless, the extent of the starting problem has been much greater than anyone anticipated and has far exceeded what could have been expected in the light of the promises made by the West German politicians.

In our opinion, the domestic-policy aspects of unification have been tackled far less successfully than the foreign-policy aspects. Sixteen million people who had escaped from fascism only to find themselves trapped in another totalitarian system surely deserve more than a receivership and a social plan. The mistakes and missed opportunities of the present economic policies have been little short of disastrous, and if these policies are allowed to continue they will pose a serious threat to social stability in Germany.

These considerations provided the motivation for writing this book. We wanted to investigate the economic problems and the political alternatives associated with unification as objectively as we could, without denying our personal commitment. Such a goal is certainly easier to achieve in the peace and quiet of an academic ivory tower than in the hurly-burly of government office. We are not unaware of the constraints under which politicians have to operate; however, *we* are not subject to such constraints, and that is our fundamental advantage. The reader must decide whether we have been able to make good use of it.

The most important part of the book is chapters 4 and 5, where a "social compact for the upswing" is worked out. If this compact were introduced, it could, we believe, put an end to the struggle over distribution and speed up the transformation of the communist economy into a market economy. The core of the compact is a shift in emphasis from factor prices to initial endowments. Labor and management agree to a moratorium on wages, and, as compensation for the wage freeze, the workers are given shares in the property formerly owned by the state. We argue that such a social compact would be a fair and reasonable response to the ending of the communist property arrangements, and that it would get the upswing in East Germany underway far more quickly than the present economic policies can.

The idea of writing the book was conceived in 1990 in the United States, where we were guests at Stanford and Princeton. We were able to work peacefully there, far removed from the pressure of events in Europe but still in touch by fax. Our work received further encouragement from invitations to give lectures on the problem of German reunification at the Center for Economic Policy Research in Stanford and at the Woodrow Wilson School in Princeton. There were also invitations to lecture on the subject from the University of Michigan and from the Congressional Budget Office and the Council of Economic Advisors. A long discussion paper (Sinn 1990), presented at a conference organized by Paul J. J. Welfens at the Johns Hopkins University, was the next step. The present book is an expansion and development of the latter paper.

When we were in the United States we became aware of the great interest there in the question of German unification. We were pleasantly surprised to find that this interest was accompanied by considerable sympathy and, indeed, frequently by approval and admiration. For the first time in the postwar period, new images of Germany are being superimposed on the negative ones that are the legacy of the fascist past. The East German revolution has become a moral asset from which we *Wessis* have received benefits far exceeding the costs of unification. We thank our hosts not only for the warm reception they gave us, but also for opening our eyes to this aspect of unification.

Thanks are due to our colleagues on the Wissenschaftlicher Beirat beim Bundeswirtschaftsministerium (Advisory Council of the German Ministry of Economics), with whom one of us has worked in preparing four reports on German unification (Wissenschaftlicher Beirat 1989, 1990, 1991a,

1991b). The work on these reports is reflected in the book, but the opinions expressed are our own and not those of the Advisory Council.

The suggestions made by university colleagues, politicians, and experts from ministries and research bodies were especially helpful, as were the references to relevant publications and the numerical data they gave us. In particular, we would like to thank Jürgen Becher, Peter Bernholz, Knut Borchardt, Edwin von Böventer, Michael Burda, Doris Cornelsen, Oldrich Dědek, Rüdiger Dornbusch, Werner Flandorffer, Wolfgang Franz, Richard Frensch, Peter Friedrich, Michael Funke, Franz Gehrels, Daniel Gros, Friedrich Haffner, Albert Hirschmann, Lutz Hoffmann, Christine and Gerhard Illing, Otmar Issing, Norbert Kloten, Reiner König, Hans Möller, Jürgen Müller, Manfred Neumann (Nuremberg), Manfred J. M. Neumann (Bonn), Wolfgang Nierhaus, Alois Oberhauser, Andreas Polkowski, Wolfram Richter, Albrecht Ritschl, Detlev Karsten Rohwedder, Paul Samuelson, Karlhans Sauernheimer, Winfried Schmähl, Günther Scholz, Bruno Schönfelder, George Shultz, Matthias Schürgers, Wolfgang Seifert, Horst Siebert, Olav Sievert, Hubert Temmeyer, Christian Thimann, and various colleagues in the Statistisches Bundesamt (Federal Statistical Office) and the Bundesanstalt für Arbeit (Federal Labor Office).

Special thanks must go to our research assistants in Munich. Ronnie Schöb, Marcel Thum, and Alfons Weichenrieder sometimes had to play detective when preparing and collecting the numerical and historical data, and they did this most enthusiastically. Ingrid Wutte typed the various drafts of the manuscript with great care and precision.

The figures in the statistical appendix must be interpreted with great caution where they relate to the GDR. These mistakes cannot be blamed on those who helped us. We bear the full responsibility.

As the proofs of the German edition were being corrected, news came of the abortive putsch in Moscow. Now the first steps in the direction of a market economy can be taken there, too. We share the happiness of all those who will be able to participate in the real perestroika.

This book is dedicated to our children. As yet they may be too young to understand fully the things that have happened, but we hope that they will come to appreciate the new-found freedoms in Europe and that they will always be conscious of their responsibilities to the neighbors with whom they are sharing such an eventful history.

Munich, August 1991

Preface to the Second German Edition

The fact that the first edition of this book was out of print just a few months after its publication presented us with the opportunity to publish an updated and revised second edition while the topic is still relevant. This second edition is structured somewhat differently than the first. Following a suggestion from Norbert Andel, we have moved parts of chapter 5 to chapter 2. Above all, the second edition offers more polished and more detailed arguments which make use of new views and of new information that has become available since the first edition. We also have updated our data and references.

We received many letters in response to the first edition, and the reaction by the news media and by policy-makers was astounding. We are grateful for all the opinions received, for the many discussions, for the invitations to speak, and also for our conversation with President von Weizsäcker. Most of the reaction has been favorable and in agreement. However, some people were skeptical or disagreed completely. The political classifications of our book ranged from "conservative-technocratic" to "socialist leanings." The truth is that we use strict libertarian market arguments, which are common in the field of economics. Such arguments cannot readily be classified within a two-dimensional "left/right" scheme, let alone identified with the position of any particular political party. Thus, whoever faithfully employs this reasoning to resolve economic questions along political lines will often find himself in conflict with conventional views.

We have also received many useful detailed comments on our first edition, some of which have been directly incorporated into this edition. For such comments, we are particularly thankful to Peter Hampe, Juli Irving-Lessmann, Wilhelm Krelle, Wernhard Möschel, Tyll Necker, Jürg Niehans, and Alois Oberhauser. We received help with updating the data and with additional work from University Assistants Kai Konrad, Angela Lechner, Stephan Panther, Ronnie Schöb, Marcel Thum, and Alfons Weichenrieder, as well as from research students Petra Gruber, Ulrich Hange, Markus Herr, Tina Ivančič, Marcos Krepel, Markus Krieg, Christian Specht, and Claudio Thum. The manuscript was typed once again, with great care, by Ingrid Wutte. We are very grateful to all these helpers.

Munich, May 1992

Editor's Note

In this edition, the abbreviation "GDR" is used to refer specifically to the so-called German Democratic Republic (the postwar, pre-unification political entity of East Germany; the Deutsche Demokratische Republik).

The unified German state has carried over from the former West Germany the formal name Bundesrepublik Deutschland, conventionally translated as "Federal Republic of Germany" and abbreviated in English as "FRG." In this book, where that abbreviation is used it is usually for the sake of parallelism with "GDR"; in such contexts it means the pre-unification Federal Republic.

Somewhat more loosely, the terms "East Germany" and "West Germany" are also used, and the people of the two areas are often referred to as "East Germans" and "West Germans." In English these usages are all but unavoidable.

The words "Western" and "Eastern" are sometimes used as shorter equivalents of "West German" and "East German." Elsewhere, "Western" is used in its broader sense. Similarly, the words "West" and "East" are often, but not always, used as synonyms for "West Germany" and "East Germany." Context should preclude any real confusion.

Jumpstart

1　Revolution and Unification

To Market with Marx

Marx was right. It really was necessary to stand Hegel's philosophy of history on its head. Existence determines consciousness, and not the reverse. The end of communism has shown this very clearly.[1]

Economic power and material success, not ideologies, determine the way the world functions. Ideological superstructures, whether they take the form of the state, of religion, or of property-rights systems, cannot continue to exist when they are in conflict with the material economic base and with the requirements of an efficient use of scarce economic resources. Marx's theory of revolution derived from this perception. He argued that, as a result of improvements in science and technology, the material base undergoes a process of change, but the ideological superstructure does not; it cannot evolve. In the process of historical development, such disjunctures cause tensions and contradictions, which eventually are released by revolution. The revolution forces the superstructure to adapt to the base, while further changes in the base create new contradictions.

Marx and his followers believed that the structures of a capitalist market economy were in conflict with the economic requirements of a highly specialized industrial society. Thus, they argued, capitalism would be subject to increasingly frequent and increasingly severe economic crises, inevitably resulting in a communist revolution.[2] It was argued that, over time, the accumulation of capital made possible by the expropriation of surplus value created by labor would cause the average rate of profit to fall. The

---

1. Marx 1859, p. 9; Marx 1873, p. 27; Hegel 1821, p. 19.
2. See Marx 1873, Tugan-Baranowski 1905, and Luxemburg 1921. Interesting discussions of the alternative theories of the change in systems in the light of the collapse of Eastern Europe are to be found in Tietzel et al. 1991, Wagner 1991, and Watrin 1990.

falling rate of profit would make entrepreneurs unwilling to undertake sufficient investment, and the end result would be the collapse of the whole system.[3] Alternatively, it was expected that a chronic shortage of demand would appear under capitalism, and that this would be temporarily alleviated by an imperialistic expansion into world markets. Such an expansion could not continue indefinitely, and when it came to an end the crises that followed would sound the death knell of capitalism. The "iron laws of economics" would ensure capitalism's destruction.

These fears have not materialized. Despite the rapid accumulation of capital, the average rate of profit has shown no tendency to fall. Technological progress and growing populations have prevented profitable investment opportunities from becoming exhausted. Even if they were to dry up, all that would happen would be the emergence of a stationary state with production solely for the purposes of consumption and replacement investment. The same applies to the underconsumption theory. Say (1803) showed that in a closed economy aggregate income would be sufficient to buy all the goods and services supplied. It is obvious even to freshman economics students that capitalism does not need external markets to survive.

Communism, and not capitalism, collapsed because its ideological superstructure and its organization of the production process were in conflict with its material base.

In communism, the returns to labor are pooled and then shared according to need. Such an organizing principle may be suitable for a small pre-industrial domestic economy, but it is quite unsuitable for a highly specialized industrial economy. People who make an extra effort will be unable to enjoy many of the benefits of this effort, because so many other people are entitled to draw from the pool. No one is willing to continue making that additional effort, and the community's activity slows right down to a minimal level. If we are talking about the "iron laws of economics," one of them surely must be that the destruction of economic incentives, which occurs under communist rule, creates a contradiction between the ideological superstructure and the material base and thus brings on the revolution.

If people were truly altruistic, achievement incentives would be unnecessary. All would behave correctly and work just as hard as if they were entitled to the whole fruit of their labor. Communist ideology, unlike that of Christianity, assumes that people are fundamentally good; but unfortu-

---

3. For a critique and further references on the "law of the falling rate of profit" see Sinn 1975.

nately they are not—they are fundamentally selfish. An economic system based on wishful thinking rather than on a realistic view of human nature cannot hope to succeed.

A market economy is based on a realistic view. If a Martian were to visit Earth and observe what was going on, he might well believe that everyone was an altruist. At first sight everybody would appear to be doing things solely for other people. However, on closer inspection he would notice that almost nothing was done without the expectation of a return. What appeared to be altruism was, in fact, people acting in their own selfish interests. When exchange is based on well-defined and well-observed property rights, giving is voluntary. What is received in return is always sufficient— and often more than sufficient—to compensate for the disadvantage of giving up something, whether that something is a good, a right of use, or a service.

Property rights and freedom to exchange create the achievement incentives that outwit selfishness. They also make it possible to fine-tune the selection of efficient economic activities. Whatever passes the market test of free exchange will be selected; whatever does not will be rejected. Most of the goods that could be produced are never produced, and most of the production processes that are technically feasible are never used. Only a few of the possibilities are selected by the market, and those it selects are the most efficient.

The incentive and selection functions of private economic exchange are the secrets of success of the market economy. They explain why this form of economic organization harmonizes so well with the requirements of industrial mass production. It is one of the ironies of history that the "anarchistic" markets so strongly criticized by the Marxists have been able to command and control economic activities whose achievements overshadow by far what even the best planners have ever been able to achieve. This has been the major cause of the great gulf in prosperity between the West and the East, and it was this gulf that finally incited people to take to the streets. The failure of the communist states to perform as efficiently as the Western countries is not explained by lack of natural resources, by corrupt political leaders, by cultural backwardness, by intellectual shortcomings of the population, or by a too-high level of reparations, though some of these may have contributed. The decisive factor is that the rules of the game of a capitalist market economy are far better suited to industrial mass production than those of the communist command economy. It is for this reason that a market economy can deploy productive forces far more efficiently than a communist one.

It is sometimes argued that the major reason communism collapsed was a political one—that the totalitarianism and the denial of civil rights were more important than the economic inadequacies in bringing about its downfall. This can, at best, be only a half-truth, for it overlooks the strong interaction between economic performance and the ability of a government to tolerate the effects of democratic processes. There was little in the communist ideology of the nineteenth century to suggest that it was intrinsically anti-democratic or opposed to the exercise of human rights.[4] The ultimate goals of both communism and democracy were liberty and equality. Indeed, in many countries, including Germany, they were seen as similar political evils, each posing a threat to social stability. It was only when communism was put into practice in this century that the desperate maneuvers of communist governments became increasingly incompatible with the values of democracy and that the injustice, terror, and cruelty we now associate with its name became dominant. Dictatorship is not an accidental accompaniment to communism that can be attributed to the specific conditions in the Soviet Union or even to particular individuals. It is a necessary consequence of the lack of economic incentives and of economic inefficiency. Because economic incentives were lacking, the people's economic behavior had to be ruled; and because economic efficiency was lacking, the rulers had to use force to smother the protests of the masses. Economic inefficiency resulted in dictatorship, and both of these were instrumental in the collapse of communism.

A fundamental contradiction between the material base and the ideological superstructure was characteristic of all communist economic systems. Such a contradiction brought about the Eastern European revolutions of 1989. The ideological superstructure of market capitalism was ushered in by those revolutions, and the contradiction was overcome. Marxism was confirmed by its own defeat.

Submitting to the Iron Laws

Mikhail Gorbachev, General Secretary of the Communist Party of the USSR, who had been well schooled in the philosophy of dialectical materialism, recognized that the collapse of communism was inevitable and acted accordingly. His observation that life penalizes those who arrive too late,

---

4. The term "dictatorship of the proletariat," which is part of the vocabulary of communism, is often misunderstood. It means the freeing of the oppressed masses through revolutionary struggle and not the crushing of the former ruling classes.

like Eduard Shevardnadze's comment that history never vowed loyalty to any constitution,[5] is quite compatible with the classical statements of Karl Marx (1873, p. 15 f.), Rosa Luxemburg (1906, p. 162 ff. and p. 180 f.), and others to the effect that politicians might be able to alleviate the birth pangs of a new system but can never stem the tide of history.

The Kremlin must have suspected quite early that history was planning the reunification of Germany, for in the spring of 1989 rumors that the Soviets might be willing to make concessions here were already circulating. The American press took up these rumors, and a widespread discussion about reunification ensued, with most of the national newspapers taking part.[6] Even earlier, in May 1987, Count Lambsdorff (a leading member of the German Liberal Party) was being quoted as saying that Gorbachev was about to revive Stalin's initiative of 1952 and make an offer regarding reunification.[7] All this was officially denied, and Gorbachev dismissed the topic by relegating it to the processes of history. At the Helsinki Conference on European Security and Cooperation, the East German leader Erich Honecker predicted that the Berlin Wall would still be standing in 100 years. The statements quoted above, however, indicate that, despite their denials, the communist leaders were preparing to bow to the inevitable when the time came.

The incredible ease with which the Eastern European revolutions and German unification were effected can in part be attributed to a deep-rooted fatalism regarding the forces of history and to the communists' thorough knowledge of, and almost reverential respect for, revolutionary processes. The fall, without bloodshed, of the regimes of Kádár, Jaruzelski, Husák, Zhivkov, and Honecker, and their replacement by democratic governments, would be little short of miraculous if the cadres themselves had not been so thoroughly trained in Marxist ideology. When the revolutionary masses took to the streets and the leaders realized that the people's movements were in total opposition to them, it seemed pointless to try to swim against the tide of history. The ever-more-insistent cry "We are the people," heard in Leipzig during the Monday demonstrations, shook the communist leadership to the core.

---

5. Gorbachev on his state visit to the GDR on October 7, 1989, and Shevardnadze, the Soviet foreign minister, on his state visit to Bonn on January 18, 1988.

6. E.g. *Washington Post*, May 7, 1989; *New York Times*, May 15, 1989. At his accreditation in Bonn in the spring of 1989, US ambassador Vernon Walters expressed his belief that Germany would be united during his term of office. At the time, the ironic comment was made that no one in Bonn had realized that a US ambassador was appointed for such a very long term.

7. The *Bildzeitung* and the German radio station Deutschlandfunk, May 13, 1987.

There was no shooting in Leipzig because *communists* rejected the blood-shed that Honecker seemed to be prepared to accept. The group around Egon Krenz, who took over from Honecker, claim to have been a moderating influence, and the Russian military commander certainly refused to use force. What happened in most other Eastern European countries was no different. Who would have believed that the communist rulers would lay down their arms so easily!

China and Romania are significant exceptions to the general pattern, but they are exceptions. What is surprising is that in many countries there were no violent and brutal clashes between revolutionaries and rulers. Fatalism with respect to the processes of history, which is an integral part of communist ideology and which has its origin in a firm belief in the laws of dialectical materialism, may well have been a decisive factor in ensuring that these revolutions remained bloodless.

German reunification policy was one of the beneficiaries of this fatalism. When the policy-makers knocked on the doors of the Kremlin, they found them already open—indeed, more open than the doors to 10 Downing Street or the Elysée Palace. The extent of the concessions made by the Soviet Union exceeded the most optimistic expectations. This is true both of the speed of rapprochement between the two governments and of the conditions negotiated in the "2 + 4" Treaty. A typical example is the agreement by the Soviets to the united Germany's being a full member of NATO, although the German foreign minister had publicly offered to settle for a more limited membership.

It is obvious that the concessions the Soviet Union was willing to make contributed to the brilliant success of German diplomacy; however, it would be naive to attribute these concessions to incompetence on the part of the Soviet negotiators, as critics of Shevardnadze's foreign policy have done. They represent, rather, a sensible and intelligent response to the inevitability of the "iron laws of economics."

Voting with Their Feet

To argue that communist fatalism facilitated the revolution is not to imply that it was the ultimate cause. The people themselves, deprived of their rights and condemned to poverty, finally swept communism out the door. The pressure they exerted began with the Monday demonstrations in the GDR, which started in Leipzig on September 4, 1989 and then spread rapidly to many other cities and towns. Eventually, even the cautious Berliners demonstrated. Hundreds, then hundreds of thousands, and finally millions were demonstrating for their rights. Week after week, peaceably but persistently, they took to the streets, their slogans becoming increasingly insistent and assertive. At first the demonstrations were about freedom to travel; then came attacks on the government and the Stasi (the State Security Service), and finally demands for reunification. "We are the people" became "We are *one* people."

The reason for the East German people's rebellion is found in their political repression under totalitarian rule, intensified by the economic inferiority of their system. Dissatisfaction increased dramatically after the government loosened its media policy and people were able to see on their television screens the luxurious living standards of their Western relatives. It is possible that the problem engendered by the difference in living standards might have been less severe if the communist government had been able to indoctrinate the people with a self-denying idealism that would have made them resistant to the lure of material prosperity. However, it did just the opposite, by continually claiming the eventual superiority of the communist system in the production of material goods. Using highly speculative and questionable statistics, the government of the GDR represented the living standards of the workers as being, in many respects, equal to or better than those of the FRG. Where the shortfall was all too obvious, the alleged high growth rates of labor productivity in the GDR were referred to. These, it was claimed, would soon overcome the shortfalls. (It was never mentioned that these growth rates were highly misleading, as minor changes in product quality were arbitrarily converted into grossly overestimated changes in quantity.) With their attention continually being directed toward the material aspects of life, in the end even the most convinced communists could not avoid seeing how great the difference in living standards actually was. In 1989, the average real wage level of the GDR was at most one-third that of the FRG.

What finally set off the rebellion was the tightening of restrictions on travel to other Eastern Bloc countries. The government of the GDR had felt obliged to impose more severe restrictions because some of these countries were being increasingly used as springboards to the West. In this way, thousands of people had succeeded in escaping in 1989, even before the wall was opened, and the situation appeared to the East German authorities to be getting out of hand. The lack of a language barrier meant that there had always been a strong incentive for East Germans to migrate to West Germany. From the time the GDR was established in 1949 until the wall went up on August 13, 1961, a total of 2.7 million people emigrated. Over the next 28 years, the iron curtain effectively reduced the number of emigrants to 600,000. However, after Hungary made the first holes in the Iron Curtain, in May 1989, there was no holding the escapees anymore. Holes appeared everywhere in the curtain and a mass exodus began, even larger than the one before the wall was built.

Tightening the visa conditions and border controls faced by those East Germans who camouflaged themselves as tourists and tried to escape to the West through Hungary did little to stem the tide. The reaction of the refugees was to crowd into the German embassies in Prague and Warsaw in such numbers that the authorities were left no choice but to evacuate them. The government of the GDR was partially successful in blocking this escape route, but its success triggered the Monday demonstrations. These demonstrations put such pressure on the government that by November 9, 1989 it was forced to open the border to West Germany.

The decision to open the border was presumably made in the hope that allowing people the right to travel freely would stabilize the communist regime. That hope proved to be false. Instead of stability, it brought about an even larger exodus. As Tiebout (1956) and others had long before suggested they would, people voted with their feet and thus gave a powerful boost to the existing lack of confidence in the GDR regime. Day after day in the months that followed the opening of the border, thousands of East Germans went across to the western part of Germany.

The migrants from East Germany have posed no real problems for West Germany. Despite widespread opinion to the contrary, their numbers each year have never exceeded those of migrants of German origin from other Eastern European countries (see figure 1.1). Since 1987 the policy of perestroika had precipitated large flows of emigrants from the Eastern Bloc countries, forcing the West German government to set up housing schemes and other services to take care of their needs. It was known that more than 2 million potential emigrants were living in the Soviet Union. These were people, officially classified as German, whose ancestors had settled in Russia under Catherine the Great and had been deported to Siberia by Stalin, some from the "Autonomous Socialist Soviet Republic of the Volga Germans" and others from German enclaves in other Soviet republics. It was also known that hundreds of thousands of people, counted as Germans according to the FRG's immigration laws, were living in Romania, Hungary, Czechoslovakia, and Poland.[8] The German authorities were clearly

---

8. In 1970 the Research Institute for World Refugee Problems estimated the number of Germans in Poland to be 1.5 million. See Bundeszentrale für politische Bildung 1989, p. 32. A detailed study of the migration flows can be found in Fleischer and Proebsting 1989.

Thousands per year

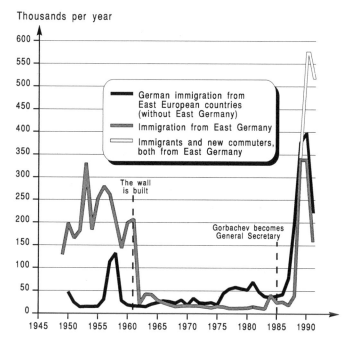

Figure 1.1
The flight from communism. Sources: Bundesausgleichamt, Statistical Report 2/89 and
information provided via telephone, January 1992; IAB, *Werkstattbericht* no. 4, December
15, 1991, p. 33; *DIW Wochenbericht* no. 3/92, January 17, 1992, p. 21n. *Note:* All graphs
show flows rather than stocks. "New commuters" is, accordingly, defined as the annual
increase in the number of East Germans living in the East and working in the West
("Pendler").

aware of, and well prepared for, the flood of immigrants that could be
expected to result from Gorbachev's liberalization of Soviet emigration
policy. This claim is in no way refuted by the FRG's dramatic highlighting
of the exodus of refugees from the East as a means of speeding up the
"2 + 4" negotiations.

The opening of the border was, however, a catastrophe for the East
German government. For one thing, it intensified the economic problems.
Many key positions in the public services and in industry suddenly became
vacant, and there was no chance of filling these vacancies in the short
run. In addition, the communist state lost at one blow the repressive measures it had depended on to control its people since its inception. When
trouble threatened, the East German people now had the option of taking
themselves off to the West. They had thus become immune to intimidation

by the authorities, and they no longer had to fear the consequences of opposition.

The problems were compounded by the fact that millions of people who themselves had no wish to move to West Germany made use of the new travel opportunities and returned home with heightened desires for material goods. The complimentary 100 deutschmarks given to everybody by the West German government enabled them to taste the delights of Western consumer society and to see for themselves that what they had been shown on Western television was no mirage. The desire to partake in the blessings of an affluent society was fortified and proved to be quite incompatible with the continued existence of the GDR.

The Road to Union

When the border was first opened, most people could not have predicted either the nature or the speed of future developments. Hardly anyone thought that reunification was inevitable, let alone that it would happen so soon. (The word "unification" was not yet being used.) Many people were, however, speculating about whether (in Willy Brandt's words) what "belonged together" could manage to "grow together."

The new East German communist premier, Hans Modrow, had taken a first step toward unification when he suggested a "partnership treaty" between the two states in his policy speech on November 13, 1989. What really led the way to a reunification policy, however, was the "Ten-Point Plan" that Helmut Kohl, the West German chancellor, presented to a startled Bundestag on November 28, 1989.[9] The plan took up Modrow's suggestion for a partnership treaty but went even further by talking about "confederative structures" and the establishment of a "federation" between the two parts of Germany. Although the words were selected with care, the Ten-Point Plan proved to be the signal for a wide-ranging debate over reunification, in Germany and in many other countries. The topic domi-

---

9. The surprise was especially great because in his first spontaneous reaction to the dismantling of the wall Kohl had not exactly been enthusiastic. He had given the impression that he would follow the Adenauer tradition of being unwilling to take up an active policy of reunification. (Venohr [1989, pp. 145–147] gives particulars of documents held in the Public Record Office in London which compromise Adenauer. See also letters to the editor in the *Frankfurter Allgemeiner Zeitung* by Osterrieth, Vogt, and Venohr on April 19 and May 16, 1989. According to the documents, Adenauer was against reunification even under the conditions of free elections and complete freedom for the German government to conduct its own affairs.)

nated discussions among politicians, in economic and political advisory bodies, and in the media for months. The first economic body to take up the Ten-Point Plan was the Advisory Council of the FRG's Ministry of Economics. On December 16 it recommended uniting the two parts of Germany "under a common political roof."

The announcement of the Ten-Point Plan was an adroit and daring political move. Kohl had deliberately not consulted the British and French governments in advance. He wanted to keep them from influencing the content of the plan and to circumvent the delaying tactics foreshadowed in various statements by Margaret Thatcher and François Mitterrand. The move was a smart one, as it meant that afterwards the European allies would only be able to complain about the form of the plan and not about its content. The content was quite consistent with the idea of German reunification to which lip service had frequently been paid. It was also consistent with statements made in various treaties and agreements which had to do with Germany—for example, the Germany Treaty of 1952, a 1954 declaration by the Western powers concerning the entry of Germany into NATO, and the European Community's 1956 Treaty of Rome. The Germany Treaty had even specifically included German reunification as a political goal.[10]

Under these circumstances, France and Britain could hardly avoid giving their approval to German unification, although this certainly went very much against the grain—particularly for Mitterrand, who up to the last minute had tried to pursue an active anti-unification policy, visiting both the East German leaders and Gorbachev. After a brief delay, the British and French governments agreed to the West German suggestion for a meeting at which the two German states and the four occupying powers (Britain, France, the United States, and the USSR) would negotiate the abolition of

10. Article 7 of the agreement states that "until a peace treaty is concluded, the undersigned countries [the United States, Great Britain, France, and the FRG] will work together to achieve by peaceful means their common goal—a reunited Germany, with a liberal democratic constitution similar to that of the FRG, which is integrated into the European community." A similar statement is contained in a declaration by the governments of the United States, France, and Great Britain announcing the immediate entry of Germany into NATO. In point 4 of the declaration given on October 3, 1954, the Allies asserted that "the creation of a free united Germany by peaceful means remains a fundamental aim of their policy." With regard to the Treaty of Rome, the reunification provisions are reflected in two resolutions of the Bundestag on July 4, 1957, and in a statement by the leader of the German delegation on February 28, 1957 (see Grabitz 1983, comment on article 227, paragraph 1). In addition, in an appendix to the treaty an explicit agreement is made not to interfere in internal German trade.

those occupation laws that still remained.[11] They continued to support this goal until it was achieved with the ratification of the "2 + 4" Treaty on September 12, 1990.

The United States had no such reservations with regard to unification. The wave of enthusiasm for the German revolution that quickly spread over large parts of the US certainly owed something to the fact that around 60 million Americans are directly descended from German immigrants. Now that large numbers of Germans were engaged in a struggle for freedom from a dictatorship, many Americans of German descent were again happy to acknowledge their ancestry, although up until then they had preferred to keep quiet about it. Language students crowded into the Goethe Institutes, and the German flag, now frequently shown on television, again became quite respectable. Leaving aside immigrants who had fled from the Nazis and who understandably had reservations about the matter, it was evident that the majority of Americans were strongly in favor of German unification. The US government did everything in its power to comply with the wishes of the American people and vigorously supported Germany's policy.

Events in Germany moved rapidly after the publication of the Ten-Point Plan and the agreement on a partnership treaty. The Volkskammer (parliament) of the GDR passed a series of reforms, desperately trying to rescue what it could of the collapsing state. East German citizens were now allowed to privately own the means of production, joint ventures with Western firms were permitted, and Western banks could now set up branches in East Germany. The productive assets owned by the state were transferred to a newly established resolution trust, the Treuhandanstalt, whose official task was to maintain, reorganize, and privatize East German industry.[12] Particularly important was the decision to hold the first free parliamentary elections in the history of the GDR—these were subsequently held on March 18, 1990.

By yielding to the pressure of circumstances, the East German government was doing everything it could to save itself, but every step it took

---

11. Interestingly enough, Mitterrand's agreement was given when Kohl agreed to the Maastricht summit, where the abolition of the deutschmark and the creation of a new European currency was to be settled.

12. See Beschluss zur Gründung der Anstalt zur treuhänderischen Verwaltung des Volks-eigentums (First Trusteeship Law), March 1, 1990; Gesetz über die Gründung privater Unternehmen (Private Firms Law), March 7, 1990; and Verordnung über die Gründung von Unternehmen mit ausländischer Beteiligung (Foreign Participation in GDR Firms—Ordinance), January 25, 1990.

in the direction of reform simply raised people's expectations without improving in the slightest the government's already slim chances of survival.[13] For a while it seemed as if the people would be satisfied with being allowed to watch West German television, then they seemed to be content with internal reform, and after that they wanted a confederation with West Germany. Finally, when this appeared to be within reach, the goal shifted to full unification. In parallel fashion, the people's sympathies quickly shifted from one political group to another. At first allegiance was given to the writers and theologians who had joined together to form the "Bündnis 90," then it was transferred to the SPD (Social Democrats), and finally to the Ost-CDU (Eastern Christian Democrat Union). At the beginning of 1990 the opinion polls were still showing the SPD in the lead, but in the election the overwhelming majority of the votes went to the party which the people had been persuaded to think would be the one most likely to achieve an economic upturn. On April 12, 1990, the East German chairman of the CDU, Lothar de Maizière, formed the GDR's first freely elected government.

The SPD Bundestag representative Ingrid Matthäus-Maier had been demanding the setting up of a monetary union and the introduction of the deutschmark as the official medium of exchange in the GDR. Chancellor Kohl was quick to adopt this suggestion, and his promise to implement it as soon as possible was a decisive factor in the electoral victory of the CDU. Kohl succeeded in carrying out his promise despite strong opposition from all parliamentary groups and from the Bundesbank, and on July 2 the transformation of "eastmarks" into "westmarks" wanted by the East Germans was effected.

The conditions of the monetary union were set out in the so-called "first state treaty" between the two Germanies. This treaty also brought an "economic and social union" into effect. East Germany adopted West Germany's social security system (although not its level of social benefits) and most of its economic laws. Free trade and commerce between the two German states was agreed to, most prices in East Germany were freed just before the treaty came into force, and East Germany's system of luxury taxes and price subsidies was dismantled.

---

13. Thus providing a new application for Tocqueville's (1856, p. 223) characterization of the French revolution: "Le mal qu'on souffrait patiemment comme inévitable semble insupportable dès qu'on conçoit l'idée de s'y soustraire". ("The evil which is borne with patience when it seems unavoidable, becomes intolerable when people begin to believe they can escape from it.")

The crucial last step toward union was made with the second state treaty, the "Unification Treaty." It was signed on August 31 and came into force on October 3.

Initially it was thought that the treaty could be drawn up by making use of the possibilities provided by Article 146 of the FRG's constitution and combining the positive elements of both state structures to form a completely new state. However, this method would have involved a complicated process of negotiation and, after unification, a long experimental phase during which a multitude of existing laws would have had to be amended. The pressure of time precluded the use of this strategy. Instead, it was decided to use Article 23 of the constitution as the basis for unification. This article gave the GDR, or any part of it, the right to join the FRG with equal-partner status provided it accepted the conditions set down by the FRG. Unification by way of Article 23 reduced the negotiating costs to those of determining the transitional arrangements that the communist state structure would have to meet in adapting to the West German legal system. With minor exceptions, the existing laws of the FRG were taken over unchanged and now apply in the territory of the former GDR. The name of the expanded state is Bundesrepublik Deutschland (Federal Republic of Germany), the same name the Western state had used before unification.

The most important transitional laws set out in the Unification Treaty are those relating to the transfer of the state-owned economy into private hands. The de Maizière government had been in favor of financial compensation for dispossessed property owners because it wanted to facilitate new investment and to keep as much as possible of the value of the state-owned businesses for the East German people. The federal government, however, strongly influenced by foreign minister Hans-Dietrich Genscher, decided to press for "natural restitution" (i.e., handing back the physical property to its original owners). The collapse of the East German economy that followed the introduction of free trade, combined with suspicions already being expressed that de Maizière had worked with the Stasi, reduced the bargaining power of the GDR to such an extent that it was unable to resist the pressure from the Western side.

Only the Soviet Union had sufficient bargaining power to ensure that its wishes were met. It made its willingness to sign the 2 + 4 Treaty dependent on agreement that the property *it* had expropriated before the establishment of the GDR in 1949 would not be returned to its original owners. Natural restitution was therefore only to apply to property taken away by the communists after 1949. (The United States later pressed successfully to have the period between 1933 and 1945 considered so that property expropriated by the Nazis could be given back.)

In addition to the concessions associated with the expropriation of property, a series of further concessions were required by the World War II victors. These included the financing of housing for the Soviet troops that were to be repatriated, the limitation of the German armed forces to 370,000, and, most important, the final renunciation by Germany of its territories east of the Oder and Neisse rivers.

In a border treaty with Poland completed shortly after unification Germany formally gave up its claim to the eastern territories, and in the Unification Treaty it was stated that German unity would be "complete when this treaty came into force." Most of Pomerania, Silesia, East Brandenburg, and East Prussia—the land of Nicholas Copernicus and Immanuel Kant— no longer belongs to Germany under German law. In fact, realistic chances of getting back the eastern territories had disappeared with the expulsion of between 10 and 12 million Germans from the area during and shortly after the Second World War. The absence of a peace treaty, however, had meant that Germany had not previously needed to relinquish its claims formally, not even with the signing of the non-aggression pact with Poland by the Brandt government in 1972. A formal renunciation of the German eastern territories was the price that had to be paid for unification. Many Germans would have preferred a true *re*unification of prewar Germany; however, this proved impossible, and in the light of German history this was probably a good thing.

Table 1.1
Chronology of important events, 1985–1991.

3/11/85	Mikhail Gorbachev elected General Secretary of Communist Party of Soviet Union.
5/13/87	Rumors about Soviet offers with regard to reunification and cutbacks in armed forces.
10/27/88	Gorbachev relegates reunification to the processes of history.
1/19/89	GDR President Erich Honecker's speech in Helsinki: The Wall "will still be standing in 50, indeed in 100 years. . . ."
spring 1989	Widespread discussion of reunification in American press.
5/2/89	Hungary pulls back the Iron Curtain. Citizens of GDR start to escape across the Hungarian border.
5/7/89	The Warsaw Pact retracts the Brezhnev Doctrine of limited sovereignty for the socialist countries.
5/7/89	Results of municipal elections in GDR are falsified.
August 89	FRG's embassies in Budapest, Warsaw, and Prague closed on account of overcrowding by refugees.

Table 1.1 (continued)

8/19/89	Mass flight by "tourists" from GDR at celebrations on Hungarian border.
9/4/89	Monday demonstrations at St. Nicholas Church in Leipzig begin.
9/11/89	Hungary allows GDR refugees to officially cross over into Austria. This is followed by successful flight by way of the FRG's embassies in Warsaw and Prague.
10/7/89	Gorbachev's state visit to the GDR: "Life penalizes those who arrive too late."
10/9/89	Bloodshed in Leipzig avoided at the last minute.
10/18/89	Egon Krenz becomes president of Staatsrat.
11/9/89	The internal border between the two Germanies opened.
11/13/89	Hans Modrow becomes premier of GDR and suggests a partnership treaty with the FRG.
11/28/89	Helmut Kohl's Ten-Point Plan.
12/4/89	The Central Committee and the Politbüro of GDR resign en masse. Krenz resigns as president of Staatsrat.
12/20/89	Modrow and Kohl agree on a partnership treaty.
1/12/90	Private ownership of the means of production allowed in GDR.
1/25/90	GDR introduces freedom of occupational choice and permits joint ventures.
2/7/90	Kohl makes an offer of a single currency area to GDR.
3/1/90	Establishment of Treuhandanstalt (First Trusteeship Law).
3/6/90	Separation of the central and commercial banking functions in the GDR. Private banking permitted.
3/7/90	Conversion of state enterprises into corporations and restitution of small businesses taken over since 1972.
3/18/90	Free elections for GDR Volkskammer.
4/12/90	de Maizière's government formed.
5/5/90	"2 + 4" negotiations begin.
5/6/90	Local government elections in GDR.
5/16/90	West German federal and state governments agree to set up a German unity fund of DM 115 billion.
5/18/90	Kohl and de Maizière sign the state treaty to establish an economic, monetary, and social union.
6/17/90	Volkskammer passes Second Trusteeship Law.
6/17/90	"Right to work" deleted from GDR constitution.
6/22/90	Price controls removed in GDR.
7/1/90	Treaty for economic, monetary, and social union and Second Trusteeship Law come into force.
7/2/90	Currency conversion.
7/16/90	Kohl and Gorbachev meet in the Caucasus. Agreement on German unification.
7/22/90	The Volkskammer passes the law to establish new states. The election of the Landtage (the state parliaments) on October 14, would reestablish the states of Saxony, Saxony-Anhalt, Mecklenburg–West Pomerania, Brandenburg, and Thuringia.

Table 1.1 (continued)

8/31/90	Unification Treaty concluded.
9/12/90	"2 + 4" Treaty concluded in Moscow.
10/3/90	German unification—Unification Treaty takes effect.
10/14/90	Election of East German state parliaments.
11/14/90	Germany concludes treaty with Poland defining borders.
12/1/90	Elections in the whole of Germany for the Bundestag.
3/4/91	"2 + 4" Treaty ratified by Supreme Soviet of USSR.
3/15/91	The "2 + 4" Treaty comes into force with the lodging with the German government of the document ratified by the Supreme Soviet. The Federal Republic of Germany attains full sovereignty.

2   Germany and the World

Germany a Superpower?

Will the economically larger united Germany be tempted to push for super-power status? This question is causing a good deal of concern among many of Germany's competitors and neighbors—rightly so, if the international press is to be believed. Their worry is understandable in view of the trouble Germany's expansionary aims caused for the rest of the world in the not-too-distant past, but it receives little support from the economic realities. In many respects Germany's economic situation is very different from what people commonly believe it to be.

It is true that in 1989, the year before unification, the FRG had the largest trade surplus in the world.[1] This surplus amounted to $72 billion (versus Japan's $65 billion), and regrettably it led even some sober and respectable German research institutes to acclaim Germany as the world's champion exporter. However, to think that this now makes Germany an economic superpower is to misunderstand how international trade functions. The foreign-trade balance is a mirror image of the capital-transactions balance, and the latter strongly influences the former. The German export surplus reflected a record capital outflow of almost $68 billion. Not only did this outflow of capital dry up after unification, but, since the beginning of 1991, Germany has become a net importer of capital, with a negative balance on current account.[2] This deficit is no more a cause for concern than the surplus was a cause for celebration. Germany needs imported capital to help finance reconstruction and consumption in its eastern Länder (states), which it is unable to support entirely with its own resources. The

---

1. See OECD, *Main Economic Indicators*, March 1991, p. 25.
2. *Monatsberichte der Deutschen Bundesbank* 43, no. 12, December 1991. See also figure 2.6 below.

foreign-trade data show that the market is responding rationally to this need.

If a possible role for Germany as a superpower cannot be inferred from the trade statistics, it might perhaps be derived from the national-product and population statistics; however, these figures also provide little support for the idea. In 1989 the Federal Republic's GNP was approximately $1.2 trillion—far smaller than that of Japan ($2.8 trillion) or the United States ($5.1 trillion). Even if the GDR's per-capita output in 1989 had been equal to that of the FRG, the combined GNP of the two Germanies would have been no more than $1.5 trillion. This would still have been only the third highest GNP of the OECD countries, a little more than half of Japan's and not even one-third of America's.

Germany's relative importance in the European Community has also changed little as a result of unification. Before unification, West Germany's share of the EC's "national product" was 25 percent. After unification, it will not rise to more than 30 percent, even under the assumption of equal productivities.

Currently the assumption of equal productivities seems remote, to say the least. Labor productivity in West Germany is indisputably among the highest in the world. GNP per worker was close to $44,000 in 1989, the same as in the United States and only $2000 less than in Japan.[3] There is no significant difference among the three values when random exchange-rate effects are taken into account. However, labor productivity in East Germany is significantly lower. According to the official East German statistics, and assuming a purchasing-power parity of 1:1 (see chapter 3), productivity there was approximately 50 percent of the West German level before unification. Initially, detailed studies by the DIW (the German Institute for Economic Research) appeared to confirm this figure.[4] The Bundesbank, however, considered 40 percent to be more realistic,[5] and the Kiel Institute of World Economics suspected that labor productivity in the GDR may have been as low as one-third of the FRG's level.[6] More recent estimates by the DIW provide support for these suspicions, and investigations by

---

3. Calculated from the OECD's *Main Economic Indicators*, March 1991, and from table 1 of Sachverständigenrat 1990. Unlike the per-capita figures, the hourly productivity figures show a significant lead for Germany, which is reflected in substantial wage differentials. This is because the number of hours worked there per annum is low. German workers have six weeks of annual vacation and many religious holidays. See figure 5.4.

4. *DIW Wochenbericht* no. 14/90, April 5, 1990.

5. *Monatsberichte der Deutschen Bundesbank* 42, no. 7, July 1990, p. 15.

6. See Schmieding 1990 and Siebert 1990.

Table 2.1

	FRG[a]	Spain	France	Poland	GB	Italy
Population (1988–89; millions)	79	40	56	38	57	57
Area (million hectares)	35.7	50.5	55.2	31.3	24.4	30.1

Source: *Statistisches Jahrbuch 1990 für das Ausland*, table 2.1; appendix A of this book.
a. After unification.

Akerlof et al. (1991) even imply productivity levels for GDR manufacturing industry of less than one-sixth of those in the FRG.[7] Regardless of what the exact figures are, it is clear that there was, and still is, a substantial difference in labor productivity between West and East Germany, and this will certainly push the productivity of Germany as a whole well below the internationally competitive level. A long catching-up process will be necessary before the gap is closed.[8]

Its relatively small population is the main reason why Germany could not become a superpower, even with the productivity gap closed. This statement may seem rather strange in view of the fact that Germany, with 79 million people, has the largest population of any country in Central or Western Europe. In a larger context, however, the statement does not appear to be so odd. Germany's population is less than one-quarter of that of the European Community as a whole, and less than one-third of that of the United States. It is far below that of Japan, which has 123 million people, and Russia, which has 147 million.

What is more, the countries that historically have coveted superpower status have mostly been those with fast-growing populations. Germany's low birth rate makes the suggestion that it wants to become a great power even more absurd. In recent years, it has had the lowest birth rate in the world. Unless there is some significant change in Germany's reproduction rate in the near future, by the year 2040 its population will have fallen by 15 million—an amount approximately equal to the present population of East Germany.[9] Even if all the Germans now living in former Eastern Bloc

---

7. See chapter 5, footnote 12. See also Filip-Köhn and Ludwig 1990.
8. See chapter 5 for further details.
9. *DIW Wochenbericht* no. 8/90, February 22, 1990, and no. 23.24/90, June 14, 1990; HWWA, *Strukturbericht 1987*. The estimated decrease in the German population is 15 million, even with immigration of 5 million. Immigration by a further 15 million foreigners (i.e., by about one-fifth of the present German population) would naturally prevent the decrease without a change in the fertility rate. It is doubtful, however, that such a high rate of foreign entry would be tolerated by the rest of the German population.

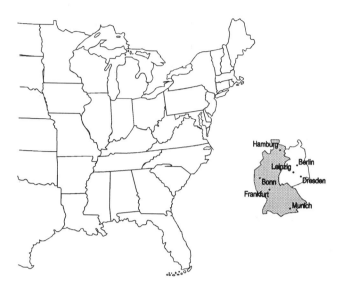

Figure 2.1
Geographic comparison of Germany and a distant competitor.

countries (2–3 million) were to emigrate to Germany, this decline would be affected little.

A geographical comparison will round out the picture. In area Germany is smaller than California, Montana, or Texas. It is smaller than Spain or France, and only a little bigger than Italy or Poland.

One reason for the distorted view many foreigners have of what Germany is like is a widespread lack of knowledge of the size of East Germany. It is often believed that unification involved the joining together of two countries of approximately equal size. This was not the case. In area East Germany makes up only 30 percent of the whole; its share of the population is 21 percent; and its pre-unification GNP was 15 percent of the combined total.[10] Today, East Germany's GNP is only 8 percent of the total. Figure 2.2 compares the German states in terms of population and output before unification. It can be seen that the whole of the area that joined the federation has fewer inhabitants than West Germany's most populous state, North Rhine–Westphalia, and that its productive capacity was similar to that of Baden-Württemberg, West Germany's third-largest state. More detailed comparisons of the two parts of the country are to be found in appendix A, where data from a variety of sources are used to quantify some of the economic differences.

---

10. Assuming 1 : 1 exchange. See table 3.1.

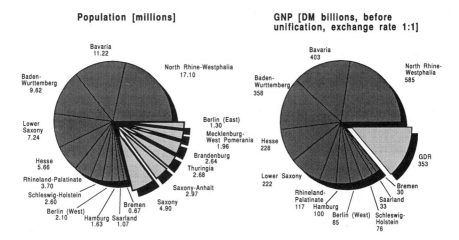

Figure 2.2
East and West Germany compared.

The Race for Prosperity

East Germany is only one of the East European countries that shook off the yoke of communism and are now taking part in the race for prosperity. They all want to achieve Western European living standards as soon as they possibly can, but their individual chances at the start of the race differ considerably. Most people would pick East Germany to be the winner, as it will be the recipient of most of the help and support being offered by West Germany. They think having a big brother should be an advantage.

Considerable financial help is certainly being given by West Germany to the other Eastern European countries. The Commonwealth of Independent States is receiving about DM 60 billion ($40 billion), and Poland not only was given a grant of around DM 120 million ($80 million) but also has had some of the debts it owed to the FRG remitted, reducing the total by half (by DM 8.5 billion—more than $5 billion).[11] Nevertheless, the payments to the former GDR are many times higher than this.

In the spring of 1990 the "German Unity Fund" was set up by the federal government and the western Länder to cover the budget deficits of the eastern states up to a total of DM 115 billion over the years 1990–1994. DM 22 billion were being made available in 1990, and DM 35 billion in 1991. Priority was given to financing social insurance (45 percent) in East

---

11. See *Handelsblatt* no. 45, March 5, 1991, and *Frankfurter Allgemeine Zeitung* no. 64, March 16, 1991.

Germany and to making up deficiencies in tax revenues caused by the tax authorities' lack of experience and expertise and the delays in introducing the West German tax system (27 percent). It is true that the German Unity Fund can also be seen as an attempt to buy East Germany's agreement not to participate in West Germany's system of intergovernmental transfers before 1995, which participation probably would have been more expensive for the western Länder. Nevertheless, the Fund is much larger than the volume of aid programs available for other Eastern countries.

In the spring of 1991 the federal government decided to introduce an additional support program, "Upswing-East," that made available a further DM 12 billion for each of the years 1991 and 1992.[12] This was intended to finance a variety of projects, including local government infrastructure investment, job-creation schemes, modernization of housing, maintenance subsidies, environmental pollution schemes, and a 12 percent investment subsidy.

The new states have also received contributions from the budgets of several federal ministries, some of them one-off grants and some of them recurring. Table 2.2 gives an overview of the combined package. The payments to the new states from official sources amounted to DM 64 billion in 1990 and DM 113 billion in 1991.[13] The latter is equal to almost DM 7000 per capita ($4700), or twice Poland's per-capita disposable income.[14] It can be expected that the 1992 transfers to East Germany will increase by another DM 25 billion.[15]

In addition to this financial support, there are two more reasons for believing that East Germany will be able to achieve Western living standards more quickly than its Eastern European neighbors.[16]

---

12. See Bundesministerium für Wirtschaft 1991.

13. For other estimates of the fiscal transfers see Heilemann 1991, p. 15; Siebert 1991b, p. 320; and Arbeitsgemeinschaft 1991, p. 22. For 1991, these estimates are DM 95 billion, DM 117 billion, and DM 135 billion, respectively. A broad discussion of the fiscal squeeze caused by unification can be found in Wenzel 1991. See Schmähl 1991 for an analysis of the problems connected with the integration of East Germans into the West German pension system.

14. Calculated on the basis of income statistics and 1988 exchange rates according to the Vienna Institute for Comparative Economic Studies 1990, pp. 57 and 382, and *Statistisches Jahrbuch 1990 für das Ausland*, pp. 177 and 287.

15. See Arbeitsgemeinschaft 1991, p. 22.

16. Some economists (see e.g. Panther 1991) have predicted a mezzogiorno effect for East Germany because increasing returns to scale imply that production will be concentrated in West Germany. Most economists have a much more optimistic view of developments in Germany; see Smyser 1990 or Albach 1991. For an extensive discussion of the transformation problems of Eastern Europe in general see Blanchard et al. 1991.

Table 2.2
Financial support planned for the new German states (in billions of deutschmarks).

	1990	1991
Federal Budget		
Social purposes	12	27
Transfers to GDR budget	10	—
Transport	—	12
Trade and industry, regional aid (incl. town planning and grants to regions)	3	5
Defense	—	4
Food production, agriculture, forestry	2	4
Other (energy, housing, education etc.)	8	12
Interest on existing debt taken over	—	3
Reduced tax revenue (increased revenue " − ")	7	− 25
Total	42	42
State Budgets (mainly forgone value-added tax)	—	6
German Unity Fund	22	35
"Upswing-East" program	—	12
East-West transfers via unemployment insurance	—	18
Total	64	113

Note: Payments from the federal and state budgets do not include payments to the Commonwealth of Independent States (CIS) in connection with the withdrawal of troops, and (to avoid double counting) also do not include allocations to the German Unity Fund, the Upswing-East program, or interest payments on borrowing associated with unification (interest payments on existing debt taken over by the federal government are included). Including expenditure financed by borrowing and the interest payments on this, as the official statistics (Finanzbericht) do, would involve double counting. The expenditure of DM 81 billion, the amount stated in the Finanzbericht, is obtained by adding the federal expenditure of DM 42 billion for 1991, the tax-revenue increase (DM 25 billion), payments to the CIS (DM 5 billion), and the double-counted interest payments (DM 9 billion). The West-East transfers of unemployment insurance payments do not include the federal government's contributions, which are already captured under "Social purposes." It is worth considering whether the deficit of the Treuhand and government loans (for example the European Recovery Program) should be counted in addition to the items listed. In our opinion this would not be justified. The Treuhand deficit should not be taken into account, because it reflects expenditures that were, or are to be, financed by the sale of East German properties (see chapter 4). Government loans should not be included, because only a possible interest-rate advantage (normally 1%–2% of the value of the loan—a negligible amount) qualifies as subsidy.
Sources: Institut der Deutschen Wirtschaft, *IWD* 13/91, March 28, 1991; Bundesministerium der Finanzen, *Finanznachrichten* 9/91 and 11/91, February 18 and 25, 1991; *Finanzbericht* 1991, p. 13; and personal communication from the Economics Ministry.

The first reason is that East Germany is the only part of the old Eastern Bloc that already has the kind of stable legal and institutional environment that investors require before they will risk undertaking long-term projects. This is the advantage of having joined the union by way of Article 23 of the constitution.

The legal system of the old FRG has been established for many years and has stood the test of time. Foreign investors from Europe and elsewhere know they can rely on the protection of this system. Other countries, such as Poland and Czechoslovakia, will have to go through a long period of trial and error, setting up and testing new laws and institutions, before they can offer investors a stable and well-functioning legal environment of the kind Germany can offer. Changing governments, political coalitions, institutions, laws, and tax systems may deter private investors, making it difficult for these countries to draw level with the West.

The second reason that East Germany has an advantage over other Eastern European countries is its tradition of craftsmanship and cooperation between skilled workers and innovative engineers. Before the war, Saxony and Thuringia were world leaders in automobile and aircraft production, precision engineering, optics, and chemicals. Junkers, DKW, Zeiss, Schott, and Leuna were known the world over for the quality and technical superiority of their products. Although the old know-how is obsolete today, the tradition of thorough occupational training and successful innovation has not been forgotten. It provides an excellent basis on which to build an economic upswing—a basis not available to other Eastern Bloc areas, except perhaps Bohemia and Slovenia.

Americans tend not to be aware of how heterogeneous Eastern Europe is, but this heterogeneity is obvious to every East European. A comparison

Table 2.3
Per-capita income in 1938 (US dollars).

Bulgaria	68
Romania	70–75
Yugoslavia	81
Poland	104
Hungary	112
Czechoslovakia	176
France	236
Germany	337

Source: Kaser and Radice 1985, p. 532.

of incomes before the Second World War may be useful in this regard. Table 2.3 shows that in 1938 per-capita income in Czechoslovakia was only 52 percent of the German level, while in Poland it was only 31 percent. This could have been due primarily to the high levels of productivity in the industrial parts of West Germany, but it was not. As table 2.4 shows, in 1936 East Germany's per-capita gross domestic product was well above the German average. In fact, as currently defined, West Germany (the British, American, and French occupation zones, including the Saarland but excluding Berlin) had a slightly smaller per-capita output than East Germany (the Soviet occupation zone). The difference in productivity was about 7 percent.

The data in tables 2.3 and 2.4 indicate how far the individual Eastern European countries must proceed along the development path before they can hope to achieve Western European productivity levels. Obviously, they must make up not only the ground they lost during the years of communist rule but also the backlog of the prewar years.

Despite its obvious advantages, East Germany too has serious problems with getting started. Not only has it been thrown overnight into the icy waters of international competition; on top of that, having a big brother has turned out to be not quite as beneficial as it at first seemed to be. The big brother insisted on the restitution of his old property rights, he demanded the right to buy his little brother's assets, and he effectively protected himself against his little brother's low-wage competition. The severe damage this will cause greatly improves other Eastern countries' chances in

Table 2.4
Per-capita GNP in 1936 (Reichsmarks).

British Zone	596
Soviet Zone	546
American Zone	427
French Zone	417
Saarland	500
Greater Berlin	697
Silesia, East Pomerania, East Prussia	229
German Reich	494
West Germany (excluding Berlin)	510

Source: Abelshauser 1983, p. 14.
Note: The numbers given measure economic performance before the war, but relate to the postwar zones.

the race for prosperity, making them far better than a casual observer might have predicted.

Hungary[17] has been steadily moving toward a market economy for more than 20 years and is said to have attracted more private Western investment in 1990 than any other former Eastern Bloc country, including East Germany.[18] It already has many of the institutions necessary for a market economy, and it has low wages, a strong agricultural sector, and good traditional trading relations with its prosperous neighbor Austria. Unlike East Germany, Hungary rejected the restitution of old property rights so that foreign investors would not be deterred by the unavoidable delays involved in reassessing those rights.[19] It has also made extensive use of joint ventures so that the Western investors do not have to carry the whole risk of the enterprise.

An even more promising candidate is Czechoslovakia. This country, which shares borders with Germany and Austria, has good industrial traditions, skilled workers, an excellent road system, and wages that are less than 10 percent of those in West Germany. In addition, large-scale privatization is being carried out rapidly. In the years to come Czechoslovakia will absorb a large share of the Western capital flowing to the East, some of it coming from West Germany. The huge wave of West German investment in Czechoslovakia is currently of major concern for the German and Czechoslovak governments. The former is worried about the resulting reduction in investment in East Germany; the latter is worried about renewed German dominance of its economy. A prominent example of the situation is Volkswagen's Eastern investment program. While Volkswagen has satisfied political expectations and has committed itself to investing DM 4 billion in Zwickau, East Germany, its real interest seems to be in Czechoslovakia, where it has taken over Skoda and opened a new plant in Bratislava. The planned joint investment in these two plants is DM 7.6 billion ($5 billion), nearly twice Volkswagen's investment in East Germany. This example may overstate the case, but it accurately describes the difficulties the East German economy is facing.[20]

In the light of this development, it is not at all obvious whether, 20 years from now, East Germany will indeed have won the race for prosperity

17. For a recent overview of Hungary's reform strategy see Hare and Révész 1992.
18. *Economist*, February 16, 1991, p. 60.
19. In agriculture, Hungary compensates the previous owners in kind, but not necessarily by returning the same properties that had been nationalized. The East German approach is to return large parts of the properties to previous owners. See chapter 4.
20. Information received from Volkswagen AG, Wolfsburg, on March 11, 1992.

among the former communist states. In the end, having a big brother might turn out to have slowed down, rather than sped up, the little brother's growth.

The Collapse

Up to 1992 there was no sign that East Germany would get off to a quick start in the market economy, let alone that there was going to be a new economic miracle. Quite the opposite, in fact. After unification the economy started moving in a downward direction. For one thing, integration into the Western economic system led to a far more dramatic collapse of the East German economy than even the pessimists had expected. In the first few months after the economic and monetary union of July 1990, industrial output had already fallen to 60 percent of the average of the first six months of 1990. By the end of the year it was down to 49 percent, and during 1991 it fell to a third of its former level. Even the gross domestic product, which is much less sensitive than industrial output, fell by 35 percent.

The effective unemployment rate rose from almost zero at the beginning of 1990 to 7.2 percent in July of that year and to 25 percent by the spring of 1991. By the end of 1991 it had reached 30 percent. The unemployed workers taking part in job-creation schemes and retraining programs are included in these numbers, and "short-time" workers are counted in full-time equivalents. Around 700,000 people who had taken early retirement up to the end of 1991, and around 540,000 commuters who found work in West Germany, are not included in the unemployment figures. By the end of 1991 the total number of persons employed in East Germany had fallen from between 9.3 and 9.7 million[21] to approximately 6 million, and when these lines were written (early summer 1992) East German effective full-time employment was no more than 5 million.

The severity of the depression in East Germany is without parallel in modern economic history. Not even the Great Depression of 1928–1933 was as bad. Then, the downturn was spread over a much longer period and, even so, the relative fall in output was smaller. Industrial output in Germany fell by 40 percent and gross domestic product (GDP) by 24 percent; in the United States the corresponding figures were 35 percent and 30 percent.

---

21. The ambiguity results from the fact that no reliable statistics existed for the secret services and the army.

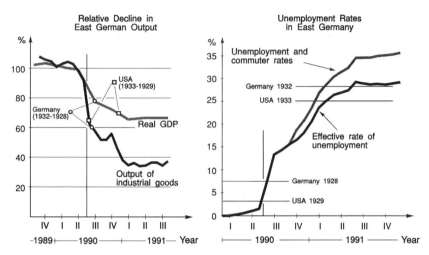

Figure 2.3
The collapse of the East German economy compared with the Great Depression. Sources of figure on left: DIW, *Volkswirtschaftliche Gesamtrechnung für Ostdeutschland*, June 6, 1991, p. 1; Institut für Konjunkturforschung, *Konjunkturstatistisches Handbuch* 1933, p. 36; W. G. Hoffmann et al. 1965, p. 829; US Department of Commerce, *Historical Statistics of the United States* 1975, pp. 224 and 232. *Note:* First six months of 1990 = 100. The numbers that apply to the Great Depression in each case compare the year immediately prior to the depression with the worst year of the depression. Sources of figure on right: Institut für Konjunkturforschung, *Konjunkturstatistisches Handbuch* 1933, pp. 13 and 15; Gemeinsames Statistisches Amt, *Monatsbericht*, December 1990, p. 12; ANBA-Jahreszahlen February 1992 (by telephone); press release, Bundesanstalt für Arbeit 36/91, July 4, 1991; Infratest, *Arbeitsmarktmonitor für die neuen Bundesländer*, figures for July and November 1991; US Department of Commerce, *Historical Statistics of the United States* 1975, p. 126. *Note:* The unemployment rate is the ratio of the officially registered unemployed to the estimated number of people in the work force (8.5 million). The effective unemployment rate includes those "employed" in job-creation schemes, those participating full-time in retraining and further education programs, and "short-time" workers, with down time calculated in terms of fully unemployed equivalents.

The catastrophic decline in production is only weakly reflected in the unemployment figures, because of emigration, early retirement, and massive subsidies given to East German industry by the Treuhand. Nevertheless, an unemployment rate of 30 percent is certainly alarming. In a country whose constitution (Article 24) had guaranteed the right to work, people are aghast at what unification has brought about.

Figure 2.3 plots the collapse of the East German economy[22] and compares it with the situation during the Great Depression.

---

22. One of the first to recognize and analyze this collapse was L. Hoffmann (1990).

The other Eastern European countries were also pulled into the turmoil of depression through their former Comecon relationships, but the developments in these countries were much less severe. The data available show that industrial output in Hungary and Czechoslovakia in the first two or three quarters of 1991 was about 24 percent below that of 1989, and that even the Polish economy—which was seriously affected—had to cope with a decline of "only" 36 percent in this period.[23] Figures like these are far from unknown in world economic history, but the collapse of an economy to one-third of its previous level, which was the case for the East German economy, involves quite a different (and in peacetime unprecedented) order of magnitude.

Despite the breakdown of the economy, the East Germans initially were very optimistic. Thanks to social transfer payments and Treuhand subsidies, for most of them things had become better than before the unification. Even if the upswing had not yet begun, there were signs that the lowest point of the slump was reached in the winter of 1991–92. By then industrial production seemed to have stabilized, the construction industry was experiencing a boom in orders, and industry's expectations about sales had at last become positive. Nevertheless, the fall in employment has continued since then, and even in the construction industry negative employment expectations are still dominant.[24] Because of the massive unemployment, the initial optimism meanwhile has given way to a certain degree of anxiety and even bitterness, which may have planted the seed for a renewed mental split between the two parts of the country.

Inherited Burdens

The unexpectedly difficult start in the market economy is certainly largely attributable to the inadequacies of the communist economic planning, which were suddenly disclosed when the East German economy was integrated into the world economy. The legacy bequeathed to their successors by the communists really did not make the start easy. Contrary to the glossy statistics published by the GDR government, the economy was a sick giant that was easily defeated in the competitive struggle between systems.

A visitor to the GDR could not fail to notice how bad the condition of the economy was, or to realize how difficult it would be for it to get on its

---

23. See OECD, *Short-Term Economic Statistics Central and Eastern Europe*, 1992, table 1.1.
24. See Ifo, *Wirtschaftskonjunktur* 1/92, p. T 21.

feet again. The GDR was a miserable country that in its last years had only just been able to stay on the razor's edge between disintegration and revival. The whole place was grey and monotonous. The main impressions received by visitors were of gloomy cities, dilapidated facades on run-down buildings, empty shelves, and potholes in the streets. It was no different with the firms—rusty pipes, machines that were due for the scrap heap, ancient office equipment, dust everywhere, makeshift accommodations, decrepit warehouses, and ramshackle factories were eloquent witnesses to the incapacity of the once-rich country to develop its productive powers. The contrast between the highly colored propaganda and the grey reality could not have been greater.

There are certainly new plants and buildings, but most of these fall well below normal Western standards. The communist government mainly concentrated its building activities in East Berlin, and some imposing buildings were put up there. The rest of the republic had to be content with prewar structures. Seventy percent of the housing had been constructed before the war, more than twice the proportion than in West Germany, and the condition of the vast majority of these buildings was deplorable. The proud old cities have decayed, and even many of the cheaply constructed concrete slab buildings of the satellite towns are ripe for demolition. In the commercial and cultural metropolis of Leipzig, the city of "Mercury and the Muses," decay and neglect were especially pronounced, and it is hardly surprising that the mass demonstrations began there.

The mismanagement by the communists also shows up in the environmental problems. Production in the GDR was far dirtier than in the FRG and other Western industrial countries.[25] Carbon dioxide emissions per capita were 3 times higher than in Japan, and 100 times more dust was produced. Sulfur dioxide emissions per capita were 7 times worse than in the FRG and 30 times worse than in Japan, mainly because domestic brown coal was burned without filtration; this was 50 percent worse even than in Czechoslovakia, and more than 100 percent worse than in Hungary and Poland. Many places did not have clean drinking water; in about a thousand districts the water was so bad that the government had to provide special deliveries of clean water for babies and small children. A third of the industrial wastewater was untreated when it left the plants, and the chemical contamination of the soil reached frightening levels. It is feared that up to 50,000 industrial sites are polluted by chemicals. Bitterfeld, Cottbus, Halle, Leipzig, East Berlin, and Dresden are among the most unhealthy

25. See Streibel 1990; Palinkas 1990; Adler et al. 1991.

cities in Europe to live in, and the uranium slag heaps of Schneeberg are miniature Chernobyls.

The long list of environmental shortcomings shows with awesome clarity the incapacity of the communist economy to compete with the market economy even in cases where the invisible hand is not available. The political decision-makers of the GDR were so overburdened just by providing for everyday needs that there was no room for dealing with environmental problems. Public protests had to be directed toward ensuring basic necessities, and no attention could be given to reducing becquerels.

Fundamental Reasons for the Collapse

The deplorable condition of the capital stock and the high levels of pollution are the most frequently cited external characteristics of the East German economy. Nevertheless, it would be superficial to claim that they are responsible for the economic collapse. There are four fundamental economic reasons behind the collapse. These affect all the Eastern European countries, but they are especially important for East Germany—the country that was most deeply committed to the communist ideology, and one that has been exposed particularly swiftly and brutally to the cold winds of international competition.[26]

Wrong Incentives

The first reason for the breakdown of the economy is to be found in the organizational defects of the firms. These resulted from incentive and wage systems that did not reflect true scarcities and did not pay enough attention to the importance of managerial functions. Among the defects were less than optimal levels of vertical integration and inadequate production scheduling, oversize warehouses, poor staff organization, lack of control on the job, use of labor for purposes other than production,[27] undeveloped marketing arrangements, and (not least) product ranges and qualities that did not fit in with the wishes of the consumers.

Firms were not simply production units where workers endeavored to make the goods the consumers wanted and received wage payments in

---

26. Thorough studies of this theme can be found in the conference volume recently published by Jens (1991). See in particular the papers by Krelle, Kantzenbach, and Diederich.
27. These included shopping done on the firm's time and party political education sessions.

return for their labor. They also had the character of social clubs where productive activities sometimes played a subordinate role. The aim behind this social-club aspect was to help prevent the "alienation of man from his labor" so deplored by Marx—and the "clubs" did accomplish this to some extent. However, the really high workplace morale hoped for remained largely a pipedream. As far as producing goods efficiently goes, ideology was no substitute for the business instinct of the capitalist who, in order to maximize his profits, optimizes the production process in all its conceivable dimensions and places great emphasis on eliminating unnecessary costs.

Wrong Institutions

The wrong incentives given *to* the firms and other economic decision-makers were even more important than the wrong incentives *within* the firms. The incentive structures under which firms and other economic agents operate are embodied in the economic system and in the institutions that constitute it. Institutions are legal and social norms, economic customs, and organizations that contribute to the coordination of plans and the spread of information. They put limits on the behavior of individual decision-makers and, at the same time, open up or preserve well-defined areas in which this behavior can be exercised. These institutions are efficient when they define the areas in a way that enables the search for individual advantage to lead to the best possible use of available economic resources in terms of satisfaction of the individual.

The institutions of the market economy evolved over centuries, and they are developing continuously. Their present form could in many respects be improved upon, but it is already so well adapted that considerable expansion of productive powers has taken place and a high level of economic welfare has been reached. The institutions of the planned socialist economy, on the other hand, were derived from primitive economic theories and were centrally decreed. They too were subject to an evolutionary adaptation process, but this process started out from the wrong basis and was not able to bring about a halfway efficient economic system within a humanly tolerable time span. As in the market economy, the economic decision-makers in the planned socialist economy were guided by the principle of maximization of utility; however, because of the wrong institutions, and thus the wrongly defined area for individual behavior, maximizing utility did not lead to the utility level that was really achievable with the available economic resources.

Lack of Know-How

The third reason for the breakdown is that technological knowledge in the GDR was inadequate. There were no market-induced incentives for discovering new knowledge in the communist system, and the transfer of international know-how was to a very large extent prevented by the Cocom rules of the Cold War years. The isolation of East Germany was partly self-induced and partly imposed from outside. Technically speaking, the GDR was using a low-level production function that prevented it from producing profitably as soon as factors of production had to be paid for at prices close to world market levels.

Wrong Prices

The fourth and possibly most important reason for the sudden collapse of the economy is the change in relative prices that occurred when East Germany became integrated into the world trading system. The Eastern Bloc's trading system, the Comecon, was a self-contained entity, with relative scarcities of the primary factors of production (capital, labor, and natural resources) different from those in the Western countries. The explicit and implicit terms of trade between the factors and between the goods these factors were used to produce were therefore also different. In addition, many of the price ratios were distorted on ideological grounds.[28] Even if an East German firm had minimized its factor cost under the exchange relationships of their own economic environment, it would not have been able to survive under the new world market conditions without substantial reorganization investment.

For one thing, the new prices and trade possibilities brought about the collapse of the trading network within East Germany and between it and the other former Comecon countries. It is always an advantage for one of the trading partners to sever old trading relationships when prices change. It will be a very difficult task to weave a new trading network that provides the single firm with the environment it needs for profitable operation.

For another thing, the new price ratios made it necessary to make changes in the factor combinations and in the range of goods produced

---

28. For a long time the GDR found it difficult to accept that the interest rate is the price of capital. An interest rate was only introduced when a new planning system (NÖSPL) was set up in the 1960s. This rate, coyly called the "production fund rate," was kept below Western levels. Other politically motivated interventions were massive subsidies and luxury taxes (see chapter 3).

which could not easily be made in the short run because of the putty-clay nature of investment processes.[29]

New factor-price ratios imply new minimum-cost combinations of the factors used. But in order for these new combinations to be introduced, there must be reorganization investment. Without reorganization investment it is impossible for East German firms to avoid losses in the new circumstances even if, despite the isolation of the old Comecon area, they had had the same technological knowledge and the same incentive and wage systems as Western firms when their plants were first established. Western firms would also have survival problems if they were faced all at once with factor-price ratios different from those that prevailed in their "putty states."

The problem of the wrong factor prices is closely related to that of the wrong goods prices in the Eastern Bloc's economic system, to which the production of the GDR combines was adapted. If the combines had chosen the range of products that was efficient under the then-existing conditions, they would have allocated the factors over the various products so as to maximize their revenues. But the allocation that maximized revenues under the old price structure did not do so under the new one. As rapid change was not possible, bankruptcies were inevitable, just as they would have been for Western firms unexpectedly faced with Eastern prices. Appendix C analyzes these relationships in more detail.

A fundamental change in the structure of East Germany's production and its foreign trade relationships is unavoidable if structures are to be established that are viable at world market prices.

Aspects of Structural Change

Structural change in the East German economy, which was described in general terms in the previous section, has many aspects. While a book could be written from a managerial perspective describing the changes necessary in production planning, organizational structure, and marketing arrangements, from the perspective of economics the changes to be emphasized are those in foreign trade and in the economy's sectoral patterns.[30]

---

29. The putty-clay hypothesis says that factors of production are easily substitutable before a production process is set up (they are then soft, like putty) but not after it has been established (they then become hard, like clay).

30. See also Kantzenbach 1990.

The Breakdown of Comecon Trade

At first sight the GDR appears to have been an active exporter. According to its own statistics, exports made up 40 percent of its GDP in 1989, and this seems very large when compared with the FRG's ratio of 29 percent.[31] However, it should be realized that a small country normally exports relatively more than a large one, because its borders are longer relative to its economic area. In comparison with the export ratios of the Netherlands and Belgium, which are respectively 60 percent and 70 percent,[32] 40 percent does not seem so very large. In addition, the exports in the official GDR statistics were denominated in valutamarks (foreign-exchange marks), which did not correspond to purchasing-power parities. Estimating the GDR's national product and exports at West German prices results in export ratios of between 22 percent and 24 percent for 1988.[33] These calculations show that, while the GDR's export activity was not small, it was not so well developed as in comparable Western countries.

About half of the GDR's exports went to other Comecon countries; the other half went to the West.[34] The bulk of the exports were industrial products, particularly machinery and transport vehicles. Imports were mainly raw materials and fuels. The country patterns of imports and exports were roughly the same, because trade agreements were bilateral, and, except for minor swings, the trade account of the GDR was normally balanced.

Trade with the FRG made up approximately one-seventh of the GDR's foreign trade. It was about DM 7 billion in the year before unification, when total foreign trade was a good DM 40 billion.[35] Trade with the Soviet Union was more important than trade with the FRG; it amounted to more than half of the GDR's total trade with the East. According to some

31. See appendix A.
32. Calculated from Sachverständigenrat 1990, pp. 325, 332.
33. See *DIW Wochenbericht* 12/91, March 21, 1991, p. 127, and Filip-Köhn and Ludwig 1990. The latter reference also calculated the labor component in the West German and East German export industries. The figures are similar: 27% for the GDR and 25% for the old FRG.
34. According to the official GDR statistics, in 1988, 46% went to Western industrial countries (including West Germany), 6% to developing countries, and 45% to Comecon countries. See *Statistisches Jahrbuch für die Bundesrepublik Deutschland 1990*, p. 653. Table 2.5 shows 58% of GDR exports of manufactured goods going to other Comecon countries.
35. *Statistisches Jahrbuch für die Bundesrepublik Deutschland 1990*, p. 653 f.; *Ifo-Schnelldienst* 18/91, June 27, 1991, p. 17.

Table 2.5
Export ratios in the GDR (percentages, 1988).

Industry branch	All countries	East	West[a]
Total manufacturing	23.8	13.7	10.1
Energy and fuel	2.1	1.0	1.0
Chemicals	26.2	11.5	14.7
Metallurgy	18.5	4.0	14.5
Building materials	9.1	4.5	4.6
Machinery and transport vehicles	36.4	29.5	6.9
Electrical machinery and appliances	25.5	16.9	8.6
Light industry	27.2	11.6	15.5
Textiles	20.1	10.2	9.9
Food	2.9	0.8	2.1

a. Including developing countries and FRG.
Source: *DIW Wochenbericht* 12/91, March 21, 1991, p. 127.

estimates, up to 900,000 jobs were directly or indirectly dependent on exports to the Soviet Union.[36]

Comecon, the Council for Mutual Economic Assistance, no longer exists.[37] On June 28, 1991, it was formally disbanded after the flow of trade had collapsed. It had set up a system of transfer prices and terms of trade that deviated markedly from world market prices and thus, as mentioned above, gave the trading partners strong incentives to break away from the old contracts.

The German government has been trying to give the impression that the breakup of Comecon was one of the most important causes of depression in East Germany. In fact, however, the causation seems to have been in the opposite direction. The sudden and complete removal of restraints on trade between the two Germanies had made East Germany the Achilles' heel of Comecon. While East Germany's exports could be maintained during the whole of 1990 thanks to generous subsidies from the federal government, the survival crisis which East Germany's economy faced after the currency conversion was transferred in all its severity to East German imports from the Comecon countries. Imports valued in deutschmarks fell just as precipitously as East German industrial production—that is, by about two-thirds from the end of 1989 to the end of 1991.[38]

36. *DIW Wochenbericht* 12/91, March 21, 1991, p. 127.
37. There is an early analysis of the significance of the collapse of the GDR for Comecon in Welfens 1990.
38. See figures 2.3 and 2.4.

Admittedly, the fall in value terms is partly due to a fall in the deutsch-mark value of the transferable ruble used as the unit of account in Eastern Bloc trade. However, as this value fell by 50 percent after the monetary union and trade with the Eastern Bloc was about 50 percent of East Germany's total foreign trade, this effect can account for no more than 25 percent of the fall in the value of imports. A real import effect of at least minus 45 percent still remains—about the same percentage as the fall in GDP.

The reduction in imports from the Eastern Bloc countries nevertheless was probably more than 45 percent, because the import boom that was occurring at the same time in Germany as a whole suggests that direct GDR imports from the West were to some extent replaced with indirect imports via West German firms which are not included in the import statistics. Thus, it seems safe to conclude that East Germany's real imports from other Comecon countries fell by 50 percent or more, while its real exports remained approximately the same.[39] The fall in exports followed that in imports with a lag of 6 months. By the beginning of 1991, German export subsidies had been discontinued, and the collapse of Comecon initiated by the stoppage of East German imports was beginning to have repercussions on East German exports. Figure 2.4 illustrates these developments.

Structural Change and Redundancy

Production that was no longer profitable and incentives to break old contracts not only undermined trade with the Eastern Bloc countries; they also affected supplier relationships and patterns of production within East Germany, and these will have to be completely reorganized during the transformation phase. Competition in the West is fierce and relentless, and in the long run it allows firms to make little profit over and above the normal interest on their own or borrowed capital. Competitive pressures result in production patterns that meet the conditions for maximizing revenues and minimizing costs and make full use of the best available technological knowledge. As long as the less mobile factors of production in East Germany can be paid less than in West Germany, it is both possible and sensible to keep on working with production patterns different from those in West Germany. (See chapter 5 for an extensive discussion of this problem.) In the long run, however, such patterns cannot survive. Internal German trade, locational competition, movement of workers, and flexible

---

39. See *Ifo-Schnelldienst* 18/91, June 27, 1991, p. 18, where it is stated that East German imports fell by two-thirds.

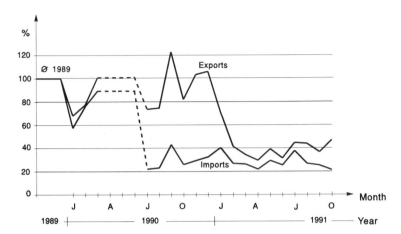

Figure 2.4
The collapse of East German trade. Source: Gemeinsames Statistisches Amt, *Monatszahlen* 5/91, p. 27, and 12/91, p. 68. *Note:* No data are available for the months of April, May, and June 1990; however, in the annual report of the Statistical Office, their average values were given as equal to (or were equated with) the corresponding figures for March. The imports and exports shown in the diagram are defined to exclude the internal German trade flows and indicate the development of the deutschmark values. The average value of imports for 1989 was set at 100.

investment decisions will force most factor and goods prices to adjust, and during this process production patterns will also adjust.

Table 2.6 provides a starting point for an examination of the long-term changes that are likely to come. It compares the sectoral employment patterns in the two parts of the country. The changes will obviously have to be very large.

Compared with West Germany, East German employment is very high in agriculture, forestry and fishing, mining, machinery production, textiles, and railways. These sectors formerly absorbed a large part of the work force in the West also. However, high wages put pressure on firms to reduce the number of employees and switch over to capital-intensive forms of production. In West Germany the labor released went into the distributive trades and the service sector, including banking, insurance, catering, and the numerous consulting professions that characterize modern economies.[40] There are also many differences in the smaller sectors caused by

---

40. In the communist ideology these sectors are "unproductive" (though not useless) and do not appear in the national accounts. Planning authorities who liked to boast of their measurable growth results were not interested in developments in these unproductive sectors. For the Marxist ideology underlying the distinction between productive and unproductive sectors see Sweezy 1959.

Table 2.6
Structural differences between East and West Germany.

Sectoral composition of labor market (percentages employed)	East Germany[a]	West Germany[b]	Redundancies[c]
Agriculture, forestry, fishing	9.9	4.2	5.7
Energy and mining	3.2	1.4	
Electricity, gas, water	1.3	0.8	0.5
Mining[d]	1.9	0.6	1.3
Manufacturing	34.1	29.7	
Chemicals, nuclear materials	1.6	2.0	—
Petroleum refining	0.6	0.1	0.5
Rubber, plastics	1.0	1.4	—
Stone and clay	1.0	0.7	0.3
Glass, porcelain	0.7	0.5	0.2
Metal working and forming	2.0	2.4	—
Steel and light metals	1.2	0.6	0.6
Machinery	5.9	3.9	2.0
Vehicle manufacture and repair	2.2	4.1	—
Electrical engineering	4.3	3.7	0.6
Office equipment, computers	0.6	0.3	0.3
Instruments, optics	0.6	0.9	—
Iron and sheet metal products	1.2	1.1	0.1
Wood and paper, printing	2.2	2.9	—
Musical instruments, toys	0.7	0.2	0.5
Clothing, leather	2.1	1.3	0.8
Textiles	2.3	0.8	1.5
Food	3.6	2.8	0.8
Construction	6.1	6.6	—
Trade	7.8	14.5	
Wholesale trade, agencies	2.8	5.1	—
Retail trade	5.0	9.4	—
Transport	6.8	5.6	
Railways[e]	2.6	1.0	1.6
Shipping, harbors	0.4	0.2	0.2
Other transport	2.4	2.5	—
Communications	1.4	1.9	—
Services, government, nonprofit organizations	32.4	38.0	
Banking, insurance[f]	0.7	4.4	—
Hotels, restaurants	1.9	3.7	—
Health and veterinary services[g]	4.1	5.1	—
Advisory services	1.4	4.8	—
Other services	3.1	4.9	—

Table 2.6 (continued)

Sectoral composition of labor market (percentages employed)	East Germany[a]	West Germany[b]	Redundancies[c]
Education and science	6.8	4.9	1.9
Social institutions	1.7	1.1	0.6
Culture, media, sport	1.4	1.1	0.3
Public administration[h]	5.1	6.6	—
Other government services (X-area)[i]	4.2	0	4.2
Churches, associations, parties[j]	2.0	1.4	0.6
Total	100.0	100.0	25.1

a. *DIW Wochenbericht* 17/90, p. 243. The DIW relies on figures from the Zentralverwaltung für Statistik der DDR, Bericht über die Berufstätigen in der DDR, September 30, 1989. Apprentices are not included.
b. Statistisches Bundesamt: *Unternehmen und Arbeitsstätten*, Arbeitsstättenzählung, May 25, 1987, Fachserie 2, Heft 4; *Bevölkerung und Erwerbstätigkeit*, Fachserie 1, Reihe 4.1.1., 1989; *Mikrozensuserhebung* 1987.
c. Positive differences between East German and West German rates.
d. Including uranium mining.
e. Including Reichsbahn-Sparkasse.
f. Including social insurance.
g. Including university hospitals.
h. Including police and ministry for social security, excluding soldiers.
i. Other government areas not included in official statistics. DIW estimate. The total number of employed according to this information therefore was 9.3 million instead of 8.9 million. (More recent estimates of the Bundesanstalt für Arbeit, Nuremberg, even imply a total initial employment of 9.7 million.)
j. Including the so-called mass organizations of the GDR.

differing relative scarcities, ideological motives (education or X-areas[41]), or simply bad planning.

In the last columns of the table, the positive differences between the East German and West German sectoral employment rates are shown. These differences provide a measure of the redundancies that must occur in East Germany if a structure similar to that of West Germany is to evolve. In total, the redundancies make up about 25 percent of the East German workforce. At first sight it may seem that this number is able to explain most of the East German employment drop. Closer scrutiny, however, shows that this is not so. For one thing, the rate of redundancies cannot be equated with the actual decline in employment, since the redundancies will not occur all at the same time. If they occur sequentially and the unemployed move continuously into other jobs, then the measured unemploy-

41. See note i of table 2.6.

ment will always be smaller than 25 percent. For another thing, the actual decline in employment has been much larger than 25 percent. As was mentioned above, in June 1992 employment in East Germany was hardly more than half of what it used to be, and yet the end of the decline was not visible. Thus, the current East German unemployment cannot be explained simply as the result of the demands made by structural change. In the chapters that follow, a detailed analysis of the possible reasons for the excessively high level of unemployment will be undertaken.

Capital for Unity

When the wall came down, labor moved to where the capital was. Now that the whole communist system has collapsed, capital has also started moving to where the labor is. Capital is scarce in East Germany, but skilled labor (or at least labor that can quickly become skilled) is abundant, and there is a potential for lucrative investment. Only with a gigantic investment program will it be possible to carry out the necessary structural changes in the East German economy. One of the safest predictions an economist could make is that the investment opportunities will be taken up as soon as the conditions for a stable market economy are established—especially clearly defined, guaranteed property rights and competitive factor prices. Capital will then soon start flowing eastward, fed by savings and depreciation originating in Western countries and diverted from rival uses there. It will take a long time before the Eastern countries are able to finance their own investments with their own savings.

Despite all its problems, East Germany will absorb a substantial part of the capital flowing eastward. With unrestricted transfer of technical knowledge and a pattern of skills similar to that of West Germany assumed, capital per head in the eastern parts of the country can be expected to eventually reach West German levels. In West Germany, the value of net fixed assets was DM 5.85 trillion in 1989—that is, with a population of 62.3 million, capital per head was DM 93,900. To reach the same level of capital intensity, East Germany, with a population of 16.4 million, will need, under 1989 conditions, a capital stock of DM 1.54 trillion.[42]

Not all of this capital stock will have to be built up from scratch. The official value of the East German stock of capital in 1989 was given as DM 1.75 trillion with an exchange rate of 1 : 1. If this figure represented the true market value, no capital would have to be imported at all; but this is, for

---

42. For the data on which these and the following calulations are based, see appendix A.

the reasons already discussed, not the case, of course. The East German capital stock is fairly obsolete and in any case was meant for methods of production that have little in common with the kind of specialization required of an internationally competitive economy. In an earlier study, Siebert (1990) conjectured that 50 percent of the East German capital stock was obsolete. According to the calculations made by the East Berlin Institute for Applied Economic Research (IAW), no less than 67 percent would have to be written off under West German accounting rules.[43] The value of the present capital stock would then be DM 578 billion, and the amount of investment required would be DM 962 billion.[44]

It should be noted that these figures have been calculated under static conditions, so that the additional investment needed to allow for economic growth has not been included. The interest-rate effects, which will appear only after capital transfer has taken place, have also not been considered. Capital will flow to East Germany not simply because it is needed, but because it is scarce and therefore can be used more profitably there than elsewhere. One trillion deutschmarks is a rough estimate of the long-term demand overhang that would have appeared under the funding conditions of 1989. It is possible that, because of the overhang, interest rates will have to increase, and this increase will both divert capital away from alternative uses in the West and reduce the demand for capital in the East until a new equilibrium between the total demand for capital and the existing capital stock is reached.

The interest-rate effect is all the more important because, during the transition to the new equilibrium, the capital market will be faced with an additional demand for public borrowing both for infrastructure development[45] and for the financing of income transfers aimed at mitigating the social hardships of the transition period. It will be many years, perhaps even decades, before adjustment to the new equilibrium is completed.

---

43. Institut für angewandte Wirtschaftsforschung (IAW), *Die ostdeutsche Wirtschaft 1990/ 1991*. Like so many other institutions, this institute will soon be closed. The successor will be the Institut für Wirtschaftsforschung in Halle (IWH).

44. See Sinn 1990.

45. The amount of capital needed for infrastructure investment is difficult to determine because the stock in the West is not reported. Assuming the same capital coefficients and the same depreciation rates as in the private sector, and a government share in GDP of one-third, the amount required becomes half that of private investment, that is, DM 500 billion. The total capital requirements for private and public purposes would then be about DM 1.5 trillion, which is very close to the estimate of DM 1.7 trillion made by the International Monetary Fund (1990).

Real interest rate [%]

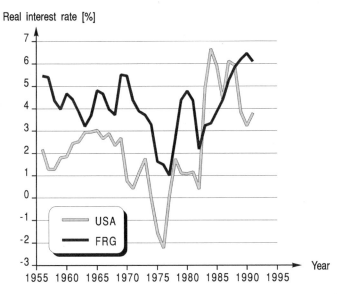

Figure 2.5
The effect of unification on interest rates. Source: OECD, *Main Economic Indicators*. *Note:*
The "real interest rate" is defined as the yield on outstanding long-term government
bonds minus the average inflation rate (consumer price index) of the previous three years
in each case.

Figure 2.5 illustrates the first effects of the high demand for capital by
comparing the development of the long-term real interest rate in Germany
and the United States. In 1991, the German real interest rate was at a
historical high of over 6 percent. To find a similar level in the past it is
necessary to go back to the early years of the Federal Republic, which was
founded in 1948. The rate has certainly not been at such a high level since
the middle of the 1950s. The German real interest rate is now equal to that
in the US in 1984, which created extremely large disturbances in world
capital markets in the years that followed.[46] As a result of the current
worldwide recession, US interest rates have fallen sharply since the third
quarter of 1990. This fall in interest rates will certainly spread to Germany,
but the differences in yields seem likely to be in Germany's favor for the
foreseeable future. The difference in yields is necessary to induce the international flow of capital to change direction.

The enormous drain on the German capital market is also reflected in the
statistics relating to the use of private savings (figure 2.6). After the expan-

46. See Sinn 1984, 1989.

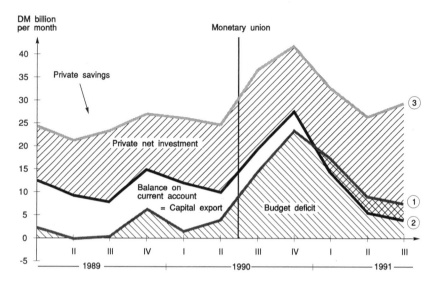

Figure 2.6
The squeeze on the current-account balance. Sources: *Monatsberichte der Deutschen
Bundesbank* 42, no. 2, February 1990, and no. 12, December 1991; Statistisches Bundesamt,
Volkswirtschaftliche Gesamtrechnungen, Fachserie 18, Reihe 3, Quarterly GDP data, third
quarter 1991; *DIW Wochenbericht* 7/92; Treuhandanstalt, various press releases. *Notes:*
Curve 1: Net borrowing in the government budget including the German Unity Fund and
the GDR budget (new borrowing from 7/1/90 to 10/2/91): quarterly data. Curve 2: Net
borrowing in the government budget plus the current-account balance as defined in the
balance-of-payments statistics. The current-account balance to June 1990 covers the
external transactions of the FRG, excluding the GDR; from July 1990 it covers the
external transactions of the FRG, including the new Länder (quarterly data). Curve 3: Net
borrowing in the government budget plus the current-account balance plus net investment
(equals private savings) (also quarterly data).

sion of the economic area covered by the statistics of the Federal Republic,
private saving, net investment, and the government budget deficit all increased, but the surplus on current account, which also measures net capital
exports, fell.[47] In January 1991 the German balance on current account
was negative for the first time since August 1985, and at the time of this
writing there is every indication that it will remain so in the medium
term.[48] Before unification, private savings had been sufficient to finance

47. When net capital exports are defined as the net increase in all interest-bearing and
non-interest-bearing claims on foreigners, the surplus in the current account equals the
deficit in the capital balance and vice versa.
48. The deficit in the current account at the beginning of 1991 also reflects the nonrecurring
German contribution to support the Gulf War, but this cannot explain the significant change
exhibited by the current-account balance since the spring of 1991.

private investment, the government budget deficit, and a record level of capital exports. After unification, the demand for these savings as a source of finance for private investment and, above all, for the vast increase in the budget deficit rose so much that nothing was left over to finance capital exports. Indeed, a net inflow of resources—capital imports—is now necessary if the domestic demand for funds is to be satisfied.

The change in sign in the current-account balance is a desirable reaction by the markets to the new capital needs in Germany. Because of its former export surplus, Germany is currently, after Japan, the country with the most net foreign assets. These were worth approximately DM 500 billion in 1990—that is, half the amount of private capital needed in East Germany.[49] It makes sense to gradually bring back the German-owned foreign assets by means of a current-account deficit. They could help rebuild the East German economy and avoid the social hardships involved in the reconstruction process.

The repatriation of the capital will be brought about through two major mechanisms. The first comes into operation when the East German demand for goods spills over from the West German market to the international market and causes a rise in imports. The additional imports have to be paid for with foreign exchange, which either has to be borrowed or has to be set free by giving up capital investment overseas. The second mechanism works through the higher level of German interest rates. Higher interest rates attract foreign money capital, but this will mean a net increase in supply on German capital markets only if the foreign currency supplied by the investors is matched by increases in German goods imports or reductions in German goods exports.

The effect of the spillover of the demand for goods is to increase the supply of marks on the foreign-exchange market, and this leads to a devaluation. The devaluation makes capital investments in Germany more attractive and induces the necessary capital imports. The interest-induced attraction of money capital, the second mechanism, increases the supply of foreign currency and leads to a revaluation. The revaluation lowers German competitiveness and reduces the current-account surplus, perhaps even pushing it down to a negative value. This either reduces the supply of foreign exchange or causes the demand for foreign exchange to increase. In any case, whatever is necessary to induce the entry of foreign money

---

49. Deutsche Bundesbank, Statistische Beihefte zu den *Monatsberichten der Deutschen Bundesbank*, Reihe 3, *Zahlungsbilanzstatistik*, no. 3, March 1991. The corresponding value for Japan is, on the basis of a rough estimate of the current-account balances, approximately DM 1 trillion. See OECD, *Main Economic Indicators* 1982, 1985, 1990.

capital into the German capital market will take place. The net effect of the two mechanisms on the exchange rate is not clear. It is clear, however, that the current-account balance will deteriorate.

The change in sign of the current-account balance that occurred in 1991 is probably the result of the operation of the first mechanism—the drain on imports. The external value of the mark has been rising since the border was opened,[50] but the rise has been unsteady and has not been very strong. Moreover, as is well known, a deterioration in the current-account balance that follows a revaluation will occur only after a considerable time lag. In the first few months, an anomalous current-account reaction has to be reckoned with because of the effect of revaluation on the dollar value of real German exports, the quantity of which is fixed in the short run. Since the deterioration in the current account appeared suddenly, it likely is the result of an increase in imports.[51]

This does not mean that the capital imports attracted by rises in interest rates played no role at all. On the contrary, they made it possible to finance the increase in goods imports. Without the interest-rate increase, the inflow of money capital would have had to be induced by a devaluation, or else the central bank would itself have had to induce it by selling foreign currency to support the mark.

In the medium term, when the present obstacles to investment have been overcome and the reaction of the current-account balance has become normal, the effects of the capital imports, attracted by expectations of high real domestic rates of returns to capital, can be expected to dominate the trade effects. The latent demand for capital with which to renovate and rebuild the East German economy is so large that a rapid unleashing of this demand will certainly lead, on balance, to a large increase in the demand for marks on the foreign-exchange markets, a correspondingly large rise in the value of the mark, and a persistent current-account deficit.[52]

The effects that can be expected are very similar to those caused in the United States by the US investment-incentive policy of the 1980s. Then, capital was attracted to the United States by artificial investment incentives established deliberately by means of the Accelerated Cost Recovery System. These incentives were the cause of the high interest rates of 1984, the

---

50. *Monatsberichte der Deutschen Bundesbank* 43, no. 12, December 1991, p. 43.

51. This is also confirmed by an empirical study made by Gros (1991).

52. In the very long term, the value of the mark naturally must fall again, and the trade balance improve, to avoid the permanent current-account deficit that would otherwise result from the reduction in the interest income earned abroad. See Wyplosz 1991 and Melitz 1991.

explosion in the value of the dollar in 1985 (the exchange rate was then 3.45 DM/$, more than twice today's value), and the persistent deterioration of the US current-account balance. Now, capital is being attracted to East Germany by natural investment incentives. The American demand for capital had a strong influence on world economic development in the 1980s. The East German demand for capital, and the demand by other Eastern European countries, will have a similar influence in the decades to follow.

3   New Money

Currency Conversion

The "disaster" (as it was later called by Bundesbank president Karl-Otto Pöhl)[1] began in the following way: The two parts of Germany were joined in a monetary, economic, and social union which came into force on July 1, 1990. The next day all ostmarks were converted into deutschmarks.[2] The number of marks that could be exchanged at a rate of 1:1 was limited to 2000 for children under the age of 15, to 4000 for adults under 60, and to 6000 for people over 59. Most of the remainder of the money stock was exchangeable at a rate of 2:1, with the exception that money acquired for speculation in the year of unification could only be exchanged at 3:1. Financial claims and debts were converted at a rate of 2:1; these were mainly firms' debts (which amounted to 260 billion ostmarks) and housing loans (108 billion). The rate for price and wage contracts and pensions was 1:1. Pensions were based on East German wages but calculated according to West German formulas.

From a political point of view, the goals of monetary union were to ensure that unification would proceed and to make it clear to the East German people that there were no longer economic reasons for them to migrate to West Germany.[3]

---

1. In a statement made to the Economic and Monetary Committee of the European Parliament on March 19, 1991. A similar comment was made by the chairman of the Treuhand, Detlev Karsten Rohwedder, on January 7, 1991—he spoke of a "catastrophic change in output potential."
2. The average exchange rate was officially calculated as 1.8:1 (*Monatsberichte der Deutschen Bundesbank* 42, no. 7, July 1990). According to alternative calculations it was 1.6:1 (Bofinger 1991, p. 3).
3. For a critical discussion of these goals see Richter 1990.

From an economic point of view, monetary union had, in effect, three aims[4]:

• The wage conversion was supposed to establish and/or maintain the competitiveness of the East German economy.

• The currency conversion was supposed to provide the combined economy with the right amount of liquidity.

• The conversion of financial claims was supposed to furnish the East German population with a fair amount of capital for their entry into the united Germany.

Achieving all three aims simultaneously would itself have been a difficult enough task; trying to do this by regulating a single policy instrument— the currency conversion rate—made it a quite impossible one. It was, therefore, hardly surprising that heated discussions took place among economists and politicians concerning the details of how monetary union was to be achieved. The solution finally reached was a compromise between the view of the government, which had officially come down in favor of a 1 : 1 conversion rate, and that of the Bundesbank, which had reservations about monetary union and would have preferred a much worse exchange rate for the ostmark.

The international press was extremely skeptical about this compromise. The exchange rate finally agreed on was seen as far too generous in view of the black-market rate, which at the beginning of the year had been 7 : 1 or higher. It was generally expected that the too-favorable rate would enable the East Germans to make very large capital gains, and that, as a result, there would be a sharp increase in demand, followed inevitably by a burst of inflation.[5]

The Bundesbank shared these fears and had argued for a very restrictive conversion policy. In the event, however, the fears did not materialize. There were certainly strong temporary substitution effects in favor of West German products in the first few months after the currency conversion, but they were neither caused by capital gains nor associated with a significant increase in the propensity to consume in East Germany. (See figure 3.2.) The rate of inflation as measured by the consumer price index in the

---

4. Good accounts of arguments for monetary union and the preparations undertaken are to be found in Burda 1990, Claassen 1990, Kloten 1991, and Lipschitz and McDonald 1990. See also Sinn 1990.

5. However, these fears were not shared by everyone. See e.g. Wissenschaftlicher Beirat 1990, p. 1498; Burda 1990; Läufer 1990.

unification year was a moderate 2.8 percent.[6] In 1991 and 1992 this rate climbed to more than 4 percent, but there were none of the dramatic developments that had been predicted. A weak economic boom in West Germany was accompanied by the deep slump in East Germany which was described in the previous chapter. Never before in the history of any industrial country had there been such a large, sudden decline in peacetime economic activity.

This chapter discusses the three aims of currency conversion mentioned above and critically examines the political means chosen for achieving them. To set the stage for the discussion, the next two sections look at the pre-unification purchasing-power parities and exchange rates.

Purchasing-Power Parities

Those who had predicted an enormous gain for East German savers, and who thought that this would result in a wave of inflation, were obviously wrong. The current deep depression in East Germany and the moderate inflation in West Germany make this quite clear. The main reason for the mistake was that nobody really knew what the values of the East and West German currencies were in terms of their relative purchasing power. Many politicians and commentators had simply assumed that this relative purchasing power was reflected by the black-market rate, not realizing that, on the eve of the collapse of the GDR, what this rate reflected was nothing but speculative expectations.[7]

It has been more and more evident that the quality-adjusted purchasing-power parity between the two currencies was, in fact, very close to 1:1 even though the black-market rate was 7:1, or even in some cases 11:1, immediately after the wall was broken down. Indeed, there is reason to suspect that the ostmark may even have been worth more than the deutschmark in terms of the basket of goods purchased by the average East German worker.[8] Table 3.1 gives an overview of some comparisons of purchasing power made by different bodies.

---

6. *Monatsberichte der Deutschen Bundesbank* 43, no. 2, February 1991, and 44, no. 2, February 1992.

7. An econometric analysis of the speculative expectations can be found in Burda and Gerlach 1990.

8. This is not to say that if unification had not taken place the free exchange rate would have been 1:1. The actual exchange rate could have differed substantially from purchasing-power parity because of capital movements and differences between baskets of goods traded and those consumed at home. See the following section.

Table 3.1
Purchasing-power comparisons.

DIW[a]	100 ostm. = 120 DM	Price changes expected from unification, East German basket of goods expected after unification
Ifo[b]	100 ostm. = 98 DM	Price changes expected from unification, East German basket of goods before unification
DIW[c]	100 ostm. = 128 DM	Actual price changes in East Berlin from January to July 1990, East German basket of goods before unification
Joint Statistical Office[d]		East German basket of goods before unification, actual price changes, from average 1989 to …
	100 ostm. = 97 DM	July 1990
	100 ostm. = 102 DM	December 1990
	100 ostm. = 109 DM	January 1991
	100 ostm. = 127 DM	October 1991
Bundesbank[e]	100 ostm. = 107 DM	East German basket of goods before unification
Federal Statistical Office[f]		Purchasing-power parity in May 1990 with adjustment for quality
	100 ostm. = 132 DM	East German basket of goods
	100 ostm. = 88 DM	West German basket of goods
	100 ostm. = 108 DM	geometric mean

a. *DIW Wochenbericht* 21/90, May 25, 1990, p. 294.
b. *Ifo-Schnelldienst* 43, 13/90, May 7, 1990, pp. 24–26.
c. *DIW Wochenbericht* 32/90, August 9, 1990, pp. 446–450.
d. Gemeinsames Statistisches Amt, *Monatszahlen* 5/91, p. 18, and 12/91, p. 62, Preisindex für die Lebenshaltung.
e. According to information from K. Köhler, member of the Board of Directors of the Bundesbank, in a public lecture given at the Economics Faculty of the University of Munich, May 5, 1990.
f. Statistisches Bundesamt, *Zahlen, Fakten, Trends: Extra* 9/90-2.

Exact comparisons of purchasing power are extremely difficult because the baskets of goods consumed in the two parts of the country differed so much. One reason for this was the difference in real incomes. Luxuries constitute a smaller proportion of purchases made from low real incomes than from high ones. Another reason was the difference in relative prices. In the GDR basic foodstuffs and other essentials were subsidized to the tune of more than 66 billion marks annually, while luxury goods were faced with special consumption taxes totaling 43 billion marks.[9] This meant, for example, that a television set cost three times as much as in West Germany,

9. See appendix A.

while a loaf of bread cost only one-sixth as much. The relative price differences were particularly striking in the case of housing. Before unification, West German households spent 26 percent of their three-times-higher incomes on rent, while East German households spent only 5 percent. To be sure, the quality of housing differed considerably; however, a comparison of housing of similar quality reveals that rents in East Germany before unification were only 24 percent of their Western equivalents.[10]

It is known that purchasing-power comparisons favor the currency of the country whose basket of goods is being used, because consumption patterns change as relative prices change. This shows up clearly in the calculations of the Federal Statistical Office listed in table 3.1. The value of the ostmark varies between 0.88 and 1.32 deutschmarks, depending on which basket of goods is used. Neither of these estimates can show precisely how many deutschmarks an East German would need in exchange for 100 ostmarks in order to buy, at West German prices, goods that would give him the same amount of utility as goods he would have bought in the GDR. If he got 132 deutschmarks he could buy exactly the same basket of goods he bought before for 100 ostmarks, but he would not want to do this. He would be better off buying more of the goods that are now relatively cheaper and fewer of the goods that are now relatively more expensive. Less than 132 deutschmarks would therefore have been sufficient to compensate him for giving up 100 ostmarks. If, on the other hand, he had received only 88 deutschmarks, he would have been disadvantaged. Only if an East German had been limited to spending his ostmarks in a way similar to the way West Germans spent their money would 88 deutschmarks have been sufficient to compensate for the loss of 100 ostmarks. However, there was no such limitation. Given East Germany's price structure and income level, the East German decided on a different basket of goods and must therefore have been receiving more value for his 100 ostmarks than he would have received for 88 deutschmarks. It therefore follows from the Statistical Office's calculations that the exchange rate that would have maintained utility levels must have been somewhere between 1:1.32 and 1:0.88. The Statistical Office established the geometric mean as 1:1.08, which may well have been a reasonable estimate of the utility-related exchange rate.

Besides the question of the different combinations of goods in the consumers' baskets, many other problems are involved in attempting to compare the purchasing powers of the East and West German currencies.

---

10. Statistisches Bundesamt, *Zahlen, Fakten, Trends: Extra* 9/90-2.

A very important one is the difference in quality of goods produced in the East and the West. It would certainly not be sensible to compare a Mercedes with a Trabant. However, as far as we know, the Federal Statistical Office did not include such comparisons in its calculations. On the contrary, wherever possible, comparisons were made between goods in equivalent quality categories, and where there were no such equivalents the quality differences were translated into equivalent quantity adjustments. It is not possible to judge whether these adjustments were the right size.

A further problem relates to the availability of goods in the GDR. It is, of course, obvious that goods that are cheap but unavailable cannot be consumed and therefore cannot distort the purchasing-power comparison in favor of the ostmark. However, rationed goods often carry with them the time costs of having to wait in line. These time costs should really be added to the prices of the goods, but as far as we know none of the studies have done this. If, for example, it is assumed that waiting time is equal to 10 percent of working time (that is, that a family with two members in the work force must spend the equivalent of one working day each week queuing up to buy things), then, including the expenditure of time, goods produced in East Germany would have cost 10 percent more. Instead of $1:1.32$, purchasing-power parity in terms of the East German basket of goods would have been $1.1:1.32$, or $1:1.2$. The geometric mean of the purchasing-power parities of the two different baskets of goods would have been $1.1:1.08$, or $1:0.98$.[11]

A third problem relates to the question of the speed at which East German prices adjusted to those in West Germany after unification. Strictly speaking, the Federal Statistical Office's purchasing-power parities show how ostmarks must be converted into deutschmarks if an East German saver who moves to West Germany is to be compensated. This exchange rate is not necessarily the same as the one that would have compensated a saver who stayed in East Germany after unification, because not all East German prices adjusted quickly to West German levels. After the initial $1:1$ conversion of ostmark prices into deutschmark prices, the deutschmark

---

11. Collier (1986) showed that East Germans would have been prepared to accept a 13% reduction in their nominal income in return for the removal of rationing. It might therefore seem that a purchasing power parity of $1:1.15$ (East:West) would have been more appropriate than $1:1.32$, but this is not the case. As the removal of rationing would have increased the weight in the purchasing-power comparison of those goods formerly supplied at less than equilibrium prices, the measured purchasing power of the ostmark would have risen rather than declined. It is wrong to assume that the percentage calculated by Collier must be subtracted from the measured purchasing-power of the ostmark in order to get its actual purchasing power.

prices of mobile goods (such as food and consumer durables) quickly reached West German levels. However, some prices, including rents and administrative fees, were temporarily frozen at their old levels for political reasons, and others adjusted slowly because commodity and labor arbitrage were hindered by transaction costs. As a result, there are still considerable differences in the price levels and structures in the two parts of the country. Most of the other comparisons of purchasing power shown in table 3.1 attempt to take this situation into account. They show the exchange rate that would satisfy an East German money owner who continued to benefit from low East German prices. With the exception of the calculations of the Bundesbank and the Federal Statistical Office, the purchasing-power parities shown in the table are therefore not exactly identical to those that are usually referred to in inter-country comparisons. They measure, instead, the expected or actual numerical price changes that accompanied unification.

The first two numbers reported in the table (Ifo and DIW) were early forecasts of these price changes.[12] The publications of the Joint Statistical Office have now made it possible to confront these forecasts with *ex post* data. These data show that the Ifo's estimate of $1:0.98$ was appropriate at the time of monetary union (July 1990) but that it has since been superseded. Over the period from monetary union to October 1991, the price index of goods supplied in East Germany rose from 0.97 to 1.27. This is equivalent to an average monthly inflation rate of 1.8 percent or an annual rate of 24 percent![13]

Such a Latin American inflation rate cannot be seen as a confirmation of the fear that East Germans would receive large capital gains from the currency conversion, which would then induce a demand-derived inflationary spiral. What it does indicate is that East German prices are going through a temporary and soon-to-be-completed adjustment process in which the price index is moving from its initial value of 0.97 toward the values calculated by the DIW and the Federal Statistical Office (between 1.2 and 1.32). The fact that the index rose by 30 percentage points within 15 months of monetary union is itself an indication that even a $1:1$ conversion rate would not have created profits for the East German savers. It does not indicate the existence of any such profits!

---

12. A critical analysis of the institutes' methods of calculation can be found in van Suntum 1990.

13. This increase in prices has not yet come to an end; rents have been rising sharply since October 1991.

While it is not possible to determine precisely the exchange rate that would have maintained the real value of East German savings, careful consideration of the available statistical data does not support the widely held view that the purchasing power of the ostmark was well below that of the deutschmark. If there was any significant difference, it was in favor of the East German currency. For all practical purposes, the assumption that the two purchasing powers were the same is, from the point of view of the East Germans, perfectly reasonable.

This finding is not in conflict with the recognition that East Germans actually rated the deutschmark more highly than the ostmark when the deutschmark was scarce and was the only means by which they could buy West German goods. Today the deutschmark is the only means by which they can buy East German goods. The purchasing-power comparison relates to the average values of the currencies when it is assumed that each currency is generally available and is the only medium of exchange in its respective country. The comparison does not relate to the marginal values that result when one currency is the general medium of exchange and the other is scarce as diamonds. The paradox of value can also show up when purchasing powers are being compared.

The Purchasing-Power Paradox

The paradox of value, which every economics student learns to resolve in the first semester, explains the high value placed by the East Germans on the deutschmark at a time when foreign exchange was rationed. It does not explain the internal foreign-exchange calculations used by the East German authorities, which were made public at the end of 1989. Officially, East Germany had always had a conversion rate of 1:1, and the price structure of its goods was set up so as to ensure that the two currencies had the same purchasing power. However, as the Modrow government eventually admitted, when East German goods were to be sold in the West, then, tacitly, much lower exchange rates for the ostmark had to be used. In this connection, among the confused jumble of exchange rates and settlement coefficients used in planning international trade, the so-called "foreign currency earnings coefficients" are particularly informative. These coefficients specified how many deutschmarks every ostmark used in Western trade could be redeemed for. In 1980 the average value of the foreign currency earnings coefficients was 0.42 for all industrial combines taken together. It fell to 0.35 in 1985, and in 1989 it was only 0.23. The coefficients applying

Table 3.2
Implicit exchange rates for GDR trade: Average deutschmark revenue per 100-ostmark expenditure in costs in GDR export sector ("Foreign currency earnings coefficient" · 100 DM).

1980	1985	1986	1987	1989
42	35	28	23	23

Source: DIW, *DDR-Wirtschaft im Umbruch*, Berlin, January 1990.
Note: The "foreign currency earnings coefficient" (Devisenertragskennziffer) is the inverse of the "foreign currency returns" (Devisenrentabilität). The "trend coefficient" (Richtungskoeffizient) often quoted in this connection is the desired value of foreign-currency returns minus 1.

to individual combines differed considerably. According to Haendcke-Hoppe (1990), the export-intensive Polygraph combine received 0.34 deutschmark per ostmark in 1989, the Zeisswerke 0.27 deutschmark, and the Mikroelektronik combine just 0.14 deutschmark.

It is to be expected that, when foreign trade is profitable and purchasing-power parity is 1:1, the overall foreign currency earnings coefficient will be 1 or more. The fact that it was so far below 1 is very surprising. How was it possible that a basket of consumption goods bought for 100 ostmarks had a value equivalent to 100 deutschmarks while goods costing 100 ostmarks to produce in the East could only manage a return of 23 deutschmarks when they were sold in the West? Is it possible to resolve this purchasing-power paradox?

One possible explanation is that the communist state held the price of consumption goods low by using subsidies financed by running down existing capital stock. According to this hypothesis, the basket of goods worth 100 deutschmarks in the West really cost 430 ostmarks to produce ($\approx$ 100 ostmarks ÷ 0.23) but was subsidized by an amount of 330 ostmarks, the subsidy being financed by not undertaking replacement investment. The subsidy made it possible for the basket of goods to be sold in East Germany for only 100 ostmarks and meant that real incomes could be higher than the level justified by average labor productivity.

No matter how well this hypothesis fits with wishful thinking in the West, it cannot be correct. If it were correct, the net subsidy on consumption goods would have to have been 3.3 times the consumption expenditure—but this was not even approximately the case. The difference between the value of subsidies (66 billion) and the yield from luxury taxes (43 billion) was only 23 billion ostmarks. This is only about 16 percent of the consumption expenditure, not a multiple of it.[14] Moreover, even though the rate of capital accumulation given in the GDR statistics was greatly overstated, it can hardly be assumed that the East German economy was contracting over the whole 40 years of the GDR's existence.

A second hypothesis suggested to explain the purchasing-power paradox is that the foreign currency earnings coefficients were wrong because the combines overstated the costs of producing export goods. It must be remembered that the foreign-trade contracts of the GDR were not made in accordance with the laws of the market, and that from the viewpoint of the export producers there was no relationship between the volume of exports and the production costs. The quantities and prices of exports were determined by government agreements and were set at levels designed to ensure the availability of foreign currency needed to buy Western imports.[15] Normally, export business was handled by special exporting organizations, which then paid the producers in ostmarks. Because the demand for their products appeared to be completely inelastic, the producers had strong incentives to claim high reimbursements by "generating" costs and by adding joint costs associated with other areas of production to the costs of exports. The accuracy of the alleged costs of exports was probably comparable to the accuracy of the costs Western firms report for taxation purposes.

It cannot be denied that this second hypothesis has a lot of merit, but it is doubtful that it can explain the large discrepancy between the purchasing-power parity and the foreign currency earnings coefficient completely. A third hypothesis can be suggested to round out the explanation. This third hypothesis is based on the fact that the prices of traded and nontraded goods differ systematically between rich and poor countries. Balassa (1964) showed that currencies of countries with low labor productivity tend to be undervalued relative to purchasing-power parity because exchange rates do not take into account the relatively low prices of the

14. In 1989 the level of consumption was 146 billion ostmarks, with a net money income of 167.5 billion and a savings rate of 12.7%. (See appendix A.) The absurdity of the capital-consumption hypothesis becomes even more obvious when the underlying level of depreciation it tacitly assumes is calculated. The subsidies required in 1989 alone would have been 482 billion ostmarks (3.3 · 146 billion), and that is equal to no less than 83% of the capital stock of the GDR. The value of this capital stock was calculated as 578 billion ostmarks in chapter 2. The depreciation rate of 85% is 17 times the total economic depreciation rate of 5% calculated for West Germany. See, for example, *Statistisches Jahrbuch 1990 für die Bundesrepublik Deutschland*.
15. See Nattland 1972.

nontraded goods. His findings may well have applied to communist East Germany.

The core of the argument by which Balassa explained his empirical results can easily be understood with the help of the following simple model: There are two countries, Eastland and Westland. Each country produces two goods—a freely tradeable homogeneous industrial good and a nontraded labor-intensive good (for example, haircuts). Factors of production are immobile internationally, and within each country there is a single wage that applies to both sectors. Labor productivity for the traded industrial good, and real wages in units of this good, are higher in Westland than in Eastland, but there is no difference in labor productivity for the nontraded good. In this model, the price of the nontraded good, expressed in units of the traded industrial good, is lower in Eastland than in Westland. The prices are proportional to the domestic wage rates in the respective countries, because the nontraded good is produced mainly with labor and the labor productivity for this good is the same in both countries. The lower wage rate in the less productive country is carried over in the form of a relatively lower price for the nontraded good.

This result has direct implications for the relationship between purchasing-power parity and the exchange rate. Because the latter reflects the purchasing-power parity of goods traded internationally, it cannot at the same time reflect the purchasing-power parity of a bundle of goods that contains both tradeables and nontradeables. A given amount of currency must have a greater purchasing power in the country with lower productivity and a correspondingly lower price for the nontraded good. In other words, a "poor" country's currency is undervalued in terms of its overall purchasing-power parity.[16]

The model's result equates with empirical reality. It is also theoretically very robust, as it can easily be extended to the case of many goods and general productivity differences. It stems primarily from the fact that the relative productivity difference for the traded good is greater than that for the nontraded good. This condition means that the external value of the the less productive country's currency is below purchasing-power parity.

It can be quite plausibly argued that the productivity condition was met in the case of the GDR. Large differences in productivity did not exist in the case of highly labor-intensive goods (such as cultural and recreational

---

16. This is one of the main reasons for the phenomenon of tourism. By turning nontraded goods into traded ones, tourists benefit from the higher purchasing power of their money in less productive countries.

goods, housing, personal services, and foodstuffs), and these goods were not traded with the West. Easily transportable industrial products were, however, exported, and labor productivity for these goods was much higher in the West than in the East because far more capital was used to produce them. Although many of the peculiarities of a centrally planned economy cannot be explained in terms of a market model, Balassa's model does appear to provide a reasonable explanation in the case of the purchasing-power paradox exhibited by the exchange rate of the GDR's currency. If the average foreign currency earnings coefficients are interpreted as exchange rates, then there is no basic conflict between the statement that the equilibrium exchange rate was 1 : 0.23 and the statement that the general purchasing-power parity was 1 : 1.

The Two Dimensions of Competitiveness

Purchasing-power parity and foreign earnings coefficients were important for the conversion of the ostmark into the deutschmark because of the necessity, on the one hand, to maintain the real wage level of East German workers and, on the other, to avoid putting too much strain on the East German economy. Some economists, including the majority of the members of the Economics Ministry Advisory Council (Wissenschaftlicher Beirat 1990), thought that a conversion rate for wages of 1 : 1 was justifiable; others, including the minister of economics and the representatives of the Bundesbank, argued strongly for a conversion rate of 2 : 1, which would have caused real wages to fall to half their former level.[17] It was thought that many wage contracts would be renegotiated soon after the monetary union, but it was generally anticipated that the process of adjustment would be slow and that, therefore, the starting level of wages would have an important role to play during an extended transition period.

All the experts agreed that priority would have to be given to finding a competitive level of wages; however, the problem was that both capital *and* labor markets would have to be made competitive. If both dimensions were taken into account simultaneously, wages would have to be low enough to make East Germany attractive to investors and to prepare its industry for a competitive struggle with West Germany, yet high enough to dam the flood of migration to the West.

The 1 : 1 conversion rate agreed to in the first State Treaty of June 1990 meant that the nominal level of East German wages was one-third of that in West Germany, and that real wages, measured in terms of consumption

17. See also Siebert 1990 or Neumann 1991.

goods, were held at the old GDR level. Because productivity in East Germany was estimated to be between one-third and one-half of that in West Germany, it was believed that this level of wages would be compatible with the survival of many of the East German firms while not providing too great an incentive for westward migration. Unit labor costs equal wages divided by labor productivity. The conversion rate therefore seemed to ensure that unit labor costs in East German industry would be equal to or perhaps even somewhat lower than those in West Germany, and that the East German economy would be competitive right from the start.

Today it is clear that the hopes for a neutral wage conversion have not been realized. The too-soft position on wages had obviously contributed to the wave of bankruptcies and dismissals that had swept over the East German economy. Two mutually reinforcing problems have become very obvious.

The first of these problems is that the initial wage levels turned out to be far too high for the former East German export industries, in which labor productivity was much less than one-third of the West German level. Although the wage conversion rate kept real wages measured by average consumer goods approximately constant, real wages measured in units of export goods rose rapidly with the currency conversion, because the exchange rate of 1:1 was higher than the internal exchange rate that had previously been used for these goods. With given deutschmark prices, the appreciation meant a sharp numerical decrease in the prices of export goods and a dramatic rise in real wages measured in terms of these goods. Because the average exchange rate before unification was 0.23 deutschmark per ostmark, the numerical export-goods prices fell by 77 percent and real wages in terms of export goods more than quadrupled (table 3.2).[18] To say that the dramatic change in the cost situation has endangered the former East German export industries is an understatement. The industries are dying. With the border between East and West gone, expanding the range of goods traded between the two parts of the country may compensate for the decline of the export industries. In principle, this expansion could enable the East German economy to benefit from the low prices of the formerly nontraded labor-intensive goods if these retained their competitive advantage—that is, if nominal wages were kept well below West German levels for the foreseeable future.

---

18. There is a major difference here from the German monetary reform of 1948. Among the reasons for the latter's success was the fact that, after an initial realignment in 1949, it was followed by a long period during which the deutschmark was undervalued. See the set of papers published in Hampe 1989. See also Siebert 1991a.

In the present political circumstances, however, the hope that wages in East Germany can be kept low is a vain one, and herein lies the second problem. In the year of unification, the East German trade unions, advised by the West German umbrella organization, successfully carried out an extremely aggressive wage policy, apparently without any opposition to speak of from the side of the employers.[19] Even before the monetary union, employees had successfully pushed for wage increases of 17 percent —a rate unprecedented in the history of both East and West Germany. After monetary union, wage and salary increases in East Germany accelerated further. Increases of between 25 and 60 percent were negotiated in the second half of 1990. The trade unions had stated that their aim was to have East German wages reach 60 percent of West German union rates as soon as possible, and by 1995 to have the same levels in both parts of the economy. (See chapter 5.)

Since labor productivity in the old firms cannot rise as fast as wages are supposed to, a continuing wave of bankruptcies appears inevitable. With unit labor costs well above (perhaps even double or quadruple) those in West Germany, the bulk of East German industry has no hope of surviving without massive help from the West. This is what the Bundesbank's president meant when he referred to the consequences of the monetary union as a disaster.

The disaster could not, however, have been avoided by simply converting wages at 2:1, as the Bundesbank and the economics minister had wanted. This would have meant that the starting level of real wages in East Germany would have been one-sixth of the West German level, but the wage adjustment would have been faster and the wage situation today would most probably have been no different. Admittedly, the lower starting level would have provided an opportunity for a wider wage spread and thus a wage structure more in line with market conditions than the one that resulted from the 1:1 conversion.

Technically, there were only two possible ways of avoiding the wage cost explosion and making it worthwhile to retain East German jobs. The first would have been not to have a monetary union at all. With an East-West German free-trade area and flexible exchange rates between the currencies, the process of wage inflation and subsequent price inflation could have been neutralized by means of regular depreciations. This solution was politically quite out of the question, for it was feared that not introducing monetary union would not only delay unification but actually prevent it.

---

19. For a detailed discussion of the problem of wage bargaining see chapter 5.

The second solution would have been to put a temporary legal limit on wage increases. Before privatization of East Germany's industries, there is no one who can legally represent the employers in wage negotiations. Putting a legal ceiling on wage increases would therefore have been economically advisable and constitutionally feasible.

Free collective bargaining is guaranteed by the German constitution. Possible limits to this were not on the agenda for the treaty negotiated between the two governments, and, even if they had been, there would have been no consensus in their favor. Because of the increasingly critical economic situation in the former GDR, there is now an urgent need to at least begin discussing some kind of wage-freeze agreement, such as the "Concerted Action" once inaugurated by Economics Minister Karl Schiller. The people of East Germany must be made aware that the aggressive wage policy recommended by West German advisors is a hindrance to them rather than a help. Such a wage policy removes any chance they may have of competing effectively with West German industry and can only result in the destruction of their jobs. The only possible beneficiaries of the policy are the West German unions and employers' organizations, because it effectively protects them from low-wage competition. Nobody in the West would have dreamed of suggesting a low-wage area along the Elbe.

Understandably, the trade unions base their argument for equalizing wages quickly on the other dimension of competitive neutrality—that is, on limiting migration. However justified this argument may be in principle, it is perverse in the present circumstances. The fact that low wages cause migration does not mean that the reverse is true, that is, that high wages will prevent migration. Wages that drive unit wage costs above Western levels lead to bankruptcies, bankruptcies mean unemployment, and unemployment provides a particularly strong incentive for migration.[20] On the other hand, though, higher wages mean higher unemployment benefits, which tend to reduce the incentive to migrate.

Whether or not migration can be expected to result from the high-wage policy, and how much migration could be regarded as reasonable, are difficult problems that will be discussed more fully in chapter 5.

---

20. This view is supported by opinion polls taken in East Germany (see Akerlof et al. 1991) and it is also evident from the West German migration figures. Cyclical unemployment indeed generates emigration: since 1950 there has been net emigration from the FRG only in the recession years 1967, 1975, and 1982. See *Statistisches Jahrbuch für die Bundesrepublik Deutschland* 1990, p. 67. However, wage-induced unemployment will not necessarily have the same effect, because of the unemployment benefits available. (For the actual figures of East-West migration before unification see figure 1.1.)

Money Overhang and Capital Overhang

The political question most discussed during the period leading up to monetary union was not the wage conversion, whose effects were expected to be temporary, but the rules for converting financial assets and savings. Along with the purchasing-power parities, the distinction between money and wealth—between the money overhang and the capital overhang—is of central importance for a judgement on the rules finally chosen.

Most communist economies had a large money overhang. More liquidity was available than was necessary for transactions (or, at least, more was available than in comparable Western economies). Price increases and reductions in interest rates, which in a market economy would quickly remove any money overhang, were ruled out by law.

At the same time, and almost by definition of a communist economy, the Eastern countries had a large capital overhang in that real capital assets exceeded marketable financial assets. There were few or none of the wide range of private financial securities that are the counterparts of the real capital stock in market economies. What securities there were—typically, savings and insurance—covered only a very small part of the capital stock. The capital stock was owned by the state and not by individuals. In broad terms, it is correct to say that in the economy of a communist country private households have plenty of money but money is about all they do have.

The GDR was no exception to this rule. In 1989, by the M3 definition (which includes savings deposits), the money supply amounted to 237 billion ostmarks.[21] This represented 142 percent of net money income, the only official national income aggregate that is comparable with OECD definitions.[22] In contrast, in West Germany the M3 money supply was only 89 percent of personal disposable income. In East Germany, therefore, there was a money overhang of 53 percent of net money income—in absolute terms, 87 billion ostmarks. The size of the money supply that would have been the same percentage of personal disposable income as in

21. Households owned cash, insurance policies, savings, and in some cases real estate. Savings were interest-bearing but, like demand deposits in banks, could be withdrawn at any time.

22. The communist countries' statistics did not include a calculation for national product according to the OECD definition because such a figure includes the "unproductive" labor in the service and government sectors. Net money income is approximately equivalent to households' personal disposable income.

West Germany was 150 billion ostmarks, not 237 billion. (See appendix A.)

Subtracting 61 billion ostmarks held by firms from the total supply of money gives a figure for the households' share of 176 billion. Adding to this 15 billion marks in insurance entitlements gives a figure of 191 billion marks for the total stock of fungible assets owned by East German households. This is only 11 percent of the official value of net fixed assets, which was given as 1.745 trillion marks. Even when the official value is depreciated to 578 billion marks, as is done by the Institute for Applied Economic Research,[23] the amount covered by private claims is still only 33 percent and the capital overhang is still 200 percent of financial assets.

The low levels of sales revenues and the generally depressed conditions in East Germany may raise doubts as to whether a capital overhang really existed, but it is important not to draw hasty conclusions from the current market situation. Today's wages are not the same as those that existed in the GDR, and the burden of restitution claims, together with the sales practices of the Treuhandanstalt, have brought about an endogenous fall in prices for East German firms. The present low prices cannot be used as evidence for the absence of a capital overhang before unification, or to argue that there would not have been one after unification even if economic policy had been different.

The Planned and Actual Money Supplies

The political discussion in Germany concentrated almost entirely on the money overhang and ignored the capital overhang. This explains the conversion rules set out in the first State Treaty. These rules were supposed to provide an M3 money supply of DM 150 billion, the same proportion of households' private disposable income as in West Germany.

In the fourth section of appendix A, an attempt is made to work out the implications of these conversion rules on the basis of the age structure of the German population; it is shown that, if everybody had converted the maximum amount allowed, the M3 money supply would have been DM 151.4 billion.

Interestingly enough, the actual M3 money supply after unification was about DM 30 billion more.[24] The reason for this divergence is that the

---

23. See chapter 2, footnote 43.
24. *Monatsberichte der Deutschen Bundesbank* 42, No. 10, October 1990. The Bundesbank explained that it had expected an M3 increase of DM 160 billion and conceded a mistake of DM 20 billion.

Bundesbank had overlooked money hidden away in remote corners of the GDR's economy. This money was held by the foreign-trade organizations, which before unification had the status of banks but which lost this status with unification. Previously, the claims of these bodies vis-à-vis the normal banks had been treated as interbank claims and had thus not been counted as part of the money supply. When the foreign-trade organizations lost their status as banks, their claims became demand deposits with the normal banks, were included in the money supply, and had to be converted in the same way as the other components of this supply. Although this mistake was not trivial, it did not add much to the danger of inflation. DM 30 billion is only 2.1 percent of the M3 money supply of the two parts of Germany combined. In any case, the Bundesbank can always use monetary policy to correct the undesired expansion of the money supply if it wants.[25]

It is sometimes thought that, because of the collapse of the East German economy and the associated decline in GNP, there must be an additional money overhang which will have to be eliminated. This view fails to appreciate that the conversion was arranged with respect to the private households' disposable income and not with respect to the GNP (the level of which was, in any case, unknown). Despite the collapse of the economy, this disposable income has not fallen, because the gap has been financed by debt-financed government transfers from the West. For the same reason, the income-determined volume of monetary transactions has not been reduced by the decline in East Germany's productive activity. If anything, some of the transactions have been transferred to West Germany. It would certainly be a mistake to adjust to the collapse of economic activity in East Germany by means of a parallel collapse in the money supply.

Apart from the DM 30 billion not taken into account, the conversion of the money supply by the Bundesbank was technically perfect. It is true that the currency conversion was preceded by a great deal of speculative activity, because the discussion about the conversion rate was carried out in public and not, as in 1948, behind hermetically sealed doors.[26] But this was not the fault of the Bundesbank. The political conditions of 1948 simply could not have been duplicated. In all important respects, the task of eliminating the money overhang of the former GDR was successfully carried out.

---

25. This money will also disappear again when the underlying debt contracts will be discharged.
26. See Möller 1989.

East German Conversion Losses

In contrast with the money overhang, the capital overhang was not only not reduced by the currency converson, it was increased. In the State Treaties the "people's wealth" was disposed of in a way that gave the "people" practically no entitlements.

Some economists, including Kloten (1990) and the majority of the members of the Advisory Council of the Ministry of Economics,[27] had argued that the best thing would be to choose a conversion rate of 1:1 and to solve the problem of the money overhang by not allowing all money to be converted into money. They suggested that the money overhang initially be put on fixed deposit, as in 1948,[28] and later transformed into long-term assets. It was seen as only proper to transfer the real capital assets that had become ownerless with the dissolution of the communist state to savers in the form of equity rights.[29] However, the Bundesbank strongly rejected this suggestion. It agreed with those who argued that a conversion rate of 1:1 would result in a "massive purchasing-power gain" which would be certain to set off an inflationary wave of consumption spending.[30] In view of the fact that the Bundesbank had at least part of the information in table 3.1 available, this view was hard to understand at the time.[31] It is even more difficult to understand today.

Because of the intervention of the Bundesbank, the first State Treaty put limits (as described above) on the amount of money that could be converted at a rate of 1:1 and fixed a rate of 2:1 for the remainder. The result was a substantial real conversion loss for the people of the GDR. As was mentioned earlier, before unification the financial wealth of East German households amounted to 191 billion ostmarks. With full use of the conversion quota, 66 billion marks could be converted at the rate of 1:1. The remainder, 125 billion marks, was exchanged at the rate of 2:1. Because the

---

27. See Wissenschaftlicher Beirat 1990.

28. See Möller 1988, 1990.

29. A discussion of the principles associated with these problems, with special reference to the USSR, can be found in Bernholz 1991.

30. *Monatsberichte der Deutschen Bundesbank* 42, no. 7, July 1990, p. 16. See also Schlesinger 1990.

31. In the report of the Advisory Council of the Ministry of Economics (Wissenschaftlicher Beirat 1990, p. 1498) it is stated that "the majority of the Council does not fear that, with the stock variables, there is any danger of inflation with a conversion rate of 1:1 between the GDR mark and the DM. This conversion rate, taken by itself, provides no basis for such fears. The danger of inflation comes above all from too much liquidity in the GDR economy. The question of an appropriate amount of liquidity is, however, not the same as the question of a suitable conversion rate. The latter applies equally to money and to non-liquid assets."

purchasing powers of the two currencies were approximately equal, this means that East German households suffered a conversion loss of DM 62 billion (DM 3800 per person). This was almost one-third of their total financial wealth.

This figure does not, of course, represent a net loss from unification. The East German households will certainly gain more from the economic upswing (which, it is to be hoped, will soon get underway) than they lost from the currency conversion. In addition, before the upswing is achieved, a stream of transfers from West to East will add up to a multiple of the amount lost through currency conversion. Nevertheless, the conversion loss is a figure that should not be left out when the benefits to East Germany are reported in the official statistics. There are legitimate claims of the East German population that could have been met by transforming them into long-term securities without thereby increasing liquidity in the East German economy or provoking the danger of inflation.

Against this, it could be argued that the East German households could have gotten around the restrictions on liquidity by selling the securities for cash. This argument, however, overlooks the fact that this would simply have involved a transfer of different kinds of assets from one economic unit to another, leaving the total amount of liquidity unchanged. There would have been downward pressure on securities prices and a tendency for interest rates to increase. This increase in interest rates would have reduced the demand for investment goods, and if anything this would have reduced the danger of inflation.

A more important argument was put forward by the Bundesbank. The Bundesbank not only rejected a conversion rate of $1:1$, because it thought that this would result in a conversion gain. It also argued that if the debts of the East German firms were converted at this rate they would amount to an insupportable burden of DM 260 billion. Having to pay market rates of interest on this sum instead of the low rates charged by the East German Kreditbank would force many firms into bankruptcy. Avoiding this, the Bundesbank maintained, required halving the debts of the firms, and this could be done by converting them at $2:1$.

This was indeed a valid objection, and the policy recommendation was an appropriate one—all the more so as the credit conditions that the GDR's central bank had required firms to meet had been imposed for the purpose of providing the government with interest income. It was right for the government to give up this form of income after unification because the revenue it provided could now be obtained from corporate taxes.

Nevertheless, it was not necessary to solve the bankruptcy problem exactly as it was solved with monetary union. It would have been quite possible to reduce the firms' debts without overburdening the banking system and without taking DM 62 billion away from savers.

One possibility would have been to take up the suggestion made by the East German Kreditbank to halve the debts of firms but not housing loans. In this way, a good DM 50 billion could have been saved.[32] If, in addition, the GDR's foreign debt of about DM 20 billion had been charged to the government budget, where it properly belonged, and not to the banking system,[33] the total would have been DM 70 billion—more than enough to avoid the loss to the savers. The Kreditbank had argued that housing loans would make up only a small percentage of the value that property would acquire under market conditions and that overindebtedness would therefore not be a problem. This position seems a reasonable one in view of the enormous increase in real estate prices in the new German states.[34]

Another way of avoiding a conversion loss for savers would have been to trim the profit the banking system made from money creation. The way the currency conversion was carried out meant that the assets of the East German credit system were greater than its liabilities, but no consideration was given to which of the items were interest-bearing and which were not. The banking system made a considerable seignorage profit from money creation because, for all practical purposes, liabilities in the form of cash and demand deposits carried no interest while other items did. The cash value of the seignorage was equal to the present value of the missing interest on the M1 money supply (cash and demand deposits), which in turn equaled the face value of the M1 money supply.

The seignorage profit was naturally not an additional profit, and it did not accrue solely to the East German banking system. For one thing, the

---

32. According to the sources considered in appendix I, DM 54 billion; according to Bundesbank information, DM 51 billion (*Monatsberichte der Deutschen Bundesbank* 42, no. 7, July 1990, p. 16). No less than 80% of housing loans had been made to public authorities, 20% to private households. Not reducing these debts by half would therefore have burdened the households with DM 10 billion. See Staatsbank der DDR, *Jahresbericht* 1989, p. 9.

33. The estimates ranged from DM 19.3 billion to DM 21.2 billion. (See sources cited in note 32.)

34. In table B.2 in appendix B an attempt is made to estimate land values in the former GDR. According to this table, the total value of building land, using average 1989 West German prices, is DM 319 billion, and assuming that building land will take 10 years to reach West German price levels, and that in the meantime it produces no income at all, the value would still be DM 256 billion—that is, three times as much as housing loans. These are land values excluding the value of existing buildings. These considerations confirm that mortgage debt would not need to have been reduced.

Bundesbank received a share of it. For another, the East German banking system would have enjoyed seignorage profits even without the currency conversion. Under the old conditions, all demand deposits were interest-bearing; only cash was interest-free. If the East German banking system had continued to operate under the old conditions, therefore, the present value of its profit from money creation would have been equal to the value of the supply of cash; that is, it would have been DM 17 billion.

In the months following unification, the structure of the M3 money supply in East Germany gradually became like that of the West. In October 1990 the non-interest-bearing part of the money supply (M1) in the new states was DM 65 billion.[35] Subtracting the profit that the system would have made anyway (DM 17 billion) leaves a surplus of DM 48 billion. This surplus measures the present value of the additional seignorage profit that the whole banking system made from supplying the new federal states with West German money and burning the East German money. In magnitude, this comes close to the savers' conversion loss of DM 62 billion.

In accounting terms, forgoing the increase in seignorage profits for the benefit of savers would have been no problem. An additional clause in the first State Treaty could have given savers interest-bearing fixed deposit accounts and compensated the banks by giving them non-interest-bearing, nonredeemable claims on the government. (The latter would have been the counterpart of the non-interest-bearing liabilities that form the M1 money supply.)

In economic terms, there are objections to such a procedure. Every banking system needs to make profits from lending out at interest the money it creates, so it can cover its administrative costs. Without the prospects of seignorage profits, the branches of the old Staatsbank could not continue to exist and the West German commercial banks would certainly not have entered the East German banking business as enthusiastically as they did. However, it would probably not have required the whole of the increase in the seignorage profit of DM 48 billion to get the banking system on its feet. Somewhat less may have been sufficient. The Bundesbank, at least, could have given up its share to the savers. This way, the profit incentives of the private banking system would have been the same, but the amount to be shared out would have increased.

---

35. Initially, on July 1, M1 was DM 54 billion (*Monatsberichte der Deutschen Bundesbank* 42, no. 10, October 1990, p. 7. and 43, no. 2, February 1991, p. 4). The value of DM 65 billion is almost exactly equal to the theoretical value expected on the basis of the actual relationships in West Germany. As in the West, it is 36% of M3.

The Bundesbank's Gains from Unification

In the West German public discussion of the economic effects of unification, it has generally been agreed that the Bundesbank did badly with unification because it gave out "good" deutschmarks in exchange for "bad" ostmarks. This belief is based on the assumption that handing out deutschmarks involves a loss just equal to the value of those deutschmarks. Superficially this seems quite logical, but it is quite wrong.

As every economist knows, when a central bank expands its currency area and provides a new region with money it does not give away any resources. The only cost involved in giving the new region the money it needs for its transaction purposes is the cost of printing it. There would be additional costs if more money than was needed for transactions was put into circulation. This extra money would be used to buy consumption or investment goods in the old currency area, causing inflation there and thus imposing a loss on money holders. This is not a danger, however, if only the necessary amount of money is put into circulation. In this case, none of the new money is used to buy goods in the old currency area, and it remains permanently in circulation in the new region.

Central banks, however, rarely simply give their money away. Instead, they lend it at interest, just as commercial banks do with the deposit money they create. Typically, central banks rediscount the commercial banks' interest-bearing bills of exchange and sell non-interest-bearing claims for interest-bearing ones. This is the principal way central banks make money from creating money.

The Bundesbank did not give up its share of the seignorage profit associated with German unification. It did not give away any money, and it did not exchange any money. Not a single ostmark found its way into the Bundesbank's coffers. The Bundesbank faced the East German banking system in the same way as it did the West German commercial banks, allowing it to take part in the usual rediscounting process.[36]

The way the currency conversion was carried out was that the Kreditbank gave the Bundesbank interest-bearing promissory notes created just for this purpose and received in exchange non-interest-bearing cash. The Bundesbank got the full benefit of the seignorage profit from the base money it provided.

Using the West German money multiplier for the M3 money supply (the relationship of M3 to the monetary base), which before unification was

---

36. The East German banking system is supervised by the Bundesbank, but is legally independent, just like commercial banks.

5.5, the unification-induced expansion of the monetary base was DM 180 billion/5.5; that is, DM 33 billion. This figure measures the present value of the additional interest payments the Bundesbank can expect to receive from the currency conversion. Apparently a good half of the savers' conversion loss (DM 62 billion, or DM 3800 per person) was siphoned off here.[37]

There was no economic imperative to pay the Bundesbank in such a princely manner. In the discussions about the way monetary union should be effected, one possibility considered was that the Bundesbank should exchange ostmarks for deutschmarks and then simply destroy them. If this procedure had been followed and if, in addition, the increased present value of profit of the Eastern banks had been curtailed by DM 9 billion[38] and the banking system had not been saddled with government debts of DM 20 billion, then the DM 62 billion needed to avoid a conversion loss for savers would have been available—even though firms' debts and housing loans were halved.

Portfolio Reactions

The currency conversion had important effects on the economic behavior of East German households. One fundamental reaction was a change in the composition of these households' asset portfolios. Technically, the conversion consisted of transforming ostmark-denominated savings accounts into deutschmark-denominated ones. Once this had happened, people wanted to follow the Western pattern and transfer some of their money from their savings accounts to the other kinds of assets that had become available to them.

Some was changed into cash or transferred to normal demand deposits. This began to happen immediately, on the day the conversion was made, although to a lesser extent than the Bundesbank had expected. As mentioned above, the M1 money supply had grown to DM 65 billion in

37. The Bundesbank transfers its profit to the federal government, and some of this is given to the new states. If their share is proportional to their population, the net loss to East Germany is reduced to about 80% of the amounts mentioned.

38. As was calculated in the previous section, the increase in the present value of the banking system's seignorage profit was DM 48 billion gross and, after subtracting the Bundesbank's profit from unification, was DM 15 billion net. The cut of DM 9 billion would have reduced it to DM 6 billion. The present value of the total seignorage profit of the East German banking system would therefore have been DM 6 billion (curtailed seignorage from unification) + DM 17 billion (seignorage under old conditions) = DM 23 billion.

October 1990; by the end of that year it had reached no less than 95 billion.

A second reaction was to shift some of the M3 money supply into long-term interest-bearing assets which do not form part of the money supply. We can provide no precise figures for the size of this effect, though the Bundesbank believes it to be quite substantial.

The theoretical implication of these two kinds of shift is a change in the maturity structure of interest rates.[39] A tendency for long-term interest rates to fall relative to short-term rates can be expected. At every given level of long-term interest rates, short-term rates must rise to induce West German money holders to shift from highly liquid M1 money to short-term interest-bearing assets. Unless this happens, the opposite shift that the East Germans want to make cannot take place. And for every given level of short-term interest rates, the long-term rates must fall to induce the West Germans to shift out of the long-term securities the East Germans want to buy and into short-term forms of investment. None of this implies anything about how the two kinds of interest rates will move in absolute terms, but their relative movements are implied. The slope of the "yield curve," which shows the term structure of interest rates, must become lower or perhaps even negative.

A definite statement about the absolute levels of interest rates can be made only if it is noted that the central bank normally accommodates a shift out of savings accounts into M1 money in a way that keeps short-term interest rates constant at the desired level. It can therefore be expected that long-term interest rates will tend to fall rather than that short-term rates will tend to rise.[40]

As figure 3.1 shows, the theoretical expectations have been confirmed. The maturity curve of interest rates has turned in the direction expected; short-term interest rates have stayed at their old level, and long-term rates have fallen. This development is admittedly also compatible with the Bundesbank's interpretation that "confidence in the stabilizing effect of German monetary policy" has again increased,[41] but the portfolio shift by East German savers is a possible explanation as well.

If the Bundesbank's hypothesis is correct, the fall in long-term interest-rate yields only reflects the reduction in long-run inflationary expectations with a fixed maturity structure for real interest rates. The fall therefore has no real significance.

---

39. See, e.g., Nachtkamp and Sinn 1981.
40. This prediction was made in Sinn 1990; subsequent events showed it to be correct.
41. *Monatsberichte der Deutschen Bundesbank* 43, no. 2, February 1991, p. 18.

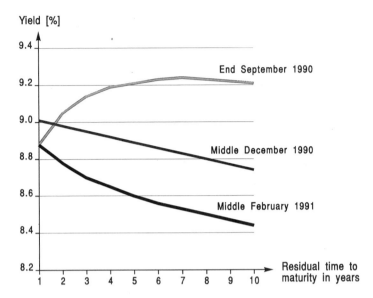

Figure 3.1
Inverse maturity structure of interest rates. Source: *Monatsberichte der Deutschen Bundesbank* 43, no. 2, February 1991, p. 17.

If, on the other hand, the hypothesis suggested above is correct, the fall in long-term interest rates is a real phenomenon that will provide a stimulus for investment. This is a desirable effect in the hangover phase the East German economy is now going through in the wake of the upheaval and turmoil of unification. The high interest rates of 1990 were an understandable market reaction in view of the expected demand for capital for reconstruction. However, in the year after unification it became obvious that East Germany was not going to get moving as quickly as had been expected. Thus, there is no longer any justification for high long-term interest rates, at least until such time as overheating actually makes an appearance. The Bundesbank, of course, can make the yield curve rise again by consolidating government debt (exchanging short-term securities for long-term ones); however, for the time being this policy is not to be recommended.

Demand Reactions

For many years, the East Germans were forced to put their money into savings because the goods they would have liked to buy were rationed. In the months before unification, the expectation that they would soon be

Table 3.3
Competitive displacement of goods from the shelves (share of Western goods in sales in East Germany in September 1990).

Coffee	Canned soups	Fruit-flavored cottage cheese	Dishwashing liquids	Cooking fat	Cooking oil
96%	94%	90%	81%	76%	41%

Sources: Nielsen, *Süddeutsche Zeitung* 46, No. 221, September 25, 1990, p. 24; *Die Zeit*, September 28, 1990.

able to buy goods once available only in the Intershops gave them an added incentive to save. It was hardly surprising that this bottled-up demand for consumption goods gave a boost to purchases of West German goods when it was released by unification.

Highly sought-after goods such as consumer electronics, coffee, tropical fruit, chocolate, and detergents were among the front-runners in the early days. In the period between monetary union and unification, West German products drove many East German goods almost completely off the shelves. Table 3.3 shows the extent to which this happened in a few particularly striking cases.[42]

This transfer of demand is due primarily to the large difference in quality between East and West German goods. However, part of it is also attributable to curiosity or to a simple desire for goods that were once almost unobtainable. Extensive advertising by West German producers was also a contributing factor. Advertising on West German television, which could be seen in East Germany, enabled West German suppliers to influence East Germans' preferences long before monetary union took place. In addition, in the second half of 1990 these suppliers spent a further DM 475 million on advertising in East Germany.

Since then, the demand for food products seems to have become more normal.[43] As supplies of Western products increased, subjective estimates of their value returned to their usual levels. At the same time, many East German producers were able to improve the quality of their goods without appreciably increasing costs. By April 1991, 150 East German firms had already been allowed to use the seal of approval of the German Central Agricultural Marketing Association (CMA) on their products. According

42. See also Dornbusch 1990.
43. See also *Monatsberichte der Deutschen Bundesbank* 43, no. 2, February 1991, p. 31, and *Süddeutsche Zeitung* 47, no. 31, January 31, 1991, p. 31.

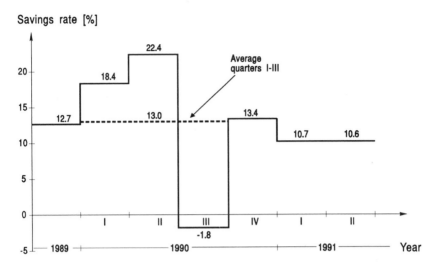

Figure 3.2
The development of the East German savings rate (three-month averages). Source:
Gemeinsames Statistisches Amt, *Monatszahlen*, December 1990, p. 58 f. *Note:* The savings
rate was 39.5% in the month preceding the monetary union (June); in the two following
months it was −9.3% and −9.7%.

to a statement by the CMA, East German consumers were no longer
demanding mainly Western products, and West German consumers were
becoming less cautious about East German products.[44] Quite remarkably,
in January 1992 a poll among East Germans showed that a comfortable
majority of the population (56 percent) preferred East German to West
German food products. One year earlier, only 21 percent of the East Germans had said that they preferred East German products.[45]

In the case of consumer durables, too, second thoughts about East German products combined with saturation effects to ensure that the mad rush
to buy West German goods was soon over. By the spring of 1991, the
flourishing trade in West German used cars had dried up and the run on
video recorders and "walkmen" was over.

The marketing problems of the East German firms have nevertheless
been difficult to overcome. Three-quarters of the East German firms taking
part in an opinion survey in January 1991 complained of marketing difficulties, and West German mail-order firms were able to book up a 41
percent increase in sales revenues over the previous January.[46] All things

44. *Frankfurter Allgemeine Zeitung*, no. 92, April 20, 1991, p. 14.
45. See *Süddeutsche Zeitung* 48, no. 15, January 18, 1992, p. 11.

considered, it is apparent even in 1992 that the manufacturing industry of the former GDR cannot keep up with West German suppliers in quality and price.

A major problem for the East German firms is to find substitutes for the lost Comecon customers. If the lack of quality could be compensated for by sharp price cuts, this would not be an unsurmountable difficulty. Even a Trabant would find its customers if it cost, say, a fifth of what a VW Golf costs. However, the combination of low labor productivity and high industrial wages that the East German firms have to cope with excludes such a solution.

Be this as it may, the interest shown by East German consumers in West German goods provides little support for the view that monetary union created conversion profits and that these profits would set off a consumption boom. Quite clearly, this interest is due more to a consumption shift from East to West than to an overall increase in consumption. This is suggested by the way the personal savings rate in East Germany has developed. (See figure 3.2.) Although the savings rate became negative in the first two months after the currency conversion, in the first half of the year it had been well above its normal level, reaching a peak of 39.5 percent in June. By the end of 1990 it was already back to its normal level. The latest figures available at the time of writing show it to be two percentage points below the 1989 average, which is not a significant change.

To be sure, the alternative view—that insufficient aggregate demand was the cause of the breakdown in East German production, and that a negative Keynesian multiplier process was the main operating force—is also not supported by the facts. Income in East Germany has been supplemented by massive transfers from the West and, despite the breakdown in production, has been raised above the prevalent income level of the time when the GDR was in existence. Clearly, enough purchasing power is available in the East.

Since the economy of the new Länder collapsed despite sufficient consumer demand, lack of such demand cannot be among the main causes of the present depression. Its main causes are the unresolved property-ownership question, sluggish privatization, and the aggressive wage policy. The next two chapters will deal with these problems.

---

46. Ifo-Institut, *Wirtschaftskonjunktur* 43, March 3, 1991, p. 21, and *Frankfurter Allgemeine Zeitung*, no. 84, April 11, 1991.

4   Privatization

Restitution and Sale

After the Imperial Edict of Restitution of 1629, Protestants in Germany asked King Gustavus Adolphus of Sweden for protection. His entry into the religious war that had begun in 1618 resulted in its rapid spread beyond the boundaries of Germany and, over the next 20 years, in the devastation of the whole of Central Europe. No such consequences are to be feared from the latest "edict of restitution" adopted in the Unification Treaty at the instigation of the Free Democrats.[1] Then, private property was to be returned to a public institution—the Catholic Church. Now, public property is to be returned to private owners. Marx had thought that the alienation of man from the products of his labor would disappear under communism; however, the alienation of "the people of the GDR" turned out to be even greater than that of their counterparts living under capitalism, and they showed little interest in what was happening to the "people's property." When the treaty was being negotiated, the public discussion focused on such issues as day care and abortion; the property issue received much less attention. Magdeburg, burned to the ground in the Thirty Years' War because it wanted a foreign power's help in avoiding restitution, is in no danger of suffering a similar fate this time.

Nevertheless, the federal government's privatization policy did precipitate a series of problems which pose a major threat to social stability in Germany. Prominent among these are the speed (or rather the lack of it) with which privatization is being carried out and the resultant obstacles to capital formation. Without privatization there is no incentive for capital formation, and without capital formation there can be no upswing. Privatization is a necessary condition for a market economy, for without well-

---

1. See the section on "The Road to Union" in chapter 1.

defined property rights there can be no efficient exchange of goods and services. There is no Third Way. Unless large quantities of capital can be rapidly mobilized to restructure the economy, millions of unemployed will be demonstrating in the streets or massive social transfer payments will be required that will put an intolerable strain on the already shaky solidarity between the West Germans and their Eastern relations.

Of the part of the East German economy that can be privatized, it is expected that 70 percent can be sold and 30 percent must be given back to the former owners through natural restitution.[2] Between 6000 and 7000 industrial combines had to be privatized. Each of these combines had to be broken up into a large number of individual firms—in all, 40,000 separate plants.[3] There were also 45,000 hotels, restaurants, and sales outlets to be dealt with. No less than 2 million compensation claims had been made, among which were 11,200 claims for the return of firms.

As of March 1992, the task of selling or leasing the pharmacies, restaurants, department stores, and shops had been effectively completed.[4] Selling the industrial firms, however, has been proceeding more slowly, especially since the "pearls" were disposed of early on. Despite the widespread publicity acclaiming the Treuhand's successes, up to the fall of 1991 (a year after unification) barely a quarter of the firms originally supervised by the Treuhand had been sold, and by the end of 1991 (18 months after the sales began) the proportion of firms sold may have amounted to about 30 percent.[5] This does not imply that the Treuhand has not done its

---

2. This is based on an estimate that 70% of productive capacity in 1948 consisted of firms that had already been expropriated by the Russians, which therefore are not subject to restitution claims. See Cornelsen 1991 and the section on "Expropriation and Restitution" below.

3. This information comes from a hearing of the board of directors of the Treuhand, held before the Economic Advisory Council of the Ministry of Economics (Wissenschaftlicher Beirat) on January 12, 1991, from information supplied by this ministry, and from Treuhand 1991a and 1991b.

4. In most cases the premises were leased and only the stock sold.

5. Despite the regular publication of detailed statistics by the Treuhand, it is difficult to establish the percentage because it relates the number of privatizations completed to a continually changing base total. The information given came from a report by Finance Minister Theo Waigel on October 1, 1991, in a speech to Treuhand employees (Bundesministerium der Finanzen, *Finanznachrichten* no. 61, October 2, 1991, p. 1), and from statistics for the Länder given in *Süddeutsche Zeitung* 47, no. 297, December 27, 1991, p. 31. In the latter case, we weighted the percentages for the Länder by the sizes of their respective populations. The Waigel figure of 25% was an aggregate for the Treuhand branches, and it was a forecast for the accumulated privatization record until the end of 1991. The figure of 30% is an extrapolation based on a press release issued by the Treuhand in December (*Süddeutsche Zeitung* 47, no. 292, December 19, 1991, p. 31). A higher percentage of privatizations (on average 35.9% to September 30, 1991) was given in the annual report of the

best within the constraints under which it has had to operate; however, absolving the Treuhand's efforts does not absolve the methods it was (politically, though not legally) directed to use.

The amount of long-term investment expected to result from the sale of firms up to the end of 1991 was DM 100 billion—that is, about one-tenth of the DM 1 trillion needed to bring capital intensity in the East up to Western levels.[6] The number of jobs secured with the privatizations up to the spring of 1992 was about 1 million. This was one-tenth of the potential workforce, or about one-quarter of the former Treuhand jobs. The number of jobs remaining with the Treuhand at that time was 1.3 million. More than 1.5 million jobs (about 40 percent) had disappeared from the statistics of the Treuhand, not by way of privatization, but through bankruptcies and dismissals. This information offers little support for the official German view that the Treuhand approach has been a success story.

Natural restitution carried out through the municipal authorities has proved to be a complete failure. By October 1991 only about 3.3 percent of the claims had been settled; 90 percent of the decisions regarding the restitution of firms were being contested and were thus not yet legally valid.[7] The mayor of Leipzig has expressed the fear that, under the present conditions, natural restitution will not be completed for decades.[8]

Sir Alan Walters, economic advisor to Margaret Thatcher, called the attempt to privatize a former communist country in 500 days "absurd" and the attempt to do this in 500 weeks "optimistic" (Walters 1990). These adjectives do not seem to be too wide of the mark in view of the current privatization record, which can only be described as disappointing.

The privatization policy should not be allowed to continue unchanged. It need not, and must not, take decades for privatization to be completed,[9] and getting rid of the Treuhand firms by closing them is no solution to the privatization problem. Part of the problem is self-inflicted and avoidable. The restitution of the physical property is being hindered by the adminis-

---

Council of Economic Experts (Sachverständigenrat 1991b, p. 70, table 11). In contrast to our numbers, which relate to the firms formerly administered by the Treuhand, the Council used the current number of firms. As the firms that were sold had been broken up into smaller units, it can be expected that the figures given by the Council place the sales results of the Treuhand in too favorable a light. See "The Treuhand's Task" below. As of June 30, 1992, the Treuhand claimed to have privatized 47% of its firms.

6. A substantial fraction of this appears to have been allocated to the semi-government energy sector.

7. *Frankfurter Allgemeine Zeitung*, no. 20, January 24, 1992, p. 13.

8. Lehmann-Grube 1991. As of June 30, 1992, no more than 8% of the claims had been settled.

9. There is, however, no hope that living conditions in the East will quickly reach Western levels even if privatization will be completed quickly. See "A Long Haul" in chapter 5.

trative and legal difficulties involved in finding out who actually has first claim on the property, while the mass sale of firms faces the obvious absorption problems of the capital markets. Neither problem was inevitable, and both could have been overcome. Even today, there remains considerable scope for policy improvements.

The Obstacle-Removal Law of March 1991 was a first small step in the right direction. This law, which was influenced by a 1991 report by the Advisory Council of the Economics Ministry, modified the restitution principle, giving investors interested in buying a property priority over the former owners in certain cases. Unfortunately, up to now the law has not fulfilled the desired expectations. Further improvement is necessary.

A second important step would be to change the method of privatization so that a firm is no longer sold for cash. Such a method will be developed toward the end of this chapter under the name "participation model." The participation model can be expected to stimulate the private interest in Treuhand properties and to speed up capital formation considerably. No legal changes would be necessary to apply it.

Apart from speeding the upswing in the East, the participation model would also bring about distributive improvements. Its essence is that the Treuhand retains a fractional ownership in the privatized firms which can later be made available for distribution to the East German population. The task of the Treuhand set out in Article 25 of the Unification Treaty and in the preamble to the Second Trusteeship Law is to give East German savers claims on the former public property to compensate them for having part of their savings converted at 2:1. This task could be carried out by means of the participation model; indeed, as things now stand, this is the only model that could ensure success.

The current policy is based on the unrealistic assumption that there is a "market for firms" on which a whole economy can be sold in a very short time. A market that can absorb such a large supply of firms so quickly just does not exist. If, nevertheless, all these firms are offered for sale at the same time, the prices will fall to ridiculous levels and what is legally a sale will become in economic terms nothing more than an outright gift. Despite the Treuhand's efforts to interest the world capital market in buying the East German economy, its hopes for realizing DM 600 billion from the sale of these firms were always utopian.[10] It would not even be realistic to expect the DM 280 billion that can be calculated from figures circulated by

---

10. From a statement made by the chairman of the Treuhand, Detlev Karsten Rohwedder, to the Viennese parliament. Reported by the news agency ADN on October 19, 1990.

the Ministry of Justice in 1991 to show that replacing restitution with monetary compensation would have been too expensive.[11] The properties sold before October 1991 generated a gross revenue of DM 15 billion. Projecting this to all the properties not yet sold gives DM 60 billion, only about 10 percent of the sales revenue originally anticipated. One reason why the expected returns have had to be so greatly modified is that the cost of restructuring the firms has been significantly underestimated. Another reason is that wage increases have been much higher than expected. A third and particularly important reason is the failure to take the law of demand into account. The principle that price falls when supply increases remains valid even when what is being sold is firms.

If selling off the firms actually made for a rapid upswing, and if speed were the only consideration, then the financial gain made by West German investors from the operation of the law of demand would have been acceptable. In fact, however, neither condition holds.

For one thing, selling the firms on the market is inferior to the participation model in terms of the speed of the upswing. It absorbs funds from the capital market that could otherwise have been used to restructure the firms and thus increase their productivity. The fall in price is a clear indication of a financing bottleneck caused by increasing pressure on the supply side. For another, the property being sold belongs to a people who had the misfortune to live in the Soviet occupation zone, who had to write off much of their human capital with the introduction of the market economy, and who suffered a severe financial loss from the currency conversion and the restitution policy. These considerations alone should rule out trying to hasten the upswing by selling off the East German economy, especially since the likelihood of success is slender. Instead of the German people growing together, two nations would remain: affluent capital owners in the West and propertyless wage earners in the East (or, in Disraeli's words, "the privileged and the people"). A selloff would be in keeping neither with the principle of equality embodied in the German constitution nor with the need to establish a sound basis for a prosperous common future.

The two-nations problem is being played down in West Germany. It is being argued there that East Germans can acquire capital by buying the

---

11. Klaus Kinkel, the former federal minister of justice, estimated that firms subject to restitution claims had a market value of DM 120 billion and, in a statement to the Bundesrat (the German upper house), argued that it was not possible to pay this amount of compensation, so that natural restitution was the only solution. (Reported by Associated Press, March 22, 1991.) If this value represents 30% of all firms that can be privatized (Cornelsen 1991), the value of the remaining 70% of the firms is DM 280 billion. See the section "Compensation or Restitution?" below.

properties the Treuhand is selling. This argument is as naive and unrealistic as the remark attributed to Marie Antoinette—"If they have no bread, let them eat cake." There is no way the East German people can buy anything of value offered in the sales—not because communist inefficiency made them too poor, but because they have no financial wealth over and above what they need for transactions (see chapter 3). If, as part of the conversion process, they had at least been given financial claims to the value of the money overhang, they would have been able to successfully compete for the assets offered by the Treuhand. But this was not done. It is hardly surprising, therefore, that up to the spring of 1991 only 5 percent of the industrial properties had been sold to East Germans. Realistically, the only chance prospective East German buyers had of acquiring assets was to lease pharmacies and shops of less than 100 square meters.[12]

A more honest way of looking at German unification may be to interpret it as an insurance contract, as Schrettl (1991) does. According to this interpretation, the West Germans provided their East German countrymen with insurance against the income risk of a systemic change in exchange for an insurance premium in the form of East German capital and real estate. From the point of view of the "insurers" this interpretation may be correct; whether it is also correct from the point of view of the "insured" is open to doubt. In any case, no one publicly informed the East Germans that they would have to pay for unification with their communal property.

Privatization policy can also be considered in relation to the extremely aggressive wage policy pursued by the trade unions (see chapter 5). It may, perhaps, be argued that it is necessary to use one of these policies to offset the other; but even if this is true the inexorable law of the market must not be overlooked. The market will not permit the mistakes of the privatization policy to be made good by excessive wage demands, for when wages outstrip productivity both jobs and firms are destroyed. Nevertheless, the impossible is being attempted, the struggle over distribution is fierce, and the government is standing idly by, doing little to help find a solution. In the next chapter we suggest a moratorium on wages as a means of ending the struggle. Such a suggestion is an appropriate complement to the privatization model developed at the end of this chapter.

---

12. Data on East German restitution claims are not available to us. However, in the light of the history of expropriation described in the next section, it is reasonable to assume that, with the exception of the properties nationalized in 1972, most restitution claims have also been made by West Germans. Either expropriation was followed by emigration or emigration was followed by expropriation; in either case most of those who benefit from restitution are West German residents.

Expropriation and Restitution

The Federal Republic had always claimed to be the only legitimate state on German territory. The decision to reverse the expropriation by, and the compulsory sales to, the communist government therefore seemed logical from a legal point of view. It was also in keeping with the simple sense of justice evidently held by the more than two-thirds of the Bundestag representatives who voted in favor of the Unification Treaty.[13]

The introduction of the principle of natural restitution ceded legal priority to the former owners of property in the dispute over the legacy of the communist state. It was certainly assumed that monetary compensation could be paid to the former owners in exceptional cases (for example, where urgently needed investment projects deemed to be in the public interest were involved, or where a property had been resold "in good faith"), but the treaty made it quite clear that, in principle, the former owners had the greater rights. A legal claim made by a previous owner put an immediate ban on the disposal of the disputed property and allowed a great deal of pressure to be exercised.

The strong position of the former owners is also evident from the coverage of the restitution claims on enterprises provided for in the Property Law. It would have been possible to introduce a provision limiting restitution claims to the value of the property at the time of confiscation, but this was not done. Instead, a much wider claim was provided for, whereby the whole firm must be given back to the former owners, even where subsequent investment has increased the firm's size. Initially, the text of the law gives a somewhat different impression, for in section 6 it states that "substantial" improvement or deterioration of a firm is to be made good by payment of compensation. However, the normal situation, where no compensation is payable, is defined such that a firm with an approximately constant debt-equity ratio must be given back just as it is. The communist government financed much of its capital accumulation by withholding wages: the East German share of wages in GDP was 40 percent, while in the West it is 52 percent.[14] Even capital financed this way must be handed over to the former owner if the firm has grown steadily without changing

---

13. The relative nature of this sense of justice becomes obvious when it is considered that no attempt was made to compensate for the loss of life, quality of life, freedom, or income suffered by East Germans. One alternative for redressing these losses would have been to share out the assets left after the communist state was disbanded to *all* those who had suffered them.
14. Calculated from appendix A.

its balance-sheet structure.[15] The amount of capital accumulated by the firm is quite irrelevant.

In principle, the restitution provisions apply to all property nationalized since the establishment of the GDR in 1949 as long as it was still in government hands at the time of unification. In detail, the following cases can be distinguished[16]:

• Property left behind by refugees between 1945 and 1953 which was confiscated without compensation. It is estimated that this case covers 31,000 real estate properties and nearly 3000 firms.

• Approximately 80,000 real estate properties owned by refugees who left the GDR after 1953. These were initially administered by a government trustee, but many were later transferred to the government when the exorbitant fees charged caused the property to become overindebted.

• A good 100,000 real estate properties and 2000 rights of ownership on industrial property owned by West Germans before 1953. Like the properties mentioned in the previous case, these were administered by a trustee but could be confiscated if they became overindebted.

• Just under 70,000 real estate properties which became the property of West Germans after 1953, mainly through inheritance. These were not initially administered by the government, but in many cases they became overindebted and were then transferred into government hands.

• About 12,000 small industrial firms whose owners were forced to sell to the government during a large-scale nationalization program in 1972.

The restitution rules make exceptions for nationalized land with single-family houses, which had normally been passed on to private individuals. Initially all that was transferred was the right of use, but with the collapse of the communist state many such properties were quickly sold to the users. In these cases, the right to restitution is determined by a "cutoff date" rule. Although what the term "acquisition in good faith" covers is very unclear,[17] it can be assumed that any property for which an application to purchase had been made before October 19, 1989 will remain in the pos-

15. See Gesetz zur Regelung offener Vermögensfragen (Property Law), section 6.3, where a "substantial improvement" is defined such that a firm had a smaller net worth *relative* to its total balance sheet at the time of expropriation than at the time of restitution.

16. These details are based mainly on information in Penig 1991. See also Möschel 1991, Kroeschell 1991, and Schulte-Döinghaus and Stimpel 1990.

17. There are lawyers who seriously argue that no acquisition from the GDR government was made in good faith because the purchasers must have known that it had been illegally expropriated. See also footnote 33.

session of its present owners. A property for which no application for purchase had been made by this date must, in principle, be returned to its former owner. However, the real right of use remains valid if this was held before the cutoff date. In many cases this makes the ownership relations extremely obscure. Typically, the land itself is given back to the former owners, the buildings remain the property of the users, and the former owners can claim monetary compensation.[18]

The complicated legal situation has made disputes between current users and former owners likely. A broad-based economic upswing must be supported by building and construction activity, but this activity is being held back by the legal uncertainties. For example, in the city of Magdeburg no fewer than 11,000 claims for restitution were made for the 18,000 private pieces of land, and by the end of 1991 only a few of these claims had been settled.[19]

Under the terms of the Unification Treaty (Schedule III), the extensive expropriations made by the Soviet occupation force before the establishment of the GDR are not subject to restitution claims.[20] This exception was included in the Unification Treaty at the behest of the Soviet Union and with the support of the East German negotiators.[21]

All large firms, many medium-size ones, and all banks, insurance companies, mines, and Nazi-owned properties were confiscated by the Soviet occupation force. A total of 10,000 firms were nationalized. It is estimated that, at the time the GDR was established, 70 percent of East Germany's industrial output was being produced by nationalized firms. About 20 percent of the output was produced by firms initially taken over as reparations by the Soviet government and subsequently transferred to the GDR government in 1953.

The Soviet Union, like Great Britain and the United States, carried out land reform in its occupation zone, but it did so on a much larger scale and far more rigorously.[22] No less than 4300 Nazi-owned properties, and all farms and forests of more than 100 hectares (amounting to 3.3 million hectares, or 42 percent of privately owned agricultural and forest

---

18. See Vogel 1991. In spring 1992 a law was in preparation that would impose a tax of 33% on the market value of the property returned, payable by the claimant. The tax revenue is to be used for compensation payments which are planned to be 130% of the property's "unit value."

19. ARD television program "Bericht aus Bonn," February 28, 1992.

20. This was again confirmed by the Federal Constitutional Court on April 23, 1991. Cf. Heldrich and Eidenmüller 1991. See also footnote 23.

21. See "The Road to Union" in chapter 1.

22. In the British and American zones a total of 144,000 hectares were expropriated, of which 72,000 were given to settlers from Eastern Europe (Aussiedler).

land), were nationalized.[23] Under the slogan "Junkerland in Bauernhand" ("Squires' land into peasant hands"), all the old feudal structures whose influence had permeated rural life in Brandenburg, Mecklenburg, and West Pomerania were removed with the land reforms. The land was split up into smaller lots, and two-thirds of it was transferred to 550,000 small (sometimes novice) farmers—among them 83,000 refugees.[24] Many of these farmers, like those whose farms were less than 100 hectares and so not nationalized, were the legal owners of their land during the whole time the GDR existed and may even remain so today.[25] When the farming cooperatives known as Landwirtschaftliche Produktionsgenossenschaften (LPG) were founded, these and other small farmers had the right to dispose of their land taken away; however, their legal title to it was not disputed. In total, 73 percent of the agricultural land in the GDR remained in private hands despite the foundation of the cooperatives.

The Unification Treaty differentiated between the period 1945–1949 and the period from 1949 to the disestablishment of the GDR. The "Law for the Settlement of Unresolved Property Questions" subsequently passed by the Bundestag also considered the period 1933–1945 (Property Law, section 1, 6). At the request of the United States, the right of restitution was extended to this period so that the ideologically motivated expropriations of the fascist government, which were mainly from Jews, could be reversed. It is said that there are streets in the central parts of Dresden and Leipzig where nearly all the properties must be given back to former Jewish owners. The Jewish Claims Conference on Germany has asked for the return of 3000 plots of land in East Berlin alone.

Invisible Hand in Chains

The disastrous consequences of the totalitarian regimes are like a curse hanging over the East German economy, a curse that is proving extremely

23. Calculated on the basis of estimates of land, privately owned or eligible for privatization, in East Germany, given in appendix B. At the beginning of 1991 a law was being worked on in the German Ministry for Agriculture that would allow the former big landowners to buy back their land under favorable conditions. Typically a price of DM 0.75 per square meter is charged for agricultural land, which is one-quarter of the West German market price, and the Treuhand offers generous credit arrangements to overcome the liquidity constraints of the former owners. The purchasers pay the market rate of interest but can claim a refund from the Federal Government. The Treuhand expects that some 500,000 hectares are involved here. See *Süddeutsche Zeitung* 48, no. 57, March 9, 1992, p. 23.
24. See Penig 1991, Weber 1982, p. 30 f., and Kruse 1988, p. 136.
25. On the intense legal debate over the exact nature of these property rights, see the literature cited in the previous footnote.

difficult to lift. According to the Treuhand, there are very few firms that are not subject to some kind of claim for restitution.[26] Many a firm faces several claims at once, though most affect only parts of the firm and not the whole.

The economy of the GDR was restructured several times after nationalization, and finally was organized into production combines. These combines (which are not firms in the Western sense, but which correspond rather to whole branches of industry) have been disentangled by the Treuhand and split up into a continually increasing number of corporations.[27] In many cases, the former ownership structure cannot be reconstructed. Some parts of the nationalized firms had been split off and merged with other firms, some parts had been closed down, and some new parts had been added as part of the process of technological change. It is often no longer possible to match previous ownership with firms in their present form. The result is a tangled web of restitution claims that will take years to sort out through the courts.

The problem is exacerbated by the fact that ownership of a firm usually goes hand in hand with ownership of real property. To work out who owns what it is necessary to check the entries in the official land registers, but these registers were not maintained under the communist government. Many of them have disintegrated or disappeared, and in those that remain many entries are illegible and others have been blacked out or falsified. Registration offices were set up again after unification but are not yet functioning well enough to cope with the flood of applications they are faced with. Even when it is obvious from the registers who can claim ownership of a property, a host of other legal and practical problems make progress toward restitution extremely difficult.

One problem is that, in most cases, the heirs and not the former owners will be the beneficiaries of restitution. The heirs have often had no contact at all with the management problems associated with their legacies. It is quite intolerable that a twenty-year-old student can take over a small or medium-size firm in East Germany, try out his entrepreneurial skills for a few years at the expense of the employees, and then, after the firm fails, realize that he has bitten off more than he can chew.

A second problem is the extremely generous way restitution is defined. As was mentioned above, both the value of the property at the time of

---

26. According to a statement made at a hearing of the Economics Advisory Council on January 12, 1991, by Mr. Schirmer, a member of the Board of Directors.
27. See "The Treuhand's Task" below.

nationalization *and* the capital accumulated since then are supposed to be given to the former owner. This generosity makes the claimants eager to hold onto their property, and they are all too often not prepared to accept the compensation offered to them by the Treuhand.

A third and particularly difficult problem is that several parties may be claiming to own a property, and all of them will consider themselves entitled to restitution because they all believe to have acquired the property in good faith. Consider the following example: A small retail firm was originally owned by a Jewish family who sold it to a member of the Nazi party before leaving Germany. After the war, the buyer fled to West Germany, leaving behind the property, which was then taken over by the Soviet occupation forces and later by the GDR government. The property was then sold to an East German citizen, only to be repurchased by the government under the forced sales program (Zwangsverkäufe) in 1972. Finally, it was resold to a different East German citizen when the Modrow government brought in its privatization laws shortly before unification. In this example, there are four potentially legitimate claimants. According to the law, the first legitimate claim must be recognized—but it is not at all clear which one this is.

The uncertainty associated with property ownership presents a serious impediment to investment. Investors are not willing to restructure the disputed properties until they can be sure that they really own them. Banks hesitate to give loans because, until the ownership situation is resolved and the registration offices are functioning properly, mortgages cannot be registered. Time and money that otherwise would be available for restructuring the firms are being invested in settling legal disputes. The Unification Treaty unfortunately did not succeed in creating a market economy; it created an economy of rent seekers who are all devoted to playing zero-sum games.

The most basic requirement for a market economy is a system of secure, well-defined property rights. How these rights are distributed is of secondary importance.[28] Market exchange can bring about efficiency, and the invisible hand can carry out its coordinating function, only when property rights are unambiguous. Natural restitution has brought not clarity but uncertainty, ambiguity, and confusion. It has manacled the invisible hand. Releasing it will take up much valuable time and will delay still further the economic upswing in East Germany. In a paper examining the restitution principle, the Kronberger Kreis (1991), a private economic research group,

---

28. See Coase 1960.

expressed the opinion that "the hand of the lawmakers was not guided by the wisdom of experienced lawyers." We can only add that it certainly does not appear to have been guided by the wisdom of experienced economists either.[29]

Compensation or Restitution?

Attempting to turn the wheel of history back to 1933 was a major blunder of the unification policy. It led (in the words of Treuhand chairman Detlev Karsten Rohwedder) to a "paralyzing stranglehold" on the East German economy, which could have been avoided if payment of compensation had been chosen instead of natural restitution. Restitution might have been allowed in exceptional cases, where it was not contrary to the public interest; as a general rule, however, it has been a disaster.[30]

The big advantage of compensation would have been the separation of the issue of investors' property rights from disputes over the level of compensation payments. Claims for compensation would have been directed toward the government and would have posed no threat to investors. The disputes could have gone on till doomsday without holding up investment.

A decision to pay compensation would have required no change in the constitution. An appeal to the urgency of the need to boost economic activity would have been sufficient to justify it, for this was clearly paramount in the public interest. The only constitutional aspect of the decision was that the Unification Treaty had to be passed with a two-thirds majority, but this was required regardless of whether compensation or restitution was chosen.

Time consistency of the economic policy, often emphasized by economists, would have been no problem either. It is certainly true that a government that shows no respect for property rights loses credibility and scares away savers and investors, but no one in his right mind would have blamed the Federal Republic for the expropriations of the Nazis and the communists. There would have been no loss of confidence in the government if the compensation solution had been chosen, especially in view of the impossibility of clarifying most of the old ownership questions.

The most serious argument against compensation, and one that the former Federal Minister of Justice, Klaus Kinkel, kept emphasizing, is that it

---

29. For an early criticism of natural restitution see Sinn 1990.
30. Among the exceptions would certainly have been the small industrial firms sold compulsorily to the government in 1972.

would have been too expensive. This argument seems to assume that compensation is paid whether or not a property is sold and regardless of when it is sold. It loses its validity, however, if compensation is linked strictly to the act of sale, as it could be. The government agencies that are currently supervising the properties to be privatized could be required to use either restitution or sale, whichever promises to be faster in any particular case. When sale seemed the faster method, the revenue received could then be used to pay compensation to the previous owner. This way there would be no question at all of a fiscal burden.

The counterargument to this is that the market prices obtained in this way may not be fair prices (Verkehrswerte), because the large quantity being supplied is depressing them. This argument is certainly correct, as will be shown below. It seems very strange, however, that it should be used by those who vehemently deny any tendency for an endogenous fall in prices to occur when they are defending the current sales policy of the Treuhand. A double standard is clearly involved here.

Fortunately there is a quick privatization method that largely avoids the fall in prices. The second half of this chapter will deal with this. Although the method was designed primarily as a replacement for the sales method, we will argue that it also opens up an escape route from the legal blind alley in which the restitution policy is trapped.

Loosening the Chains: The Obstacle-Removal Law

The economic, political, and scientific communities have been strongly critical of the federal government's privatization policy because of the problems and difficulties described above, and they have not been impressed by the government's narrow legal views.[31] As a response to these criticisms, the Bundestag passed the Obstacle-Removal Law (Hemmnisbeseitigungsgesetz), which amends the Property Law.[32] This new law does not call into question the principle of natural restitution, but it does loosen it by giving more rights to investors in a number of important cases.

• Up to December 31, 1992, the investor will have priority over the former owner in the allocation of firms and real estate unless that owner can credibly guarantee to undertake an equivalent amount of investment. If

---

31. See Wissenschaftlicher Beirat 1991a or Sinn 1990.
32. Gesetz zur Beseitigung von Hemmnissen bei der Privatisierung von Unternehmen und zur Förderung von Investitionen (Obstacle-Removal Law), March 15, 1991.

the former owner is not allocated the property, he will receive monetary compensation.

• The former owner cannot obstruct the real legal transactions of the authority with the right of disposal over the property when these have the aim of furthering investment. In the case of firms, the former owner must promise that he will continue operating the firm if he wishes to exercise his rights. Objections by the owner and action to contest the authority's decisions cannot delay the transactions.

• Investors and restored owners who do not keep their word can be forced to return the property.

It was hoped that the new rules would substantially improve the efficiency of the legal situation. They were designed to limit the ability of former owners to hold back a property and refuse to take compensation payments in the hope of making speculative gains. They were supposed to prevent the handing over of properties to people who are unable or unwilling to either carry out the necessary entrepreneurial functions themselves or arrange for someone else to do so. And it was hoped that they would speed up the transfer of properties to competent investors and foster recovery.

Unfortunately, these hopes have by no means been realized, and the old owners are still in a position to block the allocation of properties to competent investors. Three main problems are involved. First, the former owner must be found and identified before a property can be allocated to an investor so as to give the owner a chance to make an investment offer himself. Second, the investor is deterred from preparing the restructuring proposal required because he knows that the former owner can take over his plans at any time. Third, the former owner has more than enough opportunity to delay making his bid and thus can effectively block the sale of the disputed property.[33] The strong position of the former owners has resulted in a lively trade in restitution claims. In many cases the investor has a chance only if he acquires the former owners' restitution claims. In principle this is a welcome development, because it helps to loosen the investment blockage a little; however, it is not yet possible to speak of a real solution.

---

33. In a precedent-setting decision in July 1991, the Federal Constitutional Court confirmed a ban on the disposal of a now very valuable piece of property in Dresden, acquired in the GDR period, for which the former owner had made a restitution application. (Bundesverfassungsgericht, AZ. 1 BuR 986/91.)

In an attempt to do something about these problems, a further amendment to the Property Law is being contemplated which will marginally reduce the rights of the restitution claimants.[34] It is doubtful, however, whether this can bring about a solution, as the German government is still committed to the principle that gives restitution priority over compensation. Every case where an exception is made must be justified separately. The government is trapped by its own prior decision and is unable to respond appropriately to the exigencies of the times. It is quite obvious that it is going to take a long time for the chains on the invisible hand to be loosened in East Germany.

The Treuhand's Task

The Volkskammer passed the First Trusteeship Law on March 1, 1990. Its aim was to pave the way for a market economy made up mainly of government-owned firms. The Treuhand, a government-owned resolution trust, was established and given the ownership of 8000 firms that had been national property. Although the firms were turned into legally independent corporations (KG, GmbH, and AG), the main object of the exercise was not privatization but the preservation of the state-owned properties under the conditions of a market economy. Privatization was only intended to apply to small firms that, under protest, had been forcibly sold to the government in 1972.[35] The Treuhand seems to have been intended to be a vehicle for traveling along the Third Way.

The situation changed only when the Second Trusteeship Law was passed by the first democratically elected parliament in East Germany on June 17, 1990. The agency's task now became the "privatization and reorganization of the people's property," and this was confirmed in the Unification Treaty.

The plan was to privatize about 6100 of the 8000 firms, the remaining 1900 being public utilities that were to be handed over to the local government authorities under the provisions of the Municipal Property Law of July 6, 1990.[36]

---

34. A more "radical" change has been demanded in the "Declaration of Magdeburg," signed by the mayors of the cities of Leipzig, Halle, Potsdam, Frankfurt an der Oder, and Magdeburg and by representatives of Berlin, Chemnitz, and Görlitz on February 18, 1992.
35. Gesetz über die Gründung und Tätigkeit privater Unternehmen und über Unternehmensbeteiligungen (Private Firms Law), March 7, 1990, and Verordnung über die Umwandlung von volkseigenen Kombinaten, Betrieben und Einrichtungen in Kapitalgesellschaften (Ordinance for the Conversion of Combines etc. into Companies), March 1, 1990.
36. A detailed discussion of the tasks of the Treuhand can be found in Möschel 1991. See also Bös 1991b and Sinn 1990 (section 4).

When the Unification Treaty came into force, the Federal Ministry of Finance became the legal supervisor of the Treuhand. By April 1991 the Treuhand had about 3000 employees. Measured by the number of firms involved, it is the largest holding company in the world.

The Treuhand interprets its privatization task as requiring it to sell outright the firms entrusted to it. Normally it requires payment in cash, and rarely does it allow a credit purchase. It only very reluctantly agrees to a participation sale, where some of the shares in the firm are sold to one or more purchasers, and only once has a firm been sold through the stock exchange. It is, however, ready to meet the wishes of the purchasers with regard to divestment, and where necessary it will sell the profitable parts of a firm individually.

The 8000 enterprises set up initially were the result of breaking up the enormous combines that had encompassed whole branches of industry. Even these enterprises were, in many cases, too large to be sold as whole units. Included among the 8000 enterprises were 120 combines that had not been broken up and that therefore could not be sold. Many other enterprises, too, were much larger than comparable ones in the West—especially those with exceptionally high levels of vertical integration. The number of plants under the Treuhand's administration (40,000) gives the upper limit to the number of firms that can be created.

Because of the necessity of breaking up the large firms into saleable units, the number of firms to be privatized rose continuously in the first four quarters following the passing of the Second Trusteeship Law. Up to March 1991, about 1300 of the 4000 industrial firms that were established in July 1990 had been sold. At the same time the number of firms not yet sold had increased from 4000 to 9000.[37]

In addition to firms, the Treuhand owns or manages enormous areas of land, totaling 4 million hectares. This is 40 percent of East Germany's land area, and 50 percent of its private and privatizable land. Most of it consists of forests which are to be transferred to the municipalities. The trust owns 1.7 million hectares of agricultural land. In absolute terms this is equal to almost the entire land area of the Rhineland-Palatinate. In relative terms, however, it is only 27 percent of East Germany's agricultural land.[38] As was already mentioned, most agricultural land remained in private hands even after the farming cooperatives were established. The most valuable part of the Treuhand's property is its urban real estate (land and buildings).

---

37. See Deutsche Bank 1990. According to its definition, industrial firms are all those in the productive sector excluding the energy and fuel industry.
38. See Treuhand 1991a and appendix B.

Adding up to at least 270,000 hectares, this is equal to more than half of the area that is or could be privately owned.[39]

The Treuhand is not directly responsible for the reprivatization of the 12,000 small firms compulsorily sold to the government in 1972. These are the responsibility of the Länder, and by now many of them should have been returned to their former owners despite the legal difficulties. The return of these firms had already been decided by the GDR in March 1990.[40]

There have been 33,000 intergovernmental applications to the Treuhand for the return of property. These relate to almost a million properties, and include some of the 1900 public utilities that are to be returned to the municipal authorities. In some cases the applications go far beyond what can reasonably be considered to be the concern of the regional bodies. It is said that some municipalities have put in claims for such things as movie theaters, bookshops, and bakeries. Most applications, however, relate to real estate and forests which were formerly owned by the municipalities or which are to be transferred to them under the provisions of the Municipal Property Law of July 1990.

Reorganization with Privatization

The Unification Treaty (Article 25, paragraph 1) charges the Treuhand with "the competitive reorganization and privatization of the businesses formerly owned by the people." Before it can accomplish this, the Treuhand must decide whether a firm will be able to survive or whether it will have to be closed down. To provide a basis for this decision, and to give some indication of what the selling price should be, the Treuhand required the firms for which it was responsible to file opening deutschmark balance sheets starting from July 1, 1990. The original deadline of October 30, 1990 had to be extended to June 30, 1991, and for big firms it was extended to January 31, 1992. By May 1991, 60 percent of the firms had filed balance sheets, and 6 percent had been examined and approved by the Treuhand. At that time around 300 firms had been identified as not viable and had been closed down.[41] In the second half of 1991 the examination of the opening balance sheets speeded up, and since then the number of bankruptcies has increased steadily.

---

39. Ibid. and table 4.1.
40. Gesetz über die Gründung und Tätigkeit privater Unternehmen und über Unternehmensbeteiligungen (Private Firms Law), March 7, 1990.
41. See Treuhand 1991a and *Süddeutsche Zeitung* 47, no. 111, May 15, 1991, p. 29.

Under Article 25 of the Unification Treaty, the Treuhand takes over a firms's interest obligations to the Deutsche Kreditbank (the former Staatsbank) and to other banks up to the time it approves the opening balance sheet. After this is approved, the Treuhand can reduce or increase the firm's debt in a way designed to compensate for the often arbitrary assignment of liabilities by the communist authorities. Viable firms whose debts are too high receive an interest-bearing claim on the Treuhand; firms whose debts are too low are required to take on an interest-bearing liability. The Treuhand initially had a credit line of DM 25 billion for this and other purposes, but this credit line has been continually extended. It is expected that the excessive subsidies the trust has to pay to prevent further industrial collapse will have accumulated to a Treuhand debt of hundreds of billions of deutschmarks by the end of the century.

Although the filing of opening balance sheets and the debt-compensation procedure are prerequisites for privatization, they do not constitute reorganization in the sense intended by the words "competitive reorganization." Whether it should be the responsibility of the Treuhand to reorganize the firms in the sense of undertaking reorganization and restructuring investment is an extremely controversial question. Most German economists prefer spontaneous privatization without reorganization, arguing that the new management is better suited for the reorganization job than a government trust.

The sequence implied in the Second Trusteeship Law, which sees reorganization preceding privatization, is the traditional way of proceeding. It was the way chosen in Britain for the privatizations of the Thatcher era and in Chile for the reversal of the Allende nationalizations. The latter is the most extensive program of privatization that has yet been carried out.[42] In an important paper, Alan Walters, Mrs. Thatcher's former advisor, made a strong plea for the traditional sequence. In his opinion, reorganization must precede privatization; otherwise there will not be enough private buyers interested in the firms. He wrote: "So-called spontaneous privatization can be broadly characterized as the existing managements stealing the capital and running off with it. This is roughly speaking what spontaneous privatization amounts to in the Eastern Bloc."[43] Government supervision

---

42. See Bös 1991a and Luders 1990.
43. Walters 1990, p. 7.3. He went on to talk about the countermeasures being taken by the Polish and Hungarian governments, but he did not specifically mention East Germany. The many reports of sharp practices and underhanded dealings now appearing in the press indicate that Walters' fears are also relevant there. The manager of a Treuhand branch commented on German television on August 13, 1991 that he has to spend two-thirds of his time uncovering criminal activities.

of reorganization worked well in Britain because the state enterprises were given new managements and because a firm commitment had been made that the enterprises would be privatized within a given period of time. Walters argued that the prospect of privatization in 4 or 5 years was enough of a threat for the management and the employees to ensure that a thoroughgoing reorganization could be carried out. He offered British Telecom, British Airways, and British Steel as successful examples of this strategy.

Most economic advisors in Germany see the situation differently. They do not like the Treuhand's having the task of reorganization, because they fear that subsidies aimed at keeping inefficient firms in operation will be introduced on a large scale. They believe that private owners are more likely to be able to reorganize their firms successfully than a government agency. Reorganization through privatization is the principle prescribed by the Council of Economic Experts (Sachverständigenrat 1990) and by the Ministry of Economics Advisory Council (Wissenschaftlicher Beirat 1991a).[44] Whereas Walters' view is based on his own practical experience of the British privatizations, these bodies base their opinions on the exceptionally large number of firms awaiting privatization in East Germany.

While in Britain there were a few dozen firms to be privatized, and in Chile there were 500, in Germany there are tens of thousands.[45] The sheer magnitude of the task makes it difficult to imagine how a centrally managed attack on the problem of privatizing the whole economy of the former GDR could succeed. The Treuhand would be facing the same kind of logistical problems that led to the collapse of the communist economy. East German firms would try to keep going as long as they could with the old structures in order to avoid the hardships involved in thoroughgoing reorganization. The danger would be that firms would first exhaust their own resources and then use political pressure to obtain subsidies from the West in order to evade the obligation to reorganize.

Nothing remains, therefore, but to privatize as quickly and as extensively as possible. When the firms are privately owned, the owners will work out the best strategies and put them into operation as soon as they can. Of course, market imperfections in the transition phase will keep them from making completely optimal economic decisions, but there is good reason to believe that they will make fewer mistakes than a government

---

44. See also Möschel 1991 or Kronberger Kreis 1991.
45. Cf. the figures cited in section "Restitution and Sale" at the beginning of this chapter and those cited in the previous section ("The Treuhand's Task").

superagency would. Decentralized reorganization through market forces is clearly the better alternative for East Germany.

Even if this is correct, such a policy would do nothing to solve the problem Walters thinks is so important: How are enough interested potential buyers to be found? That this really is a problem is painfully obvious from the data on the number of completed sales given at the beginning of this chapter. What happens if half the economy proves impossible to sell? Should giveaway prices be accepted? Should anything that cannot be sold be closed down? Is it reasonable for millions of people to lose their jobs because no buyers can be found for the firms that employ them? The Council of Economic Experts (Sachverständigenrat 1990, chapter 4) is strongly in favor of this solution, partly because it trusts the market to make the right decisions and partly because it can see no other privatization alternative that will sufficiently stimulate the interest of investors. The severity of the consequences implicit in the sales strategy does, however, give rise to doubts about its desirability.

The relevance of a market test in the present situation of severe disequilibrium in the labor market will be denied in the next chapter, where the conditions under which such a test is appropriate are spelled out. The remainder of this chapter will be devoted to an analysis of the reasons why sales revenues have been so low. We shall develop a privatization model that shows how the interest of private investors in the Treuhand properties could be stimulated. The successful restructuring of East Germany would become much more likely if this model were to be applied.

The Junkyard Hypothesis

The parties to the Unification Treaty apparently assumed that a large amount of revenue would be generated by the sale of the Treuhand's assets. Article 25, paragraph 3 of the treaty stated that the "people's assets" were to be used "wholly and exclusively for the benefit of undertakings" in East Germany. In addition, the Trusteeship Law listed a series of functions for the institution which clearly assumed that it would receive substantial revenue from sales. These include the interest obligations mentioned above in connection with the drawing up of firms' opening balance sheets and the task of reducing the indebtedness of the agricultural sector. The disappointing sales revenue reported earlier, which is just 10 percent of what the Treuhand had expected to receive, makes the possibility of generating substantial revenue in the future seem extremely remote. The

Council of Economic Experts implied that the old proverb about counting chickens before they are hatched is clearly relevant in this case.[46]

There are many reasons why the sales revenues have been so meager. These can be divided into two categories. The first category is associated with the low efficiency of the post-communist economy. The second category includes reasons that stem from government policy, either the policy of unification in general or the specific method of privatization used by the Treuhand. This section deals with the first category and challenges the popular view that these reasons constitute the sole explanation for the poor sales record. The next section deals with the policy-related causes. An analysis of the causes of the poor sales record is a necessary preliminary to any attempt to develop a method for vitalizing the privatization procedure.

The reasons for the low efficiency of East German firms are the same as those that led to the sudden collapse of the East German economy after economic and monetary union had been established in the summer of 1990. These reasons were discussed in detail in chapter 2, so here it is only necessary to recall them. The main points are the following:

• The sudden change in goods and factor prices that accompanied the integration of East European firms into world trade. This change destroyed the East European trading networks and rendered old production patterns inefficient. Particularly important here is the speed with which wages adjusted toward Western levels.

• The lack of know-how brought about by self-imposed isolation.

• The adjustment to an inefficient set of institutions that had no similarity to those of a market economy.

• The false incentives for employees and managers created by the wage and salary payment systems.

The disastrous condition of the East German capital stock and the extensive environmental damage, both of which are highly visible, are outward signs of the low efficiency. It is clear that both of these problems have affected the willingness of potential buyers to invest in East German firms. As was mentioned above, the residual value of the capital stock has been estimated to be at most one-third of its book value (that is, no more than DM 580 billion) even before the costs of repairing environmental damage have been subtracted. It is thought that up to 50,000 polluted industrial sites will have to be cleaned up.[47]

---

46. Sachverständigenrat 1990, chapter 4, p. 231, subparagraph 518.
47. See Streibel 1990.

The role of the environmental pollution as a factor in the limited sales success of the Treuhand is nevertheless not as obvious as it might appear at first sight, because the Treuhand itself is paying for most of the cleanup costs. Purchasers will only have to take on a residual risk, the level of which is determined by the Treuhand's sharing the expenses and putting a ceiling on its own contribution so as to give the buyers an incentive to choose cost-effective cleanup methods rather than "luxurious" ones. The sensational reports appearing in the media and the horror stories told by buyers trying to drive prices down may give the impression that the whole of East Germany is a gigantic junkyard, but this is not so. The typical piece of industrial land in the former GDR is neither radioactive nor saturated with arsenic and dioxin. The main problem is the lack of filtration plants for sewage and waste gases. Experience in the West shows that this type of problem can often be eliminated quite quickly and at surprisingly little cost. Polls of East German investors have shown that environmental problems are perceived as less of an impediment to investment than the bad state of the public infrastructure, the incompetent public administration, or the legal uncertainties.[48]

It seems pretty clear that the structural shortcomings and the inefficiency of most East German firms meant that their market value would be zero, or even negative, if they were to continue to operate in the old way. The Treuhand would then have to pay the buyers to persuade them to take over the firms, even if the buyers were omnipotent universal financiers facing none of the liquidity problems discussed in the next section.

This does not, however, say much about what actually determines a potential purchaser's willingness to pay for a Treuhand firm, for no new owner would consider operating the firm in the old way. What is still missing from the analysis is a consideration of the role of investment in the reorganization of the firm. Such investment, aimed at ridding the firm of inefficiency and giving it a structure appropriate to the new competitive conditions, is the only way to achieve loss-free production. Taking over Western know-how, setting up new incentive systems, improving the quality of the products, reorganizing operation sequences, changing the product range, and removing production bottlenecks are among the immediate measures private entrepreneurs will have to take. Although these measures cannot guarantee that devaluation of previously invested capital will be completely avoided, in many cases they do promise a positive cash flow for the buyer in the medium term and a positive capital value for the invest-

48. See Sachverständigenrat 1991b, p. 76, figure 18.

ment. This capital value is the net present value of the cash flow the purchaser can expect from investing in reorganizing the firm if he does not have to pay for taking it over. If this capital value is positive, then the investment is worth undertaking, and offering a positive price for the firm is worthwhile.

The capital value of the reorganization investment is at one and the same time the present value of the potential earnings of the old capital and the amount of revenue the Treuhand could receive by selling the property under ideal competitive conditions. A price lower than this would mean that an economic profit could be made, so purchasers would bid against one another for the property and the profit would fall to zero. In an ideal competitive bidding process, the purchaser would be compensated for all his costs (including imputed interest and a risk premium on the equity invested) but the pure profit from the reorganization investment would go to the Treuhand. The investor can perhaps make a profit equal to his cost advantage over the next-best bidder; however, when there are large numbers of bidders—and this must be the case if the best reorganization strategy is to be discovered—the cost advantage can be expected to be very small and the Treuhand will be able to skim off nearly the whole of the reorganization profit. Anyone who argues that in a market economy the reorganization profit must go to the investor has not understood the basic principles of such an economy.

It is evident from this discussion that, although firms are at present incurring losses, the revenue the Treuhand can expect from selling may well be greater than zero. How high this revenue is likely to be cannot be inferred, however. Only the bidders know how they propose to reorganize the firms, and only competitive bidding can extract this knowledge from them.

It might be thought that the firms' opening balance sheets could be taken as indicating their value, but the system of compensating claims and liabilities described in the last section makes this extremely unlikely. The exact rule for calculating the amount of compensation is that a firm whose equity exceeds the value of its real estate must accept a liability, and that firms that are worth restructuring but whose equity value is negative are awarded compensating claims.[49] It is obvious that this provides strong incentives to understate the firm's value. The communist managers have been given a chance to demonstrate their skills in falsifying balance sheets one last time. The opening balance sheets certainly cannot provide the Treuhand with

---

49. See Dietl and Rammert 1990.

Table 4.1
Land owned by Treuhand.

	Area (million hectares)	Western prices (DM billion)	Present values with 10-year fallow period (DM billion)
Agricultural land	1.72	53	43
Forests[a]	0.51	6	5
Urban land	0.27	256	205
Total	2.50	315	253

a. After transfer of 1.45 million hectares to public ownership.
Source: Treuhand 1991a; authors' calculations from data in appendix B (below), where the method of calculating the prices is given. In 1991, the Treuhand was working on a detailed survey of real estate ownership. According to information given out on June 20, 1991, the actual amount of urban land owned by the Treuhand can be expected to be 0.4 million hectares—even more than reported in the table. Using this information would increase the total land values reported in the two latter columns by DM 123 billion or DM 98 billion, respectively.

reliable reference points for its price-setting policy. At most, these balance sheets might one day be useful for convincing the public of the success of the Treuhand's sales policy.

A better idea of the value of the Treuhand's properties can be gotten from table 4.1, which lists the land it owns. The table reports lower limits for the land values that would emerge under ideal market conditions. These lower limits are, however, only hypothetical ones, because (as will be explained below) there are many important policy-determined reasons that would prevent them from being realized when the properties are actually sold.

As has been mentioned, the most valuable part of the Treuhand's property is its real estate. Using 1989 West German prices, the value of the Treuhand's urban land (housing and industrial) amounts to DM 256 billion. If it is assumed that prices in East Germany will take 10 years to reach the then-prevailing West German levels, and if the land generates no rental revenue in the meantime, the present value of the Treuhand's urban land is still DM 205 billion. Similarly, the potential value of the Treuhand's agricultural land is between DM 43 billion and DM 53 billion. Including the forest land that does not have to be given back to the municipalities, the total value of the land owned by the Treuhand can be estimated at a good DM 300 billion using West German prices, and at about DM 250 billion using prices that would be appropriate if the land produced no revenue for 10 years. (Note that these figures refer to the land values only, and exclude any buildings. Note, too, that the underlying West German prices are distorted downward because they apply only to the land actually traded, most of which is in marginal locations.)

The Treuhand is obviously not presiding over a treasure trove; however, it is just as obviously not presiding over a junkyard, as many journalists and politicians would have us believe. The junkyard hypothesis completely overlooks the facts that the ideal market value of the Treuhand's properties is equal to the capital value of the reorganization investment and that the land value alone is much greater than the value that can be extrapolated from the revenue generated by the properties sold.

Six Reasons for the Endogenous Fall in Prices

The gap between the hypothetical and the realized prices of the Treuhand properties, which according to the Treuhand's own estimates is about 90 percent, needs explaining. Six possible endogenous explanations relating to the policies of the government and the Treuhand are discussed in this section. The reasons considered can all operate at once and can be mutually reinforcing. Assessment of their quantitative significance must be left to future econometric studies, which will (it is hoped) be based on better data than are now available to us. The reasons are complementary in the sense that removing only one of them will not result in a substantial increase in revenue even though the presence of just one of them may be sufficient to frustrate sales. We will discuss these reasons in what seems to us to be the reverse order of their importance, though in doing this we have no wish to preempt the reader's own assessment of the matter.

The list of reasons given here is by no means exhaustive. In fact, two of the most important reasons are not included. One of these is the fact, discussed above, that in many if not most cases restitution claims continue to apply to Treuhand properties even after they are sold. The other is the far-too-large increase in East German wages, a problem that will be analyzed in detail in chapter 5.

First Reason: Restricting Market Power

Under ideal market conditions, the Treuhandanstalt should aim to sell its properties to the highest bidder. It can be assumed that the highest bidder would have the best plan for restructuring the firm and would use the capital stock acquired in a way that would maximize the social surplus. However, there are two problems that can prevent the agency from allocating the property to the highest bidder. The first of these is the strengthening of market power. All too often, West German industrial firms are interested in buying up potential East German competitors in order to gain a foothold in additional markets in the East and to preserve their own market power. In many cases, the East German producer is downgraded to a mere sales office, with a minimal staff engaged simply in keeping up customers' records, and in some cases the East German plant is simply shut down to get rid of a potential competitor. The Treuhand is right to guard against such dangers when deciding who the purchasers are to be. It would surely make little sense to encourage mergers that would later be disallowed by the Cartel Office.

Second Reason: Employment Guarantees

The second problem associated with selling to the highest bidders, and thus maximizing sales revenues, is that the Treuhand sees guaranteeing job security as an important part of its task. Because unemployment has been rising so rapidly in East Germany, it requires potential buyers to commit themselves not only to investment plans but also to guaranteeing jobs for some of the firm's employees. The buyer who agrees to do this may obtain the contract even if he is not the highest bidder.

This policy may seem dubious from an efficiency point of view because it obstructs privatization and runs the risk of slowing down structural change by tying workers to unprofitable sectors. There may be some justification for the policy, however, if wages are higher than equilibrium levels, which can result in poor reorganization decisions and in the dismissal of too many workers. (These difficult questions will be discussed in more detail in chapter 5.) It is, in any case, clear that sales revenue is being reduced by wage subsidies that otherwise would have to be financed through the government budget.

Third Reason: Financing Unification by Borrowing

In the period leading up to unification, there was a hot debate as to whether unity should be financed by government borrowing or by increased taxes (see table 2.2). The first method could be justified by the public-finance argument that a one-time-only government expenditure should be financed by borrowing so as to spread the burden over successive generations (intergeneration equity). The argument in favor of increasing taxes to pay

for unification was that both government expenditure and private investment had to be financed and that it was important not to crowd out the
latter. Most economic advisors tended to discount this argument on the
ground that the German capital market is open to the world capital market.
It was assumed that the withdrawal of capital-market funds by the government would have little effect on German interest rates because domestic
funds would be replaced immediately by capital imports at the expense of
investment in the rest of the world.

In the event, credit financing of German unity was the method chosen.
It is now obvious, however, that the expectations associated with the
decision to use this method have not been realized, and that the capital
market has become very tight (see figures 2.5 and 2.6). The increase in the
budget deficit led to a large reduction in capital exports and eventually to
capital imports, as was desired, but it also increased the interest rates even
more than had been feared. For the first time in many years, German
long-term real interest rates exceeded the US rates, and eventually they
reached the level of the exorbitant 1984 US rates. The shambles the latter
had made of the world capital markets is well known.[50]

The high interest rates not only put an undesirable brake on investment;
they also narrowed considerably the Treuhand's revenue prospects, because they reduced the market values of the firms it was trying to sell.
Under ideal conditions, the market value of a firm equals the present value
of the cash flow it can generate, and this present value is a relative rather
than an absolute measure of profitability. It responds just as strongly to
changes in the interest rate used for discounting the future cash flow as it
does to changes in this cash flow itself. If the interest rate rises, the present
value of the future cash flow falls and so, too, does the maximum price a
purchaser is prepared to pay for the property.

Although the value of the capital stock in both East and West Germany
is affected, it is important to realize that the discount-rate effect is necessarily greater for East German capital, and that the present value of its earnings may well be pushed down below zero. The reason is that the West
German capital stock, which is optimally adjusted to present economic
conditions, does not have to be resuscitated by reorganization investment,
as does the East German stock. The former produces a steady positive cash
flow whose present value can never become zero or negative no matter
how high the discount rate may be. By way of contrast, the cash flow of
the East German firms starts out negative, because reorganization and

---

50. See Sinn 1988, 1989.

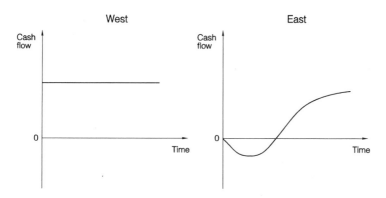

Figure 4.1
Comparison of cash flows.

restructuring investment must be undertaken; only later will it become positive (see figure 4.1). Even a small rise in interest rates could make the present value of this cash flow—the capital value of the reorganization investment—negative.

The extent of the danger that a rise in interest rates will cause the capital value of the reorganization investment (and thus the present value of the potential earnings of the Treuhand properties) to become negative can also be seen by comparing the interest rates in the capital market with yields on West German investment. In appendix A it is calculated that the real *average* rate of return on all private West German capital, including real estate, is 7 percent. Compare this with figure 2.5, where it is shown that real long-term interest rates in Germany rose above 6 percent in the year of unification and in 1991. This comparison indicates that many West German firms would certainly have negative capital values and would not be set up if the investment decision were being considered today. Only the fact that the expenditures involved have now become sunk costs ensures their continued existence.

The fact that present reorganization investment in East Germany must meet much stricter profit criteria than past West German investment is partly the result of an arbitrary policy decision. If the cost of unification had been financed by taxes instead of by borrowing, then consumption would have been lower, aggregate saving higher, and interest rates lower than they are now.

These statements will appear obvious to practical businessmen, but economists will want them explained further because they will immediately think of Ricardo's equivalence theorem (1817, p. 245).[51] According to this theorem, people see no difference between financing government expenditures by taxes and by borrowing, because borrowing means only a temporal displacement of the tax burden, with present values unchanged. They choose the same consumption path regardless of the method of financing used, so aggregate saving and the interest rate are the same in either case. It is now known that this theorem has very limited empirical relevance. Why this is so is also known. At least five important reasons can be suggested to explain why financing transfer payments to East Germany by borrowing led to higher consumption, lower aggregate saving, and higher interest rates than financing them through taxes would have:

• Private households did not understand that the two ways of financing government expenditures are equivalent. They adapted their consumption to their current levels of disposable income and did not take into account the fact that, because future disposable income would be reduced by the need to service the debt, it would have been wise to lower their present consumption accordingly.

• Private households expected that financing by borrowing would be compensated for in the future by reductions in government expenditures rather than by tax increases, because they believed that a growing debt burden would impose budgetary discipline on the government. If debt financing means that taxes can be permanently avoided, private households can afford a higher permanent level of consumption than they can with tax financing.

• Debt financing allowed credit-constrained private households to consume more than they could have if taxes had been increased. If taxes had been raised, these households would have had to curtail their present consumption. With credit financing of government expenditures they were given the option of meeting their future tax obligations by reducing their future consumption, and they decided to take up this option.

• To the extent that the burden of financing by borrowing was expected to fall on future generations, no need was seen to arrange for debt servicing by forgoing present consumption. (There may, of course, have been parents who wanted to share their children's future debt burden by bequeathing them more and so reduced their own current consumption, but certainly not all parents were so altruistic. In any case, not everyone has

---

51. This theorem was reconsidered in a popular article by Barro (1974). A detailed theoretical discussion of the pros and cons can also be found in Gandenberger 1972.

children. Debt financing involves a redistribution from ongoing family dynasties to those that have come to an end. This redistribution raises aggregate consumption because the present representatives of the two types of dynasty have very different propensities to consume.)

• People who believed that future debt service associated with government borrowing would be paid for by consumption taxes did well to avoid them by bringing their consumption forward.

These arguments make it obvious that the hope that debt financing would not put a greater burden on the capital market than tax financing was doomed from the start. It must be assumed that the decision to borrow raised interest rates, put an unnecessary brake on investment activity, and destroyed some of the value of the potential earnings of the Treuhand properties.

Fourth Reason: The Portfolio Effect

The first three reasons for the endogenous fall in the price of Treuhand properties would still be valid even if the Treuhand were trying to sell only a few firms. The remaining three reasons apply specifically to the effect on prices of its offering a large number of firms for sale all at once. They explain why, as in other cases, the law of demand must be respected when the goods in question are firms.

An important price effect results from the risks associated with buying the Treuhand properties. Unlike the returns from interest-bearing financial assets, the cash flows generated by these properties are far from certain— and the uncertainty is much greater than for West German firms. Property rights are unclear, and the costs of repairing environmental damage, the extent of the firms' legal responsibilities, and the future course of wages are all unknown. These, together with the uncertainties associated with the establishment of complementary industries, all add to the risks the purchaser of a Treuhand firm must face.

The risks mean that the buyer will not simply use the capital-market interest rate to discount the expected future cash flow, but will take them into account either by adding a risk premium to the discount rate used or by lowering the expectations of what the returns will be. The extent of the necessary adjustments will be closely related to the number of properties on offer. The individual buyers will become more risk-averse the larger the commitment they must make, and highly motivated, venturesome buyers will become scarcer and scarcer as the number of firms up for sale increases.

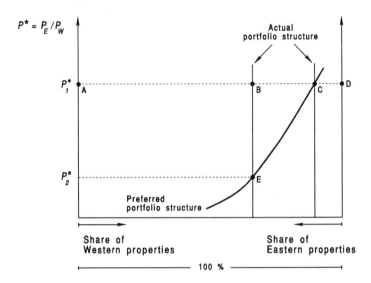

Figure 4.2
Property portfolio and Treuhand policy.

Purchasers will become less interested and more hesitant, and will require higher and higher risk premia.

The Treuhand is obviously being confronted with a typical portfolio problem. The more properties it puts onto the market, the higher the expected rates of return must be to induce buyers to include these properties in their portfolios. Other things being equal, higher rates of return will be expected only if the property prices fall.

The nature of the portfolio equilibrium is illustrated in figure 4.2, where we determine the relative market values of properties available in East and West Germany assuming that their quantities can be measured in terms of their constant book values. The shares of the West German and East German properties in the total privately owned book values are represented, as percentages, along the horizontal axis, the Western share being read from left to right and the Eastern share from right to left. By definition, the distance between the vertical axes is equal to unity (or 100 percent). In contrast, the market prices of the East German properties relative to the Western ones, $P^* = P_E/P_W$, are measured along the vertical axis.

The rising curve shows the owners' preferred portfolio structure as a function of the relative price of the East German properties, P^*. The higher this price, the larger the preferred share of West German properties and the lower the preferred share of East German properties in the overall portfolio. The vertical lines through B and C represent variants of the actual portfolio structure. The price is at an equilibrium level where the actual and preferred portfolios are equal. Where they are not equal, a disequilibrium exists and the price must adjust until they become equal.

If the Treuhand is selling only a few properties, and if the share of these properties in the total portfolio structure is given by CD (the share of West German properties being thus AC), the equilibrium price is given by P_1^*. If the supply is increased, the relative price falls, the extent of the fall being given by the change in the actual portfolio that results from the sale of the properties. For example, a policy that increases the relative share of East German properties from DC to DB causes the relative price to fall by BE, that is, from P_1^* to P_2^*. The fall in price analyzed here occurs not because the quality of the properties on offer has declined but because the absorptive capacity of the market for investment properties is limited.

It is possible, of course, to disagree with this conclusion, given the fact of open world capital and risk markets. Theoretically, East German properties could be bought by purchasers from all over the world, making up such a small proportion of each of their portfolios that the risks are diversified away. The relationship between quantity and price described above would then no longer hold. Unfortunately, however, such a diversification of the Treuhand risks does not occur.

The main reason for this is that in practice only whole firms are being offered for sale by the Treuhand.[52] Small shares, which could easily be integrated into a great many portfolios, are not available. The Treuhand has only twice considered selling a firm through the stock exchange, and has actually done so only once. The reason for its caution is that an amendment to the Stock Exchange Law (Börsengesetz) that would have made it possible to sell East German firms on the stock market was not among the many new laws passed in association with unification. It would have been quite easy to bypass the normal creditworthiness requirements and introduce a junk-bond rule for East German firms along American lines. In the absence of such a rule, East German shares cannot be issued and thus direct access to the risk-capital market is closed off.

Only indirect access remains as a possibility. West German buyers could issue shares in their own firms and by this means break up the risks they take over with East German firms. Under ideal conditions, this method

---

52. Under the pressure of public criticism, the Treuhand has recently considered changing its policy by using the services of investment funds. However, so far this policy is the exception rather than the rule.

could prevent them from requiring an increase in the risk premia. The problem with this is that in Germany, unlike in other countries, only a minority of firms are public corporations whose shares are quoted on the stock exchange. The limited diversification capacity of the German capital market is particularly obvious in a comparison with the United States. There the market value of the corporations was 69 percent of 1989 GNP, but in West Germany in the same year this value was only 25 percent of GNP.[53] Assuming that capital coefficients are similar, this means that the proportion of the capital stock that is potentially subject to portfolio diversification is more than $2\frac{1}{2}$ times as high in the United States as in Germany. The differences appear to be even bigger when it is recognized that in Germany only about one-quarter of the corporations are publicly traded and that of these just one-tenth (about 60 companies) have widespread ownership in the sense that there is no majority owner. In comparison with the United States, the German risk market is completely underdeveloped.[54]

The fact that small shares in East German firms are not available is only one reason why their risks cannot be diversified. Even if shares in these firms could be sold on the stock market, some of the risks could not be atomized because they are correlated, both among themselves and with overall capital-market risks. The risk that the upswing will be delayed affects all East German firms, and these firms are also affected by general business-cycle risks that apply to firms whose shares are already part of the purchasers' portfolios. If only for this reason, it is impossible to avoid the conclusion that the more Treuhand properties to be integrated into investors' portfolios, the lower the obtainable prices will be.

Fifth Reason: Credit Constraints

Even if there were no problems associated with the limited opportunities for risk diversification, other things would make it difficult for the market to absorb all the Treuhand properties at once. One of these difficulties comes from constraints on buyers' ability to borrow. It is precisely because less reliable borrowers are not deterred by high interest rates and are not easily identified that credit rationing has become a major allocative mechanism in the credit market.[55] Anyone who wants to finance the purchase

---

53. See OECD, *International Financial Statistics*, December 1990, pp. 242 and 554, and *Handbook of World Stock and Commodity Exchanges*, 1991, pp. 180 and 373.
54. Cf. Edwards and Fischer 1992, chapter 3.
55. For an outline of the theory of credit rationing see Baltensperger and Devinney 1985.

of a capital good by borrowing must contribute a certain proportion of the purchase price from his own resources; 100 percent loans are not obtainable. This fact is especially significant for the sales policy of the Treuhand since it prevents potential buyers from being able to raise as much financing as they would like.

The problem is exacerbated when, as is often the case, unresolved property relationships prevent the use of the property as collateral for a loan. Potential restitution claimants often block the discharge of debts on the property, and in many cases the registers in which mortgages and other types of loans are entered are not yet, or are no longer, available. Also, the entry of a loan on the property may be ruled out because the ownership of a building being sold does not coincide with the ownership of the land. Conditions essential for a properly functioning credit market are just not met in the new Länder, and it is obvious that the Treuhand's sales cannot be carried out as they would be under textbook conditions.

The number of buyers interested in a particular firm is limited by the location, the range of products, the production process used, the kind of customers, and many other details. Potential buyers who do not have the necessary know-how, or who are not geographically mobile, are ruled out from the start. This limitation would not be any problem if the remaining buyers could borrow as much as they liked from the capital market. Their willingness to pay for a Treuhand firm would then be determined exclusively by its potential earning capacity.

The situation is different where there is credit rationing. In this case, there is an upper limit on the amount the buyer has available to spend; it is determined by his own resources and by the proportion of the planned expenditure the bank will let him borrow. The quotient of the purchaser's own funds and the minimum equity-asset ratio the bank requires him to have is the upper limit on what he can spend in a particular property category. This upper limit on expenditure in a particular property category is not the same as the upper limit on the revenue the Treuhand can obtain from it. The expenditure that must be financed also includes the reorganization investment required to make firms viable. Because the aggregate volume of this investment increases as the number of properties increases, while the upper expenditure limit available for a property category is constant, the price the Treuhand can get from selling its properties must fall and may eventually become zero or even negative. For the whole range where credit rationing applies, the demand curve is strictly inelastic: the more properties the Treuhand sells, the lower its aggregate revenue will be.

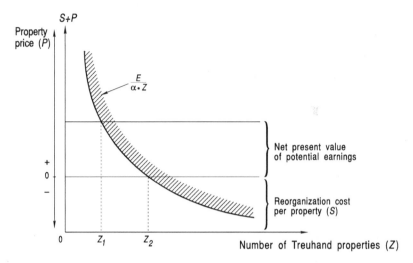

Figure 4.3
Credit limits and ability to pay. *Note:* If E is the amount of equity funds the potential buyer has available, α the minimum equity-asset ratio required by the bank, S the restructuring cost per property, P the price of the Treuhand properties, and Z their number, then, because of credit rationing, it holds that $\alpha \cdot (S + P) \cdot Z \leqslant E$. Solving for P gives the credit limit $P \leqslant [E/(\alpha \cdot Z)] - S$, illustrated here by the downward-sloping curve.

Figure 4.3 illustrates this relationship under the simplifying assumption that properties within a particular category are homogeneous: they all require the same amount of expenditure for reorganization, and the resulting cash flows all have the same present value. As was explained above, the capital value of the restructuring or reorganization investment is the same as the present value of a Treuhand property's potential earnings net of the cost of this investment. The revenue from sales can be expected to equal this present value only if the number of properties supplied is small enough to keep the credit limit from being a binding constraint. In the figure, this is the case when the number of properties supplied does not exceed the quantity Z_1. Quantities greater than Z_1 must sell for prices less than the net present value of their potential earnings, and if the quantity exceeds Z_2 only negative prices can be obtained. Although the present value of the properties' potential earnings is positive, the Treuhand cannot expect a positive revenue from the sale—and it is quite possible that, instead of receiving a payment from the buyer, it may have to pay someone to take over the firm.[56]

---

56. For further studies along these lines see Schöb 1992.

In part, the problem of the credit limit, too, can be traced back to the fact that the Treuhand is selling whole firms and not small shares in them, so that the opportunity to spread the sale over many buyers does not exist. This aspect of its sales policy limits the potential buyers to those who are willing to take on the running of the firms themselves. In practice these are West German firms from the same branches of industry and, in particular, the East German managers of the firms being sold. The West German firms must intend to expand and must be large enough to cope with the requirements of their commitment. In particular, they must have available unallocated equity funds not already tied to their normal business purposes. Some firms, but certainly not all, will be in this position. Well-run firms that have arranged their balance-sheet structures so as to maximize their tax advantages will have financed their operating capital largely by borrowing and will not have large amounts of surplus equity. If these firms want to commit themselves to operating in East Germany, they must build up additional equity funds by retaining profits or, more expensively, by issuing new shares.

The lack of capital resources among potential East German buyers creates an almost insurmountable problem. For them the fact that the German economy is completely integrated into the world capital market is no help at all, because they own almost no equity which they could use as proof of their creditworthiness. This situation did not come about because the GDR economy was badly managed; it is simply the result of the extremely cautious way the Bundesbank proceeded with the currency conversion. If the East Germans had been given financial claims equal to the value of the former state-owned property, they would, of course, be in a position to buy this property today. However, this did not happen. The credit constraint means that those buyers that are most strongly motivated from the point of view of insider knowledge and geographical location are, in practical terms, excluded from taking part in the Treuhand sales.

If, despite these difficulties, the principle of selling whole firms for cash is maintained, the credit constraints can be overcome only by finding a new group of buyers who have not so far been attracted by the Treuhand offerings. This is what the agency is attempting to do. The Treuhand's sales policy was initially rather passive; the agency used to wait for interested buyers to approach it. But more recently the Treuhand has taken more active measures to attract potential purchasers. It has distributed catalogs of firms on offer, advertised in the press, and taken part in industrial fairs. It has made particularly strenuous attempts to find foreign buyers. Although it has had some success, it has not yet made any great breakthrough. As before, West German firms have been involved in almost all sales, and foreign firms have played a rather minor role. Despite vigorous attempts to publicize its offers in other countries, up to October 31, 1991 the Treuhand had been able to attract foreign buyers for only 5 percent of the industrial firms it had sold.[57]

One factor that limited the Treuhand's success in attracting foreign buyers was that only in exceptional cases did it make use of investment banks with experience in international markets. According to a statement by the Treuhand, one of its attempts, which involved a lucrative hotel chain, failed because of resistance by "new coteries." These caused it the same kind of trouble as the "old coteries" of the former GDR, which strongly resisted the closing down of firms. Hopes that the Treuhand's problems could be solved with the help of foreigners have not, as yet, come to much.

Sixth Reason: The Stock-Flow Problem

The Treuhand has attempted to circumvent basic macroeconomic relationships and to call upon financial resources that just do not exist. The fact that this attempt is doomed to failure may not be noticed when the other reasons (including the legal uncertainties) drive the sale prices close to zero. Of course, sales at zero prices place no demands on capital markets. This, however, does not alter the fact that it would not have been even theoretically possible to sell off the whole capital stock of the GDR in the way proposed by the Treuhand and to collect a revenue of DM 600 billion, as was officially expected.[58] Even if the properties provided risk-free investment opportunities and were profitable under normal conditions, if there were no legal problems, and if buyers had access to as much funding as they wanted, trying to sell them so suddenly would necessarily drive the prices down to zero. The enormous quantity of funds required would push interest rates up until the market values of the properties sold approached zero.

Unlike the fifth reason for the fall in prices, which was related to microeconomic credit constraints, the sixth reason involves macroeconomic constraints. It is concerned not with the fact that individual investors cannot borrow as much as they want, but with the fact that the demand for funds worsens credit conditions so much that investors are scared off. The sixth reason is closely related to the third, which attributes the erosion of the

---

57. See Treuhand 1991b, p. 1.8, in connection with p. 1.27. A discussion of the reasons for the low engagement of foreigners can be found in Preusse 1991.
58. See footnote 10.

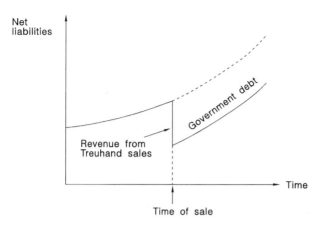

Figure 4.4
Paying off government debt with Treuhand revenue?

Treuhand values to increases in interest rates driven up by government borrowing to finance unification.

If, instead of being sold, the Treuhand properties were exchanged for other assets, such as West German capital goods or financial securities, there would be no danger of interest rates' increasing. An asset swap can be carried out quickly, in the amounts desired, without greatly disturbing capital-market equilibrium.[59] An asset swap would occur if the Treuhand used the revenue from its sales to reinvest in the capital market or to pay off some of the government's debt. In the second case, the time path of the stock of government debt would shift downward at the time of sale, as shown in figure 4.4.[60]

An exchange of assets nevertheless remains only a hypothetical possibility, because this is not in line with the Treuhand's actual policy. Article 25, paragraph 3 of the Unification Treaty stipulates that Treuhand revenues be used for the benefit of the new Länder, and the revenue from sales goes mainly to firms, institutions, and individuals who are constrained in their ability to raise credit and who have absolutely no intention of putting their

59. The portfolio argument for declining prices (fourth reason) still remains completely valid when the risks involved in buying the Treuhand properties are taken into account. The discussion in this section abstracts from this.

60. A mere reduction in net new borrowings—that is, a reduction in the slope of the path of government debt—is not sufficient to finance the purchases of the stock. In 1991 the government budget deficit was about DM 100 billion, but if the privatization program had been carried out as expected the Treuhand revenue would have been DM 600 billion, and thus the government debt would have had to fall by DM 500 billion.

newly acquired funds back into the capital market. The old saying that "money burns a hole in your pocket" is especially true of the Treuhand's income—its revenue really does breed expenditure.[61] At present this revenue is flowing, by way of cross-subsidies to firms fighting for their very existence, into purchasing consumption, intermediate goods, and replacement investment. Even if something is left over, it must be given to the state governments, and it is most unlikely that they will use it for anything other than purchasing more goods. As figure 4.4 illustrates, it is technically possible for the stock of government debt to be reduced by the value of the stock of Treuhand properties; however, this is contrary to the duties of the Treuhand as set down in the Unification Treaty, and it is completely out of the question from the point of view of the public choice theory. According to this theory, policy makers will not miss the opportunity to increase their power by spending as much revenue as they can.

This is the fundamental dilemma of the Treuhand's policy. Instead of exchanging its assets against securities, the agency wants to exchange them for goods out of current production—which means, in effect, that it plans to absorb private savings. To give way to the Treuhand's demand for goods and to provide the purchasers of Treuhand assets with the necessary means of finance, either private savings will have to rise via a decline in consumption or other savings-financed expenditure will have to be crowded out. Sound as this plan may seem at first sight, it cannot work, because savings are flows and flows cannot match stocks. If capital stocks are to be purchased from savings flows, enough time must be allowed for savings to accumulate. Unless sales are spread over a sufficiently long period of time, not enough revenue can be generated. The attempt to sell 70 percent of the East German capital stock in exchange for West German savings at a single point in time, or in just a few months, is bound to be a failure—just as attempting to fill a dam overnight with water from the river that flows into it would be.[62]

This is even more true when the river is only a rivulet. Aggregate private savings can hardly be changed through the Treuhand policy, and there are no spare savings that are still seeking investment opportunities; efforts to create them necessarily raise interest rates and reduce the Treuhand values. Under the present Treuhand policy, West German saving equals the sum of private net investment, the government budget deficit

61. This behavior of the Treuhand has caused the German economic research institutes to postulate a harder budget constraint: see Arbeitsgemeinschaft 1991, p. 29.
62. For a discussion of the macroeconomic stock-flow problem associated with the Treuhand policy see Sinn 1990, 1991a, and 1991b. See also Bolton and Roland 1992.

(excluding Treuhand revenues), capital exports, and Treuhand revenue. As figure 2.6 shows, at the start of 1991 private saving was already being absorbed by net investment and the recently increased government deficit.[63] Capital exports, which in 1990 were still DM 100 billion, had disappeared and had given way to imports of capital associated with increased goods imports. If the sales of the Treuhand were to produce the estimated DM 600 billion revenue, they would have to be financed by a *further* increase in net capital imports, or else the drain on savings by the budget deficit and net investment would have to be reduced—a rather unlikely event.

A Treuhand-induced increase in net capital imports would mean using foreign savings, either directly or indirectly, to finance purchases of the Treuhand properties. The size of the world capital market, the large flow of savings that services it, and the high mobility of international capital might in the first instance encourage hopes that interest arbitrage would make enough funds available so that the properties could be sold quickly.

Unfortunately these hopes fade as soon as it is remembered that the mobility of international financial capital is only a necessary and not a sufficient condition for the import of capital. Flexible goods flows are also necessary if capital imports are to be induced by way of higher interest rates. It is true that individual purchasers can always get foreign credit because they can induce offsetting transactions by other market participants, but it would be quite wrong to conclude that this observation is applicable to international credit as a whole. If the domestic demand for credit is to induce a *net* inflow of foreign capital, the current-account balance must react in a way that allows the foreign suppliers of capital to buy the deutschmarks they need in the foreign-exchange market. To bring about the necessary current-account reaction would require a complex chain of causes and effects. First of all, interest rates would have to rise as a result of the domestic demand for credit by the purchasers of the Treuhand properties. This increase in interest rates would then have to attract foreign capital, the deutschmark would have to appreciate as a result of increased demand for it on the foreign-exchange market, and finally the current-account balance would have to deteriorate as a result of the appreciation of the deutschmark. The deutschmarks required to finance the import of capital will be supplied to the foreign-exchange market only when the current-account balance has deteriorated.

---

63. In principle the budget deficits shown in the diagram include the cross-subsidies financed by the Treuhand revenue. However, for the reasons explained, the Treuhand revenue was negligible in 1990 and 1991.

It is extremely unlikely, if not impossible, that this chain of events would enable the Treuhand to carry out its DM 600 billion mass sales program. First, even if the current account reacted quickly enough, the capital supplied would still be a flow and the stock-flow problem would remain. Second, the mechanism described implies an increase in domestic interest rates. Even if this mechanism worked as described, an erosion of the Treuhand values could not be avoided. (To some degree this would be true even if the Treuhand were spreading its sales over time.) Third, experience has shown that the current-account balance is most unlikely to change quickly in the direction required. The quantity of goods traded internationally tends to remain constant in the short run, so that the appreciation will initially cause the value of imports to fall and the current-account balance to improve (the J-curve effect). Drawing on foreign capital to pay for the Treuhand properties would therefore lead at first to an export of capital rather than an import. Anyone who wants to dispose of the financing problem by appealing to the existence of the open world capital market necessarily comes up against this basic conclusion of international monetary theory. As the case of the United States in the 1980s showed, it can take years for the mechanism described to produce the capital imports required. The Treuhand certainly cannot afford to wait that long. Fourth, any attempt to finance Treuhand purchases by importing capital would risk being frustrated by the Bundesbank's stable-exchange-rate policy. To keep the deutschmark from appreciating, while holding the supply of money constant, the Bundesbank has to buy foreign currency in exchange for domestic securities.[64] This policy would prevent capital from being imported to finance the Treuhand's sales right from the outset.

The only way the planned revenue of DM 600 billion could bring about a current-account deficit large enough to induce the capital imports required would be if this revenue were spent directly and exclusively on foreign goods. Only in this way could the macroeconomic financing problems be solved. Strictly speaking, the stock-flow problem would still exist, because even world saving is a flow. However, as the amount of DM 600 billion is small relative to this flow, there would not be an absorption problem.

Before unification, the FRG's import rate was only about 20 percent.[65] If this rate applied to the Treuhand expenditures, then just DM 120 billion of

---

64. Technically, this policy consists of buying foreign currencies to support their value relative to the mark and combining this with a tight monetary policy to mop up the increase in the money supply brought about by the currency purchases.
65. See appendix A.

the expected sales revenue could be financed without affecting exchange rates; the question of the remaining DM 480 billion would not be resolved. It must be paid for by way of the exchange rate's effect on the current-account balance, described above. The problem of financing it would show up again in full strength. Unless all of the Treuhand revenue was converted directly into imports, the incompatibility of stock and flows, the J-curve effect, and the central bank's exchange-rate policy would again create problems.

The new German transfer problem has potentially the same dimensions as the transfer problem caused by Germany's having to pay reparations after the First World War. Inflexible international trade flows wrecked attempts to find a solution to the transfer problem then; they could certainly wreck the sales strategy of the Treuhand now.

It may be true that the combined force of all the other reasons for an endogenous fall in prices has kept the absorption problem discussed in this section from becoming a binding constraint, but this cannot be credited to the Treuhand. The whole concept of the sales policy was economically wrong. It was carried out because marginal microeconomic privatization strategies previously used in other Western countries were superficially transferred to the whole economy without even considering the existence of macroeconomic constraints.

By definition, a budget deficit is a reduction in government wealth. Treuhand revenue that is spent rather than reinvested in the capital market thus contributes to the government's overall budget deficit. In 1991, the deficit excluding the Treuhand sales was about DM 100 billion. If the Treuhand had succeeded in generating a revenue of DM 600 billion in 1991 and had used this revenue to finance the revival of East Germany, the overall deficit would have increased to DM 700 billion (25 percent of the GDP). The actual deficit of DM 100 billion was already regarded as enormous, and most observers agreed that it was a major cause of the historical peak in Germany's interest rates relative to those in other countries. Only supreme optimists could have expected the capital and goods markets to cope with an increase in the deficit spending from DM 100 billion to DM 700 billion without further increases in interest rates and without erosion of the value of the Treuhand property.

The stock-flow problem described thus far is macroeconomic in nature. A microeconomic variant of this problem is related to the individual credit constraints discussed in the previous section.[66] As explained, potential

---

66. See Bolton and Roland 1992 and Sinn 1991b.

purchasers who do not have sufficient equity capital today are unable to pay the capitalized values of the Treuhand properties. Nevertheless, these purchasers can augment their equity capital over time by accumulating savings. West German firms can retain and accumulate their profits, and East German households can build up a stock of savings from wages and transfers. If the Treuhand realizes this and sells its properties slowly enough, it can overcome the microeconomic credit constraints and free the capitalized values—however, it is then selling flows and not stocks of capital. The political aim of selling off the whole of the Treuhand's capital stock in one fell swoop can also be seen as the deeper reason for the effects of microeconomic credit constraints described above. The macroeconomic stock-flow mismatch erodes the net present values of the Treuhand assets and reduces the purchasers' *willingness* to pay. The microeconomic stock-flow mismatch leads to a collision with individual credit constraints and reduces the purchasers' *ability* to pay. Both problems create a conflict between the goal of realizing high sales revenues and the goal of privatizing rapidly and this conflict cannot be resolved when the cash-sales method is used. The Treuhand would have to resort to magic if it wanted to achieve both its aims at once.

The Participation Model

As is evident from the above discussion, the Treuhand's cash-sales strategy has severe deficiencies. It results in erosion of the prices of the Treuhand properties, and it prevents the Treuhand from carrying out the task, given to it by the Unification Treaty, of transferring shares in the state-owned property to the savers. It delays privatization, because to offset the fall in prices the Treuhand must spread its sales over a relatively long period of time. It also retards the upswing, because the buyers draw on capital-market funds that otherwise would have gone into profitable private investment.

Since selling the properties for cash makes no sense, they should be given away or exchanged for something other than cash. In the next few sections we develop a privatization model that embodies this conclusion. The heart of the model is a participation strategy by which investors and the East German population get shares in firms without having to pay any money to the Treuhand. We deal first with corporations; then we discuss the problems associated with the privatization of unincorporated enterprises and real estate. Finally, we return once again to the reasons for the endogenous fall in prices.

The Model for Corporations

Grants of shares are suitable for large and medium-size firms that can be set up as corporations. It is desirable to find a wise method of distributing the shares that will guarantee wide dispersion of ownership, establish strong owner interests, and introduce well-motivated management.

An interesting but problematic way of distributing the shares is that chosen for the "big" privatization now underway in Czechoslovakia.[67] Each citizen is first assigned 1000 coupon points in exchange for a symbolic payment of about one week's salary. Shares in firms are then auctioned, the prices being denominated in coupon points. Shares are sold in individual firms and in investment funds with well-diversified portfolios. These alternatives cater to those who want shares in particular firms and to those who are interested in getting returns that are as safe as possible.

The Czech method of privatization has a great many advantages and is worth serious consideration. It provides for a symmetrical distribution of the now-ownerless capital assets left behind by the communist state. Its standardized procedures allow a large number of firms to be dealt with simultaneously, and it makes no demands on capital-market funds.

Its major disadvantage, noted in a report of the Advisory Council to the Economics Ministry (Wissenschaftlicher Beirat 1991a), is that it does not solve the reorganization problem. Initially the old managers continue to run the firms; new owners can take over the management and develop plans for restructuring only after privatization has been completed. It is true that, in principle, there is no reason at all to fear that it would not be in the private interests of the new owners to reorganize the firms. Competent managers can be hired, and advice and other help is obtainable from management consultants. However, the advocates of the cash-sales method of privatization now being used in Germany can rightly claim that this method provides a more direct solution to the reorganization problem, in that reorganization concepts and plans are provided with the act of privatization. Normally, the purchasers are West German firms in the same branches of industry. They have access to plenty of information about how to organize the firms' operations optimally and about product ranges and trade linkages, and they can also provide competent management. The disadvantages, which in turn can be attributed to the cash-sales method, have been discussed in the previous sections.

---

67. See Begg 1991. A similar suggestion for the East German economy was made in Sinn 1990. For the reasons explained in the text, this book no longer supports a mere distribution scheme.

The participation model proposed here avoids the disadvantages of both the Czech and the German methods. It solves both the financing and the reorganization problems. The model, proposed in Sinn 1991a, was supported by a minority of the members of the Advisory Council to the Economics Ministry (Wissenschaftlicher Beirat 1991a) and has found considerable attention in the literature.[68]

As far as contacts with private investors are concerned, the model's procedures are similar to those currently used in Germany. Just as it does now, the Treuhand looks for competent investors who could provide the required know-how, capable experienced management, and the capital needed for reorganization investment. What is new is that the investor does not pay anything for the firm he is taking over; instead, the Treuhand retains a share in the firm. The investor's share corresponds to the value of the technological knowledge he provides plus the value of his own investment for reorganization purposes; the Treuhand's share, in principle, reflects the value of the firm's existing stock of capital. The Treuhand and the private investor are partners each of whom contributes his own particular type of equity to create a new firm that has a chance of surviving under market conditions.

The Treuhand is not supposed to keep its equity claim though, but to distribute it to the East German population. One way of doing this is transferring the claims to investment funds and then distributing shares in these funds to the people. The details of this part of the participation model are given below in this chapter and toward the end of chapter 5. It is important at this stage to realize that the model implies only a gift to the East German population, not one to the investor. The investor receives shares in exchange for the know-how and the reorganization funds he contributes, and the East German population receives shares that reflect the value of the old capital contributed by the Treuhand (including the investment chances this capital offers). In value terms, 100 percent of the Treuhand properties are given to the population, and yet a dominant shareholder is established who can be expected to carry out the entrepreneurial function.

The size of the retained share is arrived at by negotiation between the Treuhand and the partner firm much as the price is determined in the cash-sales method. The current procedure with the cash-sales method requires the investors to make a price offer and to specify the investment

---

68. See Bös 1991b, Bolton and Roland 1992, Demougin and Sinn 1992, Leipold 1992, Michaelis and Spermann 1991, Sinn and Sinn 1991, and Sinn 1991b. In addition, there have been many newspaper reports in the German press.

program they intend to carry out. The Treuhand then makes its choice in terms of what it sees as the best combination of these two aspects of the bid. With the participation model, the investors must specify both the percentage share they allow the Treuhand to retain and the investment program, and then the Treuhand decides. If the conditions for reasonably well-functioning labor markets are met (see the extensive discussion in chapter 5), the contract should be given to the investor whose plan can be expected to bring the highest present value of the dividends and distributions accruing to the Treuhand's retained share.

The investment plan must be specified and guaranteed much as the Treuhand now requires. In order to motivate the investor to carry out the plan in the specified way, he could, for example, be required to give back part or all of his share to the Treuhand if he fails to keep the agreement. Another alternative would be to increase the investor's share in step with the progressive completion of the announced investment plan. An increase in the investor's share must, in any case, be generally possible so as to keep alive the incentive to inject more equity into the firm in the future. The contract with the Treuhand is, in this respect, no different from the usual share contract associated with a corporation.

There should, however, clearly be a difference with respect to the control over participatory and consultation rights of the Treuhand or the funds. Because of the overriding need to provide an incentive for investors, the retained share should be held in the form of a sleeping partnership (i.e., a partnership without voting rights).[69] This, naturally, makes a well-specified right of control even more important in order to protect the sleeping equity holder against fraud and other criminal actions.

From an economic point of view, the idea of retaining nonvoting shares is similar to dividend taxation of corporations, which is known to be easy to administer and to have important neutrality properties from an allocative point of view.[70] With such taxes the government makes itself a sleeping partner of the firm. It has no influence on the decision-making; it does, however, exercise considerable control through the revenue offices and the tax laws. The economic difference between dividend taxation and the own-

---

69. The importance of this point is emphasized by Bös 1991b in a response to the first edition of this book. Elaboration on this point was not made in the first edition but was contained in Sinn 1991a.

70. Dividend taxes belong to the category of cash-flow taxes. Cash-flow taxes do not distort the investment decisions, because they imply that the government, by giving up tax revenue, contributes to the investment outlay to the same extent as it participates in the returns. See Sinn 1987.

ership of nonvoting shares lies primarily in the fact that the participation "tax" rate is individually negotiated in relation to the value of the firm and the equity and know-how provided by the investor. A further important peculiarity is that future equity injections by the investor permit the Treuhand's participation rate to fall.

It is desirable that the investor put in enough capital and know-how to make him a majority shareholder (that is, to keep the retained share below 50 percent). If at first this proves impossible, an attempt should be made to find other private participants who would then have the usual control and participatory rights. If this attempt also fails, the investor can then be offered the prospect of an increase in his share rights depending on the success of the firm which he will be allowed to manage. Until a majority shareholding is attained, the Treuhand or the fund's management naturally keeps certain participatory rights which go beyond a sleeping partnership. If no private investors can be persuaded to participate, then nothing remains but to close down the firm—always on the assumption that competitive structures exist elsewhere in the economy.

Management Buyout

Even though West German firms will still be the main potential investors if the participation model is put into practice, it must be possible for a firm to be handed over to its former East German managers if they are the highest bidders. In this case there would be no additional know-how involved, but the transfer to private ownership would greatly increase the incentive to run the firm in a profitable and cost-effective way.

"Privatization without cash sale" gives the potential East German investors a much better chance of making successful bids. It prevents the new Länder from simply becoming havens for subsidiaries of West German firms that do not compete with the parent companies and whose main role is to cushion the parents against cyclical swings.[71] If East Germany is to be restored to health, it needs genuine entrepreneurs who are willing and able to compete with the West German market leaders.

Giving away firms to their former managers is especially worth considering in the case of small companies whose investment needs are modest. The big advantage of this model over management buyouts in the literal

---

71. Despite promises to the contrary, the firm Kugelfischer closed down a recently acquired plant in East Germany because of sales difficulties. A member of the West German Betriebsrat commented that charity clearly still begins at home.

sense is that the managers do not need any funds to obtain the firm from the Treuhand. The meager funds that they can put their hands on can all be used for reorganizing the firms, while at the same time none of the "people's property" needs to be given away.

The advantages of the participation model proposed here are greatest for the case of privatization intended to arouse the East Germans' interest in entrepreneurial activities. Only those interested East German buyers who succeeded in accumulating substantial financial wealth during the Communist regime will not profit from the application of this model. They certainly have better opportunities if the Treuhand carries on with the cash-sales method. Whether this fact supports the Treuhand's policy or whether it supports our suggestion we leave up to the reader.

Handing Over the Retained Shares

A big advantage of the participation model is that it enables the Treuhand to carry out the task assigned to it—that is, where possible to provide the East German people with claims against the former "people's property." The compromise reached by the parties to the Unification Treaty (Article 25) was based on the assumption that savers were to be given such claims to compensate them for having their savings converted at a rate of 2:1. With the cash-sales method used by the Treuhand, this agreement has become a farce. There is no hope that any claims to assets worth mentioning will be available for savers after privatization is complete. With the participation model, on the other hand, there would certainly be valuable assets to be distributed, because some are retained at every step in the privatization process. The "possibility" mentioned in the Unification Treaty would become a certainty.

Little can be said against using the Czech method of distributing the retained assets, though the coupon points would have to be given away rather than sold for even a symbolic sum. (Unlike Czechoslovakia, East Germany no longer has a money overhang.) The savers' claims could then be satisfied quite simply by their participation in the distribution of the coupon points provided.

However, it is not necessary to use the Czechoslovak method to distribute the shares retained in the East German firms. Instead of first giving out coupon points and then selling shares in the firms in exchange for the coupons, it would be possible to set up regional or industry-related investment funds and distribute shares in these funds directly. The exact method of distribution is not essential to our proposal; it is a side aspect. There are many feasible ways of distributing the shares, all of them superior to the sales method. It would be preferable, however, to privatize the management of the funds in order to further reduce state's influence and to install incentives for careful monitoring of the firms. The owners of the funds' shares should be given the right to elect the funds' management.

It is even worth considering privatizing the Treuhand itself instead of creating separate funds and transferring their shares to the East German population. The regional Treuhand branches that now function as government authorities could be transformed into private investment funds and their shares distributed.

Despite the fact that the exact method of distribution is not very important, a particular method is proposed below, and it is argued there that this proposal should be combined with a moratorium on wages. As with the currency conversion of July 1990, a procedural law would have to be passed to determine the details.

It must be emphasized that, although the legislative process would take some months, there need be no delay in putting the participation model into practice. There is nothing to prevent the Treuhand from dispensing with cash payment and retaining shares in its firms now. The easing of pressure on the capital market and other advantages of the method could be realized immediately. In fact, since the first edition of this book came out, the Treuhand has occasionally used a participation model similar to the one described above. It has privatized some firms by retaining a fractional ownership instead of demanding cash, and has then transferred the ownership retained to local communities. This is certainly not the optimal way of allocating the share of ownership retained, but the new policy is a milestone on the way to overcoming the cash-sales method.

Nobody can guarantee that the shares will have a high market value. What can be distributed now is not the certainty of receiving a return but the chance of receiving one. The East Germans' legitimate wish to participate in this chance should not go unheard. This is another reason for introducing the participation model, quite apart from the efficiency reasons discussed in this section.

Some voices have been arguing that the East Germans would not be interested in getting the "junk bonds" the Treuhand could offer and that the government should "protect" these people from the disappointment such bonds are likely to cause. However, the voices were those of West German industrial interests, who may well be afraid that a different privatization method would reallocate the potential windfall profits in a way that they would dislike. The Czechoslovak experience again shows how unfounded such views really are. After a somewhat difficult start, the Czechoslovak distribution method has turned out to be a great success. No fewer than 6.5 million people, or more than 40 percent of the Czechoslovak population, had subscribed to the privatization program by the end of 1991, and the coupon prices have now risen to many times their original level. Czechoslovak Finance Minister Vaclav Klaus, who has been responsible for the privatization model, was the winner of the national elections in the spring of 1992. A similar success story would be possible in Germany if the participation model were applied. For the reasons explained above, the value of the Treuhand shares would definitely be much larger than the sales revenues the Treuhand is currently earning, and particularly large values could be expected if the participation model were combined with a wage moratorium (as will be recommended in the next chapter).

Other Properties: Credit Sales

The financing problem applies not only to corporations but also to unincorporated enterprises and all the other assets that the Treuhand must transfer to private ownership. As was mentioned previously, it seems that most of the value of the Treuhand's assets is in real estate. Precisely here it is essential for privatization to be completed quickly so that private initiative can be exercised and the upswing can get underway.

In the case of these properties, however, it is not possible for the agency to hold back shares, as it was with corporations. Defining and enforcing participation claims would require more control and more extensive bookkeeping duties than can reasonably be imposed.

Selling by crediting the purchase price provides a good substitute for retaining shares. It establishes a claim of the Treuhand on the property, which can be distributed to the East German people, and it avoids putting pressure on the capital market. Its advantage is a technical one, and it comes from the fact that claims associated with the giving of credit take the form of agreements to make fixed interest payments and are thus easy to define and enforce. Its disadvantage is that purchasers face higher risks than they would with retained shares. When a share of capital is retained, the investor only has an obligation to pay out part of the profit if any is made. Interest obligations, on the other hand, must always be paid and if necessary must be financed out of the existing capital.

Where buying on credit is possible at market interest rates, this is better for the investor than buying for cash. A buyer who does not need to borrow can put his funds in the capital market and suffer no disadvantage.

A buyer who faces credit restrictions, however, can buy a property that he otherwise would not have been able to finance. Buyers of land that they want to build on, or buyers of firms that need to be restructured, will be happy to be able to save their own resources for the investment they intend to undertake. This is especially true if the Treuhand is content with subordinated securities, as it should be.

The Advantages of the Participation Model

The privatization model proposed can do nothing about the moribund condition of the East German capital stock. It cannot get rid of the monopoly-power problem, the burdening of the properties with social plans, or the financial bottlenecks caused by the government's borrowing to finance unification. It can, however, reduce the danger of a supply-induced fall in the price of the Treuhand properties. Individual credit restrictions lose their importance, the stock-flow problem is done away with, and the sting is taken out of the portfolio problem. Thus, there is no longer any reason to privatize *slowly* in order to get reasonable prices. More funds are available at lower interest rates for the necessary restructuring of the firms. More-over, participation helps to ease the restitution problem. Last but not least, it can be used as a bargaining ploy to persuade East German workers of the benefits of a wage moratorium. The first four advantages will be discussed in the following subsections; discussion of the fifth is postponed until the last chapter.

Easing the Individual Credit Constraints

It is obvious why the participation method eases the problem of individual credit constraints. As the Treuhand demands no cash but keeps a share in the firm or a credit claim against it instead, the investor no longer has to pay twice (once for reorganization investment and once for the old assets supplied by the Treuhand). Forgoing payment in cash means, in effect, that the Treuhand is returning the purchasing price to the firm in the form of equity or debt capital. In view of the poverty of the East German bidders and the fact that it is often impossible to use the property as collateral, this will be a strong stimulus to the demand for the Treuhand properties. More firms can be reorganized because additional funds are available for that purpose, and the danger that the Treuhand properties will be given away without appropriate compensation is lessened. Credit-constrained investors

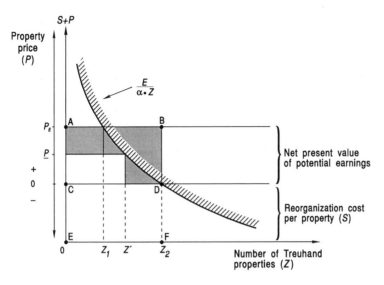

Figure 4.5
Overcoming the credit constraints.

may be willing to commit themselves to taking on the property and concede a substantial share ownership to the Treuhand, although they would not be able to pay a cash price.

The two advantages are illustrated in figure 4.5, which again uses the format introduced in figure 4.3. Assuming that the Treuhand's lowest asking price is $\underline{P}$ (which is positive but lower than the present value of earnings net of reorganization investment, P_E), then, with the cash-sales method, the number of firms that can be privatized is Z'. The only way to privatize more firms is to lower the price.

Suppose first that the purchasing price $\underline{P}$ is permanently credited with an interest equal to the market rate. In this case demand will rise to Z_2, because the funds the investor has will be just sufficient to cover the reorganization costs. The investors will make a profit of $P_E - \underline{P}$ per project. However, $\underline{P}$ is lower than it needs to be in order for the quantity Z_2 to be sold. Because the purchase price is being collected in the form of future interest payments, it can be raised to just below the level of the value of returns, P_E, without affecting the quantity demanded. Privatization through credit has, in fact, the double advantage of expanding the volume of sales —from Z' to Z_2—and increasing the Treuhand's revenue in present-value terms. The shaded areas in the figure 4.5 show the increase in the present value of revenue.

Consider now the case where a fractional ownership in the firm is retained by the Treuhand. This case is not very different from the crediting
case except that the "interest" is flexible and uncertain. Abstracting from
risk premia, the expected present value of the Treuhand revenues is equivalent to the price with the cash-sales method. As the "purchaser" does not
need cash to pay the Treuhand, a competitive bidding process can be
expected to result in the situation where the Treuhand keeps a share whose
value in terms of expected future returns is given by ABDC and the investor receives a share with value CDFE.[72] The shaded area shows the amount
by which the value of the Treuhand's share exceeds the revenue it would
receive under the cash-sales method. Once again, more revenue can be
collected than with cash sales, and at the same time the number of firms
privatized is increased.

If the number of firms to be privatized exceeds Z_2 (that is, if the expenditure required for reorganization is more than the private funds available),
the problem of the credit constraint is reduced but not eliminated. In this
case, to avoid the problem completely, the Treuhand must provide credit
for the additional reorganization expenditure needed, or it must take over
this expenditure itself and increase correspondingly either the (credited)
price that it charges or its own share. This procedure may be subject to
abuse, so direct loans and guarantees, like those offered in the various
government programs aimed at assisting the rebuilding of the East German
economy (see table 2.2), are worth considering as an alternative to having
the Treuhand itself finance the reorganization of firms.

No Stock-Flow Problem

Overcoming the individual credit constraints avoids the necessity of selling
the Treuhand properties slowly in order to give the purchasers a chance to
accumulate the needed funds out of saved income: the microeconomic
stock-flow mismatch is being mitigated or even avoided. A similar remark
applies to the macroeconomic problems.

The macroeconomic stock-flow mismatch is avoided because the Treuhand receives no cash and thus cannot withdraw funds from the capital
market. The planned deficit spending cannot take place. Interest rates are

---

72. It is assumed here that the minimum marginal equity share (α) which the banks require
is independent of the privatization method. As there are good reasons for the assumption
that this share falls when the participation model is used, one can expect an outward shift
of the demand curve; this increases both the number of firms that can be privatized and the
Treuhand's profit. See Schöb 1992.

lower than in the case of sales, and the discounted values of the firms' potential earnings (the maximum prices that bidders would be willing to pay) are higher.

This is not to say that with the participation model there is no risk at all of burdening the capital market. The burden can be completely avoided only if the Treuhand keeps the retained shares. However, if it distributes the shares to households, then the households may react by increasing their consumption and thus reducing aggregate savings. But the additional consumption will be only a flow, not a stock. Unlike the credit-constrained bodies that receive the Treuhand subsidies, households will spread the increase in expenditure which they can finance from their additional wealth over a long period of time.[73] It is true that credit-constrained households would immediately channel the full wealth increase into consumption demand and would therefore place a burden on the capital market just as high as that caused by the sales policy. However, the typical East German household is a net saver (see figure 3.2) and does not face binding constraints— notwithstanding the fact that it typically would hit against binding constraints if it tried to borrow for the purpose of buying Treuhand properties. Net savers smooth out their consumption over time, reacting to an increase in their stock of wealth with an increase in their flow of consumption. No stock-flow problem can result from asset gifts.

Moreover, giving the shares to households and explaining their values is not the same as giving the households cash. The distribution of a stock of cash will induce a flow of consumption. The distribution of ownership shares in the former national assets will have a strong signaling effect that will induce many households to keep the shares and not react at all.

To further reduce the risk of placing a burden on the capital market, a temporary embargo could be placed on the private sales of the shares. However, such a measure is rather questionable from an allocative point of view, and it is not needed in order to avoid the stock-flow problem. One argument in favor of an embargo is that the East Germans, who have just escaped from communism, need to learn how to deal with securities, and the embargo would give them time for the learning process. Unless there is a temporary ban on sales, there is a danger (though not a very great one) that inexperience could cause market values to become unstable and that before very long the majority of the shares would end up in West German

---

73. Again, Ricardian equivalence is relevant here. If households do not regard the assets they would be given as an increase in wealth, then they will not increase their consumption at all, and no burden will be imposed on the capital market.

hands. This is, of course, not the purpose behind the distribution of the shares. The temporary ban on the sales of shares in East German firms, made for paternalistic reasons, could be a useful supplement to the privatization method proposed. However, if the ban is to be imposed, it should not be a strict one. It is desirable to allow East Germans to sell their shares to finance any real investment project they might want to undertake, including repairs, construction, foundation of a business, and, last but not least, acquisition of majority ownership in a Treuhand firm along the lines described. Capitalism needs capitalists, and capitalists need capital. The participation model recognizes this fundamental truth.

More Risk Capital

From the point of view of eliminating the micro- and macroeconomic financial bottlenecks, there is no difference between crediting the purchase price of a property and retaining a share in it. There is a considerable difference between them, though, with regard to the risk aspect and the portfolio problem associated with it. A credit sale puts pressure on the risk market just as a cash sale does, but share retention reduces this pressure. Share retention mitigates the price decline because the shares bear some of the firm's risks and help spread this risk burden over many shoulders.

The nature of this effect is illustrated in figure 4.6, which is similar to figure 4.2. It is assumed that, with the sales completed up to the present, point C has been reached, and that when the privatization of all firms has been completed the actual portfolio structure will be that represented by the vertical line that passes through E. BE represents the price decline that will result if the cash-sales method is continued.

When small shares in the firm are distributed, possibly after diversification by way of investment funds, the price decline is smaller and the market moves from C to E′ instead of to E. This effect occurs because portfolio diversification eliminates risks that are uncorrelated, though not risks correlated with the rest of the capital market. If there were only perfectly correlated risks, there would be no advantage (from a risk point of view) in distributing small shares rather than selling the firm as a whole, and the price would again fall to BE. If there were only uncorrelated risks, the price would not decline at all and privatization would result in a movement from C to B. The reality is somewhere in between.

It is not only the higher prices that prove the superiority of the participation method; the increased interest shown by potential investors also indicates this. Even just crediting the purchase price makes taking over a firm a

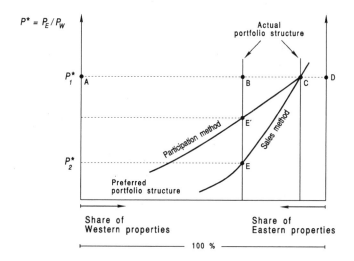

Figure 4.6
The effect of risk diversification.

more attractive proposition, because it helps overcome the credit constraints. The switch from crediting the price to retaining shares increases the attractiveness even further, because it replaces debt with risk-bearing equity capital. This brings great advantages for the investor as a result of the imperfections in the risk-capital market discussed above. Even when, on average, equity receives a somewhat higher rate of interest than debt, for the investor it still has the advantage of a higher tolerance for earnings risk. Equity has to be serviced only if profits are actually made, so the investor himself faces a smaller risk than with debt financing and will dare to undertake more profitable (though riskier) projects than he otherwise would. Overcoming the fear of risk by means of consolidating mechanisms such as insurance or the stock market plays an essential part in the success of the market economy because it frees productive resources and activates "risk as a factor of production."[74] The participation model favored here can also contribute to overcoming this fear.[75]

---

74. See Sinn 1986.
75. A formal model that proves this contention is developed in Demougin and Sinn 1992. The model shows that the participation method strictly dominates the sales method when the Treuhand sells its properties in accordance with the criterion of maximizing the present value of its expected revenue. The participation solution results in both higher returns and more investment! Indeed, under very weak assumptions, the participation model induces even more investment than giving the properties away (or selling them at giveaway prices). This is clearly an argument against deliberately selling at a loss in order to maximize investment incentives, a policy advocated by Bofinger (1991, section 3.3) and others.

An Escape Route from the Restitution Trap

As already explained, the shares retained by the Treuhand reflect the value
of the old capital brought in by that agency, and the investor's majority
shareholding represents his contribution in the form of know-how and new
equity for reorganization purposes. The shares retained are a right *in rem*
which should, in principle, be able to satisfy the right of restitution in kind.
Thus, the Länder and the local authorities, which currently hold the properties that are to be restored to their former owners, could privatize them
using the participation method before, and independent of, clarification of
the ownership rights. In a second step, the shares retained could then be
given to those who are entitled to restitution (or, if there turns out to be
no one in this category, to the funds whose shares are being distributed to
the East German population). With respect to putting the reorganization
process in motion, it will not matter how long it takes to sort out the
ownership question. The investor with the majority share will not worry
too much about who will ultimately be his minority partner.

One difficulty with this solution is that it deprives the minority shareholders of the right to vote. The "sleeping partnership" provision makes
the firms attractive to investors, but it is not compatible with the idea of
restitution in kind. For those properties that are subject to restitution, it is
therefore necessary to retain not only fractional claims on future distributions of profit but also the consultation and voting rights that normally
accompany share ownership.

A further difficulty is that the retention of shares will be possible only in
the case of corporations. As was explained above, small businesses and real
estate should be privatized by a credit method, but giving out credit claims
to the former owners cannot be considered equivalent to restitution in
kind. The participation model could therefore offer an escape route for only
some of the legal problems associated with the restitution rule. Nevertheless, if it is decided to abolish this rule, the claimants will be better off
receiving credit claims rather than sales revenues, because, for reasons
already explained, with a competitive bidding process the former would be
much higher than the latter.

Faster Recovery

The participation model can be seen as a natural response to the elimina-
tion of communist property ownership. It gives the now-unowned capital
to those who should own it, and yet it induces competent investors to

carry this capital into the market economy. It is fairer than the current sales method, it provides time to sort out the property claims, and it makes commitment more attractive to investors. There can be little doubt that going over to this method will accelerate the upswing.

Fears that the use of the participation method will reduce the incentive for future increases in equity capital are quite unfounded. For one thing, the shareholders will contribute to investment financed with retained earnings by forgoing profit distributions. For another, new equity injections by the majority shareholder will be recompensed by corresponding increases in fractional ownership, as is the case with private participation contracts. There is also no need to fear that the government's participation will enable it to exercise permanent influence on the firms. The Treuhand shares carry no voting rights, they are definitely to be distributed to the East German population, and they are to be managed by private investment funds.

Besides its many advantages, privatization in which no cash changes hands has the "disadvantage" that the Treuhand receives no revenue and must therefore reduce its subsidies to firms that have not yet been privatized. There is, however, doubt as to whether this really is a disadvantage. For one thing, because of the problems discussed above, there are clearly more efficient ways of financing subsidies than selling off the Treuhand properties; for another, going without revenue results in the availability of more rather than fewer funds for reorganization purposes. Scarce resources should be allocated to competing private ends through the capital market, not by a government planning authority such as the Treuhand. It makes little sense to propagate the market economy while bypassing one of its most important allocative mechanisms.

5   Strategies for the Upswing

A Long Haul

The political transformation of East Germany has been successfully completed. Totalitarianism has been replaced by Western democracy. However, the necessary institutional changes are far from simple, and the economic transformation is only just beginning. Thousands of old firms have yet to be privatized, many old firms will have to be closed, and new firms will have to be established. Massive sums of money will have to be invested by the government and by the private sector before the economy can become competitive. All this is necessary if the East Germans are to produce enough to support their new level of consumption.

This will be a very long haul. Political transformation will seem almost like child's play compared to economic transformation. Only someone with a vested interest in optimism could suggest that the East German economy will be able to catch up with the West in as little as "three or four or five" years after unification, as Helmut Kohl kept saying until the spring of 1992. Just getting the economy moving at full speed in that time will involve a great deal of luck; reaching Western levels is going to take much longer.

How much time will actually be needed depends above all on investment requirements and financing possibilities. In chapter 2 it was estimated that a trillion deutschmarks of private net investment is needed to bring the capital stock per worker up to the 1989 West German level. Even if the West German capital-labor ratio does not increase, it will take DM 50 billion per year for 20 years or DM 100 billion per year for 10 years for East Germany to catch up.

It is, however, not realistic to assume that capital growth in the West will cease. The increase in interest rates due to increased demand in the capital market may well slow down the rate of growth, but even so it is hardly imaginable that West Germany will stagnate, given the present dynamic European climate. Even a decline in net investment (that is, in the annual increment of the West German capital stock) does not seem very likely. Reaching today's finishing line is not enough in an economic race, for the finishing line keeps moving further away. A competitor in this race must get right up among the fast-moving leaders in order to be counted as successful.

Before unification, capital in West Germany was accumulating at a rate of DM 200 billion per year.[1] In view of the relative population, DM 50 billion must be invested in East Germany each year just for it to reach this rate of accumulation per capita. For East Germany to make up the shortfall and draw level with West Germany would require an additional investment of DM 1 trillion. To draw level in 10 to 20 years would therefore require an investment of between DM 100 billion and DM 150 billion a year at 1989 prices.

It is difficult to imagine such a large amount of investment being carried out in the foreseeable future. In terms of the net national product expected for 1992,[2] it would mean initial investment shares of between 60 and 90 percent—that is, seven to ten times the West German share.[3] This amount of investment would be far greater than what is anticipated by the research institutes, whose estimates for 1992 range between DM 50 billion and DM 70 billion.[4] Obviously, conditions must be extremely favorable if the East is to catch up with the West in only 10 to 20 years; it is likely that the catching-up process will take even longer.

The residual value of the existing capital stock left behind by the communists and now administered by the Treuhand is a major determinant of the length of time needed. The data given in chapter 2 are based on the assumption, confirmed by the Institute for Applied Economic Research (see Institut für angewandte Wirtschaftsforschung 1990), that this residual value is about one-third of the book value—that is, DM 600 billion. If, in line with the popular junkyard hypothesis, the value is zero, then under stationary conditions the amount of investment needed to catch up rises from DM

---

1. See appendix A.

2. According to the national-accounts estimates of the DIW (*Volkswirtschaftliche Gesamtrechnung für Ostdeutschland*, June 21, 1991), using the West German depreciation rate gives the net national product at market prices (based on the last six months of 1991) as DM 167 billions in 1992.

3. The final investment share would then be between 13% and 26% if a constant capital coefficient is assumed for East Germany.

4. See Ifo, *Wirtschaftskonjunktur* 4/91, table A 29, and DIW, *Volkswirtschaftliche Gesamtrechnung für Ostdeutschland*, June 21, 1991, p. 12.

1 trillion to DM 1.6 trillion. To catch up with West Germany in 10 to 20 years will require an annual investment of between DM 130 billion and DM 210 billion, which means that the share of investment in net national product is between 80 and 130 percent. These amounts are even less plausible than the ones calculated above. Fortunately, there is no reason to believe that the junkyard hypothesis is correct. However, anyone who accepts it must also accept its extremely pessimistic implications regarding the time needed for the East to catch up with the West.[5]

The time needed for catching up will depend on German economic policy. The mistake of deciding in favor of natural restitution has already caused a delay of at least two years, and the dubious sales policy of the Treuhand has contributed to making the start more difficult than it had to be. The deciding factor, however, will be the wage policy.

At present the new states, encouraged by advice from big industry and trade unions in West Germany, are all still trying to carry out high-wage, high-technology strategies similar to those in the West. Wages, it is thought, should adjust as quickly as possible to Western levels so that productivity is also "whipped up" (in the words of Saxony's premier, Kurt Biedenkopf) to Western levels. New industries are supposed to spring up in "open fields," and any suggestion that the "old junk" be renovated and put into operation again is treated with scorn. Wages, the politicians say, will in any case eventually reach Western levels; trying to keep them low would give out the wrong signals and encourage false hopes in labor-intensive industries, which in the long run are doomed. Better a quick end to the agony now than a lingering death in the future.[6]

At first sight such a strategy may appear plausible; however, its advocates are confusing cause with effect. Wage levels the same as those in the West are possible only if capital levels are also the same; but there will be capital investment in the East only if it is profitable there, and it will be profitable only if wages are low. Rising wages and declining returns are

---

5. There are politicians who, on the one hand, adhere to a kind of "catalyst" hypothesis, according to which the breath of free enterprise is enough to raise the East German economy up to the Western level, but, on the other hand, use the junkyard hypothesis to explain the Treuhand's meager sales revenues. This is a logically inconsistent position—one cannot bend reality to fit both hypotheses.

6. It seems that Biedenkopf has changed his opinion in the meantime. The message of an important speech he gave to the "Forum für Deutschland" (Biedenkopf 1992) is very similar to that of this book. This is remarkable insofar as the criticism of the high-wage, high-tech strategy given in this chapter was motivated by a debate between Biedenkopf and one of the authors which took place in Dresden in the summer of 1991. At that time Biedenkopf was a strong advocate of the high-wage, high-tech strategy.

what the market uses to put a brake on excessive capital investment. They are results of investment, not causes. If all goes well you can hope to end up with high wages, but starting with them is worse than useless.

The effectiveness of the "productivity whip" is undeniable. High wages destroy a large part of an industry; only those firms that are productive enough to be able to afford them can survive. Average productivity indeed rises, but it does so because jobs are destroyed and not because new ones are created. The average productivity of the surviving firms is "whipped up" because the less productive firms of the industry are "whipped out."

Social transfer payments and subsidies are the consequences of such a high-wage strategy. East German jobs have to be subsidized to avoid the danger of political turmoil that would follow mass dismissals, and large transfer payments have to be made to cushion the effects of unavoidable job losses. These consequences are expensive, undermine the allocative functions of the labor and capital markets, and may bring about even more aggressive wage strategies. They are tolerated in Germany at present not because they are the result of a farsighted policy of unification but because the damage caused by hasty, ill-thought-out decisions has to be patched up somehow.

One alternative to the high-wage strategy is the "maintenance" strategy, in which wages are kept low enough to make all East German jobs competitive. Quite apart from the fact that this strategy would fail because it would lead to excessive migration to the West, it would be as inefficient as the high-wage strategy. The high-wage strategy destroys everything that does not meet Western standards. By contrast, the maintenance strategy minimizes structural changes and preserves all the old fossilized structures under which the GDR suffered. Neither of these strategies can be regarded as a realistic solution to the transformation problem. If West German jobs were available without any migration costs, the high-wage strategy would be appropriate. If migration costs were infinite, the maintenance strategy would be appropriate. Since neither of these extremes applies, a happy medium must be found.

This happy medium is the strategy of "organic system transformation," in which wage rates are competitively determined by supply and demand in the labor market at every stage in the transformation process. This strategy would also result in the destruction of jobs, because competition with the West German labor market would increase East German wages and drive many of the old firms into bankruptcy. However, it would make possible a compromise between the two rival aims of making the location of production attractive to capital and making it attractive to labor. Economic theory suggests that such a compromise could well be optimal from an efficiency point of view, because labor that cannot find a better use elsewhere stays in its old employment and labor that can find a better use elsewhere is set free to move there. Pushing wages artificially above the competitive level (as the high-wage strategy does) means setting free labor for which there is no better use anywhere else, and pulling wages artificially below the competitive level (as the maintenance strategy does) means keeping employed labor for which there is a better use in the West.

Organic System Transformation

The essential characteristic of an organic transformation process is a gradual change in the price structure that keeps pace with the gradual change in the pattern of production. The prices of geographically mobile goods and factors will adjust quickly to Western levels, but the prices of less mobile goods and factors will differ from those in the West for a longer period. These differences are both necessary and desirable. Prices are the main allocative instruments through which the efficiency of the market economy is achieved and maintained. The very high costs of the unification process make an efficient solution indispensable for Germany.

It makes sense to enlist the help of the invisible hand for the extremely complex task of moving in an efficient way from a centrally administered economy to a market economy. It is impossible for a planner to work out which path is best to take, in what order the structural changes should occur, how quickly the necessary adjustments are to be made, and to what extent it is sensible to employ part of the East German work force in the West until new productive capacity can be built up in the East. Individual economic actors, however, know what is in their own best interests, and the price mechanism will ensure that they take adequate account of the interests of others when making their own plans. The price a person has to pay measures the disadvantages incurred by other people as a result of his action, and the price a person receives measures the advantages that accrue to other people. Prices internalize other people's advantages and disadvantages and provide an incentive for making a constructive contribution to the millions of individual efforts that must be made during the transformation process.

The most important price in a market economy is the wage rate. It, too, would perform an allocative function in an organic transformation process, because it would continually provide a measure of the marginal advantages and disadvantages of work and would ensure that these are equilibrated.

Initially the East German wage rate would be low, because capital would be scarce; however, as capital accumulated, the productivity of and the demand for labor would increase and the wage rate would rise. At every point in time during the transformation process, the prevailing East German wage rate would measure both the value added that a marginal worker would continue to produce in the East if he stayed there and the value added, net of transactions costs, that he could produce by migrating to the West. Workers who knew the respective wage rates and preferred to work in West Germany would be creating a net advantage for the economy, in spite of the resulting decline in East German output and in spite of the subjective and objective costs of the change. Similarly, workers who preferred to stay in the East would add more value there than they would by migrating to the West. In the initial stages, when wages in the East would be low, many people would go to work in the West; later, when wages would be higher and a greater number of productive employment opportunities would be available in the East, they (or others) would move back.

Figure 5.1 illustrates these relationships in the simplified form of a supply-demand diagram for the labor market. Employment in East Germany is shown on the horizontal axis; average wage rates there are shown on the

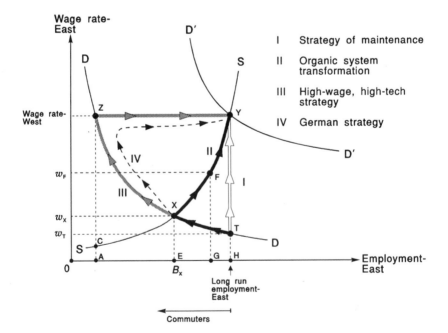

Figure 5.1
Alternative wage strategies.

vertical axis. The figure abstracts from the frictional unemployment that accompanies structural change in order to be able to focus on the wage problem and because only a small part of the actual dismissals of nearly 50 percent of the workforce can be explained by this type of unemployment (see chapter 2). For similar reasons, the discussion also abstracts from the question of economic growth in Germany.

The East German employers' initial demand for labor is represented by DD, and the East German employees' supply of labor is represented by SS. DD is the demand curve that results when spontaneous improvements in productivity (that is, improvements made possible by reorganizing production without having to undertake much in the way of capital investment) have occurred. It slopes downward because, among other things, the number of viable firms increases as the wage rate falls. The supply curve slopes upward because fewer workers migrate to the West as the wage rate rises. The supply curve can, in principle, also reflect households' decisions to exchange more leisure for work as wages rise, but the discussion abstracts from this possibility for the sake of brevity. None of the policy conclusions would change significantly if the households' labor-leisure choices were considered.

It is assumed that labor can migrate between the two parts of Germany without delay, albeit with migration costs. By contrast, the real capital stock is assumed to be rather immobile. Despite extremely flexible financial capital markets, adjustment and absorption problems imply that the East German capital stock can only gradually increase with the passage of time. To the extent that the East German capital stock increases, the demand curve DD shifts gradually outward, but at a given point in time with the then-available stock of capital the curve has a given position. The height of the demand curve at a particular level of employment measures the value added generated by an additional worker in the East, and the height of the supply curve measures the wage an additional migrant can earn in the West after his subjective and objective costs of migration have been subtracted. Under competitive conditions, the West German wage (gross of migration costs) equals the value of the additional output the migrant produces in the West. The height of the supply curve therefore also represents the increase in the West German value added, net of the migration costs, that the migrant produces.

The costs of migration are to be understood here in a very general sense. They include the subjective aversion against moving as well as the objective transaction costs involved in the move. An important part of the costs of migration is the rent increase that is connected with the decision to work

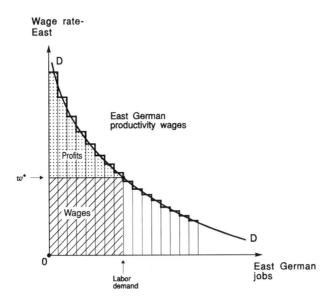

Figure 5.2
The demand curve arrived at by ranking East German jobs according to their productivity wages in a given period of time and with the then-available stock of capital. The productivity wage of a job is the highest wage that this job can tolerate without becoming unprofitable for the firm. With the given wage rate w^*, all jobs whose productivity wages are above this rate are profitable and all others are unprofitable. The sum of the productivity wages of all jobs filled is the net national product of the East German economy. Here, this national product is divided into profits and wages.

in the West. Along with the other costs of making the change, this rent increase is responsible for the fact that not everyone migrates to the West in response to even substantial differences in wage rates. We define migration in the sense of "commuting." Migrants are people who are based in the East but work in the West, commuting regularly between the two parts of the country, where the frequency may range between a day and several months. Accordingly, the costs of migration are defined on a periodic basis. They have to be incurred by an East German worker as long as he is employed in the West. In Germany, commuting in the narrow sense of the word accounts for most of the actual East-West migration.

In figure 5.1, the size of the East German work force is given by OH. It is assumed that everyone in the work force would prefer to stay in East Germany if there were no wage differential between East and West. The greater the differential, the more workers move to the West. For simplicity, the West German wage rate is assumed to be constant. Strictly speaking, this assumption is not correct, because the commuters can find employment

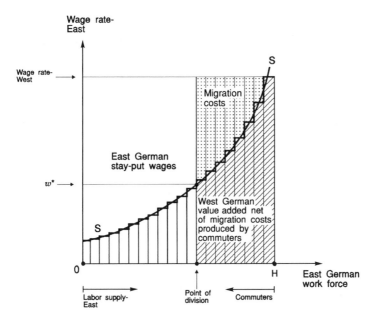

Figure 5.3
The supply curve arrived at by ranking East German workers according to their "stay-put" wages. The stay-put wage is the subjective East German wage at which a worker is indifferent between staying in the East and moving to the West. With the given wage rate w^*, everyone whose stay-put wage is higher than this moves to the West and everybody else stays in the East. The stay-put wages are equal to the difference between the given Western wage and the subjective and objective costs of migration. The higher the wage differential between East and West Germany, the more people there are whose migration costs are less than this differential and the larger the number of people who move to the West. The sum of the commuters' stay-put wages measures the national product produced in the West by the commuters (it equals their wages) net of the costs of migration. These amounts are shown by the areas labeled correspondingly.

in the West only if wages there are falling. However, the effect (analyzed in Sinn 1990) is not particularly large. Even if there were no transaction costs and migration were to continue until wages in the East and the West had become equal, the West German wage level would fall by barely 6 percent. Such a figure can safely be ignored in view of the present large wage differential between East and West Germany (see figure 5.4). With given union wages, a minimal reduction in the gap between effective and union wages will enable all those workers moving from the East to be absorbed into the West German work force.

The labor supply curve can also be interpreted as a ranking of the "stay-put wages" East German employees require to prevent them from moving, and the demand curve as a ranking of the "productivity wages" the East German workplaces can tolerate. An exact definition and interpretation of these curves is given in the legends of figures 5.2 and 5.3. The correct interpretation of the curves is essential for the analysis of the efficiency of the transformation strategy that follows.

In the organic system transformation, competition in the labor market ensures that wage rates and employment levels at any point in time are given by the intersection of the supply and demand curves; therefore, in figure 5.1, they are w_X and B_X at point X. A higher wage rate cannot emerge, because then the dismissals would exceed westward migration. The competition for jobs of the unemployed would reduce the wage rate. Neither could a lower wage rate persist, because then westward migration would exceed the firms' planned dismissals. The competition for employees of the firms would increase the wage rate. In equilibrium the wage rate has to be such that planned dismissals and westward migration are just balancing.

Before the opening of the wall, the East German economy may have been at point T, because the wage rate had to be low enough to enable that all workers are employed. After the opening, however, the large wage differential induces migration to the West equal to EH, which brings about a corresponding reduction in employment in the East. The migration immediately raises the wage rate to w_X—a level that, because of the cost of migration, remains below the West German level. Given that a wage differential persists, one can expect a large investment flow to East Germany; this gradually increases the productivity wages and shifts the demand curve from DD to D'D'. In response to the resulting increase in the equilibrium wage w_X, the number of commuters gradually falls again and employment in the East rises. These changes are shown by the movement along the supply curve labeled as path II. The movement stops in the long run when point Y is reached because wages are there the same in the East and the West and there is no longer any incentive to undertake above-normal investment in the East. As was argued above, the process of adjustment from X to Y may take two decades and the amount of investment needed to shift the demand curve from DD to D'D' will be at least a trillion deutschmarks.

At every stage in the adjustment process, the allocation of the East German work force to East and West German jobs is optimal because the marginal contribution made by an East German worker to the overall German national product, net of migration costs, is the same in the two parts of the country. Every other distribution of the work force between East and West Germany would result in a lower level of national product net of migration costs.

The Maintenance Strategy: The Path of the Other Eastern Bloc Countries

For the sake of completeness, it is useful to compare the organic system transformation strategy with a maintenance strategy, illustrated in figure 5.1 by path I. Such a strategy could be carried out in East Germany only if a new wall were built. In that case, the East German wage rate could be very low because the wall would prevent workers from leaving. In principle, the wage rate could be low enough to ensure that most of those employed before unification would also have a job afterward. Before capital accumulation started, the initial equilibrium would be at point T in figure 5.1. However, the incentive for importing capital would be very great, so the demand curve DD, and therefore the equilibrium wage rate, would move rather quickly toward their long-run positions.

Not only would this strategy be politically impossible, it would also be economically inefficient. As can be determined from figures 5.2 and 5.3, the initial size of East Germany's national product would exceed that under the organic strategy by the area XTHE in figure 5.1. However, the commuters' contribution to West Germany's national product would be lost. With the organic transformation strategy, this contribution would be equal to XYHE after the costs of migration were subtracted. Thus, maintaining the whole of the East German industry would lead initially to a net loss of XYT for the German economy. Over time, as the demand curve shifted upward, the loss would diminish; however, some loss would continue until long-run equilibrium was reached at point Y.

The maintenance strategy is certainly not relevant for Germany, but it is relevant for the other Eastern Bloc countries, where political restrictions prevent commuting to the West. The transformation of these countries' economies must, in principle, be carried out in the way shown in figure 5.1 by path I.

Initially, wages in these countries are low enough not to cause unemployment. Only frictional unemployment (discussed in chapter 2, but not considered in figure 5.1) is possible. An economic upswing with higher wages requires capital imports from the West and internal saving. Exporting labor, which would lead much more quickly to productive employment relationships, is not an option.

It was most fortunate for East Germany that it faced no such restrictions on the movement of labor. The possibility of giving up East German jobs in exchange for much more productive employment in the West promised considerable welfare gains. To what extent this possibility has been and will be realized is, of course, quite another question.

The High-Wage, High-Tech Strategy

Organic transformation is a theoretical ideal. To achieve the necessary wage flexibility and to avoid possible artificial incentives for labor migration would have required certain adjustments to the social system in both East and West Germany. Nevertheless, it would not have been impossible to use such a strategy, and in combination with a different distribution of the East German property endowments it would certainly not have disadvantaged the East German people. As will be explained in the last section of this chapter, distributively neutral policy options are still available that would at least approach organic transformation.

One alternative to organic transformation is the maintenance strategy, which was shown to be neither feasible nor attractive. Another alternative is the high-wage, high-tech strategy. In essence this means imposing the price structure appropriate to the post-transformation steady state on the East German economy right from the start and then waiting for the pattern of production to adjust. The main idea behind this policy is that all existing production units unable to survive the steady-state wages are weeded out immediately and that reorganization investments not worth making at these wage levels are not allowed to take place. Only the most modern factories meeting the highest Western standards are allowed; no intermediate solutions are permitted.[7]

In figure 5.1, path III represents the high-wage, high-tech strategy. The East German wage level is raised very rapidly to the Western level, with the result that a large part of the existing industry becomes insolvent. The level of employment in East Germany is lower than with the organic transformation strategy by the amount AE and the potential unemployment equals ZY (although, depending on the social security arrangements, unemployment may to some extent be offset by the migration of labor to the West). Those proposing the high-wage, high-tech strategy must hope that, despite the high wages, capital will nevertheless accumulate in the

---

7. A numerical specification of our model that allows a quantitative comparison of the strategies, was recently presented in an inaugural lecture at the University of Kiel (Bröcker 1992). An analytic model with migration costs was presented independently of this book by Burda and Wyplosz (1991). The latter assume market-clearing wages in the East; only the Western wages can be fixed on non-market-clearing levels in their model.

East and the demand curve for labor will eventually reach D'D', as is necessary for the full-employment equilibrium Y to be achieved.

Wage Developments in East Germany

The Germans reached a surprisingly clear decision in favor of a strategy very similar to the high-wage, high-tech one, accompanied all the way by vociferous propaganda from politicians, business interests, and trade unions. The big Western industries took up the most prestigious investment projects, proudly installing only the most modern plants. Time and again warnings had been given that East Germany could not be expected to remain an area of low wages and older, more primitive production processes. There has hardly ever been a discussion of the economic problems of East Germany in which the idea of setting up new plants in the "open fields" has not been suggested as an alternative to refurbishing the old plants. Government policy, too, has played its part by arousing expectations that incomes and living standards would rise rapidly to Western levels.

Collective wage bargaining has reflected the expectations. Even before unification, in the year 1990, industrial wages had risen by an average of 17 percent. After the economic and monetary union was established, real consumption wages remained constant but real production wages in the East German export industries more than quadrupled when calculated at the official exchange rate, which was 1:0.23 (East to West) before the currency unification and 1:1 thereafter.[8] After unification, in one wage bargaining round after another, double-digit wage increases were agreed to—rates that, if they had been demanded in the West, would have resulted in lockouts and set off screams of protest from industry. By the end of these wage rounds, East German wage rates had rocketed sky high— and this in a period when very little industrial investment was taking place. At the beginning of 1992 the hourly gross wage in East German manufacturing industry was 50 percent below the West German level, but 600 percent above the level of only two years before.

In terms of what the unions and the employers agreed to, these wage increases are only the beginning. In the metal industry wage agreement of March 1, 1991, which set the standard for other wage contracts, it was decided that the base wage rates will be adjusted to West German levels by 1994 and that all additional benefits will be adjusted by the following

---

8. See "The Purchasing-Power Paradox" in chapter 3.

year.[9] It is true that, given the present gap between union wage rates and effective wage rates in the West, the East German wage levels would then still remain below West German levels by between 15 and 20 percent. However, as explained, the movement of labor to the West may reduce this wage gap somewhat. The course may therefore be set for a substantial narrowing of the differential between East and West German wages before 1995. By way of contrast, even under the most favorable conditions possible, only a very small part of the shortfall in capital in East Germany can be made good in this time. It is impossible for East German productivity to rise fast enough to make the planned wage levels compatible with even low unemployment, let alone with full employment.

Path IV in figure 5.1 illustrates the developments in the labor market that can be expected to result from the wage policy chosen. This path is somewhat to the right of path III (which corresponds to the high-wage, high-tech strategy), because full adjustment of wages will not take place immediately, but it is certainly closer to this path than to the organic transformation path (path II).

Comparing the gross hourly industrial wage costs in East Germany with those in other countries shows quite clearly what an extreme solution Germany has chosen. Figure 5.4 summarizes the available data. The calculations assume a constant differential between effective and union wage rates in West Germany, and they include both direct wage costs and nonwage labor costs. All wage costs are calculated in terms of hourly rate equivalents, are based on actual and planned wage agreements, and are compared at 1990 exchange rates.

To interpret figure 5.4 correctly, note that the pattern of hourly wage rates says nothing directly about the pattern of real consumption wage rates. The differences in real consumption wages are certainly smaller than those in wage rates calculated on the basis of currency exchange rates, because relative prices of nontradeable goods are lower in less productive countries.[10] The latter wage rates, however, are the ones that are relevant for comparisons of international competitiveness.

Figure 5.4 shows that in the spring of 1990 hourly labor costs in East Germany were between those of Poland and Turkey. After unification, East German wages quickly surpassed those in Greece, and by the spring of 1991 more than half of the large disparity between wages in Greece and Ireland had been covered. At the time of this writing, in the spring of 1992,

---

9. See Arbeitgeberverband Gesamtmetall, *Geschäftsbericht 1989–1991*.
10. See "The Purchasing-Power Paradox" in chapter 3.

East German hourly
industrial labor costs
as a percentage of
the West German level

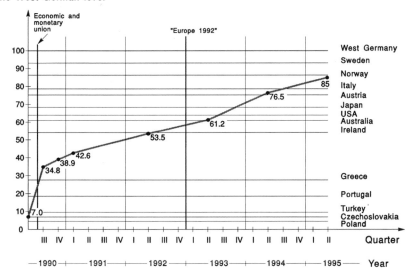

Figure 5.4
The journey through the wage hierarchy. Sources: Salowsky 1991, p. D 4; Statistisches
Bundesamt, Fachserie 16, Serie 2.1, table 8, January 1991; press release, Statistisches
Bundesamt 4/91; Clasen 1991, p. 16 ff.; Bundesministerium für Arbeit und Soziales,
*Entwicklung der tarifvertraglichen Löhne, Gehälter und sonstigen Arbeitsbedingungen im
Beitrittsgebiet seit dem 1. Juli 1990 in ausgewählten Tarifgebieten*, IIIa 1-31283-11, April 1,
1991, p. 14; *Biuletyn statystyczny* (Statistical Bulletin) no. 1–3, April 1991, Warsaw 1991;
information by telephone from the Economic Institute of the Czech Academy of Sciences
in Prague. *Note:* The international comparisons of the cost of labor are based on 1990
manufacturing industry wages and exchange rates. Labor costs consist of gross hourly
wages plus nonwage labor costs. The average West German nonwage labor cost is 85%
of the wage cost. In the absence of better information, this percentage was used for
determining East German wage costs from April 1990 to January 1991, and also for wage
costs in Poland and Czechoslovakia. The 1990 values for these three countries were
calculated from the average monthly earnings of wage and salary earners combined
because separate data were not available. Up to 1991 actual data are given; from 1992 the
numbers are estimates. The estimates assume that the step-by-step adjustment to West
German levels will be completed by 1995 in the whole East German manufacturing sector,
as agreed in the standard-setting bargain for the metal and electrical industries in
Mecklenburg–West Pomerania (March 1, 1991). It is assumed that the East German union
wage rate is the same as the effective rate. For West Germany a gap of 15% is assumed.
The wage bargain included an agreement to provide further nonwage benefits in 1995.
The cost of these benefits was estimated to equal 10% of the ordinary wage cost.

Ireland's wage level is being reached. Soon, after the internal European barriers are removed at the end of 1992, East German wage costs will have moved to American and Australian levels. Japan will be overtaken in 1993, and Austria and Italy in 1994. In 1995 East Germany's hourly labor costs will be equal to those in the Scandinavian countries.

Note that this scenario applies if West German wages do not change in relation to the rest of the world. A relative fall in West German union wages with an unchanged gap between union and effective wages would prevent East German wage costs from being pushed up to peak world levels in the way described. Under competitive conditions, this may happen eventually because supply pressure will increase in West German labor markets. However, the West German trade unions will continue to put up strong resistance for some time; thus, what is more likely initially is a narrowing of the gap between West German union rates and effective wage rates. This would push West Germany down relative to other countries, but with the present wage agreements it would have no effect on the path of East Germany's wage costs relative to those of other countries. As was mentioned above, it can be expected that the relative decline in effective wages will be less than 6 percent. It will not even be strong enough to push West Germany's wage level down to that of Sweden.

The Berkeley Study

It will be obvious to a critical observer that a wage policy that aims at pushing East Germany's hourly wage rates up to American or Japanese levels within three years of unification is utopian. Even the most extreme optimists cannot believe that industrial production in East Germany can survive such a policy. It is nevertheless instructive to look at the results of an important study made by a research group from Berkeley (Akerlof et al. 1991). This study also highlights the catastrophic nature of the high-wage, high-tech strategy chosen for East Germany.

On the basis of the input-output tables of the GDR planning authorities, Akerlof et al. estimated the cost functions of the industrial combines and assessed the effects of the high-wage policy on their ability to survive. A combine is held to be viable when its sales revenue, valued at world market prices, can cover its variable costs of production. It was found that, with the wage increases that had occurred up to October 1990, most of the combines would have gone bankrupt if they had not been subsidized. Only 8.2 percent of industrial employees could have kept their jobs if production had continued with the old technologies.

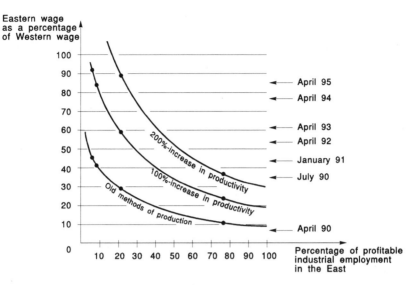

Figure 5.5
Results of the Berkeley study compared with East German wage-rate developments.
Source: Akerlof et al. 1991 (table 8) and authors' calculations in connection with figure 5.4.
Note: The curves shown here were calculated from the subsidy scenarios of the Berkeley
study. The benchmark case of a rise in nominal wages of 42%, taken as the basis, is equal
to the actual rise in hourly wage rates up to January 1991 and not, as Akerlof et al.
suppose, up to October 1990. The hourly wage rates in January 1991 were coincidentally
a similar percentage of Western labor costs (43%).

Figure 5.5 summarizes the results of the calculations and compares them
with the time path of wages in figure 5.4. The lower curve is a freehand
regression through four points that can be calculated from alternative subsidy scenarios studied by Akerlof et al. for other purposes. It can be seen
that, with the old technologies and the old organization of production, all
industrial jobs would have remained competitive, despite the opening of
the borders and the introduction of prices that were adequate to the quality
of the East German products, if wages had stayed at the April 1990 level—
that is, if nominal wages had not risen and conversion had been at the rate
of 1:0.23 (East to West).[11] However, with the wage rates that resulted
from the currency conversion of July 1990 not even 20 percent of the jobs
could have been saved.

---

11. Of course, it cannot be concluded from this that such a policy would have been efficient.
The organic transformation strategy requires some of the old industry to be closed down.
See the above discussion of the maintenance strategy.

As an alternative scenario, it may be useful to consider a situation in which labor productivity doubles. With the new market-related pattern of incentives, the technology used will not be exactly the same as before and it should be possible to bring about some initial increase in productivity very quickly and cheaply by avoiding obvious organizational mistakes. This possibility is illustrated by the middle curve. It can be seen that with wages at July 1990 levels almost 50 percent of the jobs could have been retained, whereas with the wages planned for April 1995 the percentage would once again be less than 10. Even tripling productivity, as shown by the top curve, would not help much. In this case, barely a quarter of the jobs would still remain in April 1995. For at least 50 percent of the industrial jobs to remain profitable despite the wage rise, productivity would need to grow by 500 percent, which means an annual growth rate of 46 percent from the time of unification.[12] Nothing could make the utopian nature of the wage increases demanded by the unions more obvious than these figures.

Critics of the Berkeley study have argued that the wage cost is less important for the profitability of East German industry than the demand problems resulting from the breakdown of Comecon and the low quality of East German industrial products. The importance of these effects, discussed above in chapter 2 and 3, cannot be denied. It would be superficial, however, to see a conflict between this recognition and the results of the Berkeley study. Every product has its price, and if the prices are low enough then even low-quality East German products will be able to find and defend their markets. After all, there was a great deal of trade between East and West Germany when the exchange rate was 1 : 0.23. The Berkeley study uses prices at which East German products had actually been sold to the West and compares them with the wage costs established with unification. In that way, the quality problem is adequately taken into account.

A similar remark applies to those who argue that productivity comparisons between East and West Germany, and wage recommendations based on these, are misleading because the product qualities are so different. This argument overlooks the fact that the productivities compared are measured

---

12. The order of magnitude of the productivity differences between East and West Germany cannot be concluded directly from these figures, because the spread of wages among the firms is different in the two parts of the country. If the curves in figure 5.5 were straight lines, a sufficiently large spread in the East would enable all jobs to be retained when productivity increases by 500%. However, for this to happen with convex curves an even greater increase in productivity would be necessary. It follows that the Berkeley study implicitly set the average initial productivity level in the GDR industrial sector at less than one-sixth of the FRG level.

in value terms rather than in quantity terms and thus implicitly take the quality differences into account. The low quality of East German products results in low prices, and low prices imply low productivity. By definition, therefore, productivity wages keep an industry profitable even though the product qualities may be low.

It is possible to question the justifiability of one or another of the assumptions of the Berkeley study, but its theoretical soundness and care cannot be denied. The results of the study differ so markedly from the optimistic hopes expressed by most Western economic advisors that it is obvious that an about-face in wage policy is an urgent necessity.

Employment Prohibited!

The wage bargains for East Germany come, in effect, close to a ban on employment. After 1995 only wages and technologies like those of one of the world's most productive economies will be allowed. Anything that does not meet the highest standards is definitely not wanted. It is as if the East Germans were being forbidden to continue to drive their old Trabants anymore simply because Mercedes are now available. Stay at home if you can't afford a Mercedes!

Why was this policy selected? A few apparently reasonable arguments were offered in the course of the public discussion, but on closer examination they do not prove to be convincing.[13]

One argument is that wages which will be supportable in the future should be put in place now to avoid giving investors the wrong signals when they are deciding which technology to use. If today's wages were close to present market-clearing levels, investors would make decisions that they would come to regret later when wages rise. This argument implies that the wage negotiators know the investors' business better than they themselves do; it is basically paternalistic. Experience has shown that the opposite is true. No one is in a position to be sure how the labor market will develop in the future, but no one has a greater interest in weighing the imponderables than the investor who is risking his capital. An investor who expects wages to be high in the long term will take this into account when making his choice of technology and will not allow himself to be misled by

---

13. The list of arguments given here is not exhaustive. For the sake of brevity, the purchasing-power argument, which is no longer put forward very often, has been omitted. This argument is strongly refuted in Donges 1991. A plea for a rapid wage equalization is given by Mieth (n.d.).

current low wage levels. He does not need to be taught how to do this by the wage bargainers. In view of the time spans discussed earlier, it cannot be expected that market-determined wages in East Germany would reach West German levels within the usual payoff period for industrial investment projects, which is normally less than ten years. In that time there would have been plenty of profitable low-tech investment opportunities available.

A second argument, already mentioned, is that high wages will "whip up" productivity to the levels appropriate to those wages. What this argument involves is illustrated very clearly in figure 5.5. With the old technologies and without the Treuhand subsidies, the wage increases up to January 1991 would have certainly brought about a dramatic rise in East German productivity, but at the expense of destroying 92 percent of the available jobs.

Few economists would subscribe to the view that high wages can speed the upswing. High wages not only destroy existing industries that otherwise could have survived in the transition period; they also prevent new investment. Investment in the East is not needed only in high-tech firms. Middle-of-the-road industries, handicraft firms, suppliers of intermediate products, and many other types of firms must develop, but Western-level wages will strangle many of these before they even get born. The high-tech path in figure 5.1 can be traveled very quickly from X to Z; the hard part will be from Z to Y, and that is the part that must be traveled if unemployment is to be overcome. With no wage differential between the East and the West, it seems extremely unlikely that enough capital will be attracted to make this journey successful.

A third argument for the high-wage strategy in the East is that it will stop the migration of people to the West, which is induced by the high Western wages. Because there is a single labor market in Germany, migration makes East German labor scarce and pushes its wages up. Therefore, it is said, a wage agreement that equalizes union wages is justified by the market conditions. The true aspect of this argument is that the movement of labor imposes a lower limit on wages. This effect would show up fully in an organic transformation process (see figure 5.1). If there were no westward movement, full employment could be achieved only with the wage rate w_T—that is, at point T on the demand curve DD. If westward movement occurred, employment in the East would fall by EH and the wage rate would rise from w_T to w_X. The Eastern wage w_X is below the Western wage because of the costs of migration, and it strikes a balance between the incentive to move and the trouble involved in doing so. However, the wage rise induced by the westward migration would never be able to cause unemployment. It would be accompanied not by a surplus of labor but by a shortage. The current mass unemployment in East Germany is a clear indication of the absurdity of the argument. Current wages there are much higher than would have been induced by labor migration.

The argument does apply to certain highly skilled occupations, where the combination of high mobility and large wage differences has indeed caused labor shortages. Paying West German wages in these occupations today may very well be justified. Wage policy should deal with this problem by encouraging a much wider spread of wages. In principle there is no reason why this should not be possible with the current average wage levels. A general rise in wage levels is certainly not necessary.

Wider wage spreads would be much easier to introduce if no one were to lose out in the process. There would have been an opportunity to introduce wider differentials if wage rates had been set at levels less favorable for the East German population in the beginning and then selectively adjusted toward West German levels. Today it is much more difficult. According to DIW calculations,[14] to introduce the West German wage structure now without lowering any wages would mean a rise in average wages of at least 60 percent. Advocating such a policy with a reference to the wage-spread argument cannot be justified. If productive jobs are to be kept in the East, a larger spread must include a lowering of many wages.

A wage spread is necessary not only between occupations but also, and especially, between regions. The common plea for "equal pay for equal work" (a CDU slogan in an election campaign of spring 1992) cannot be met in a competitive economy where there are migration costs. It is true that in Berlin and other areas close to the former border, where migration costs are low, the wage differential is being quickly removed, albeit partially at the expense of the West. However, it would be quite wrong to draw conclusions from this for wage policy in more distant regions. It does not follow that, because a particular wage differential is sufficient to attract labor to West Berlin from East Berlin, exactly the same differential will attract labor from Frankfurt on the Oder to Frankfurt on the Main, 400 miles away. The migration argument justifies large wage gradations between occupations and regions; however, it does not justify a general equalization of wages between East and West Germany, or even wage rises that would result in unemployment somewhere.

---

14. *DIW Wochenbericht* 32/90, August 9, 1990, p. 444.

Strictly speaking, each particular combination of profession and region
requires a special organic transformation strategy of its own. Many graphs
like figure 5.1 are necessary to analyze the appropriate wage strategies. In
areas along the former border and for mobile occupations, the supply curve
is very flat, so the path of the organic transformation strategy is hardly
different from that of the high-wage strategy. In more distant regions
and for traditional rural occupations, the supply curve could be almost
vertical, so the path of the organic strategy approximates that of the
maintenance strategy. Normally there will be a situation (as illustrated in
figures 5.1, 5.2, and 5.6) where the organic strategy is the happy medium
between two extremes, each of which results in substantial efficiency losses.
There is no longer a wall (which the maintenance strategy would have
required), and there is no perfect labor market without migration costs
(which would justify an immediate wage equalization). Berlin is not the
whole of Germany.

Is the High-Wage, High-Tech Strategy Efficient?

The loss of efficiency that would follow the introduction of the high-wage,
high-tech strategy more than offsets the unconvincing arguments in its

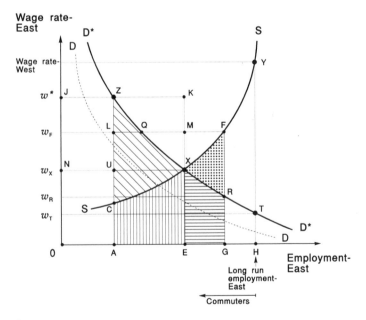

Figure 5.6
An efficiency analysis of the wage strategies.

favor. The extent of the efficiency loss can be seen in figure 5.1, but it shows up even more clearly in figure 5.6. Figure 5.1 depicts the welfare loss that results when the wages in East Germany are raised immediately to West German levels. Figure 5.6 illustrates the more relevant case where the wages are equalized less quickly. In contrast to figure 5.1, figure 5.6 refers to an advanced stage in which capital accumulation has already shifted the demand curve to D*D*. Point Z in figure 5.6 is on the "German" path IV shown in figure 5.1. Despite these differences, the following discussion applies to both of these figures.

The efficient level of employment associated with organic transformation is shown at point X. Compared with this, a high-wage strategy, with employment at point Z, reduces employment by AE and results in a reduction in East German value added equal to ZXEA. If the workers who have become redundant in the East find jobs in the West, the value added there will increase. For simplicity it is assumed that the workers are dismissed according to a "principle of minimal resistance," which means that the dismissals begin with individuals whose migration costs are low and proceed to those whose costs are higher.[15] Under this assumption, West German value added net of migration costs will increase by CXEA, and the net effect on the total German national product adjusted for migration costs is given by the diagonally hatched triangle ZXC. This triangle measures the smallest possible temporary loss of efficiency from the high-wage strategy.

The actual loss is certainly larger than that shown by the triangle, because the assumption that all labor made redundant in the East will be reemployed in the West is unrealistic as long as unemployment benefits are available in the East. Unemployment benefits are stay-put premia which prevent all those whose stay-put wages are lower from migrating. These benefits paralyze the incentive to look for jobs in the West if the difference between the West German wage and the East German unemployment benefit is less than the cost of migration. The higher the unemployment benefits, the smaller the number of people willing to take their fate into their own hands and look for jobs wherever they are to be found. In figures 5.1 and 5.6, the unemployment benefit is w_F. It limits the number of "commuters" to GH and implies that the number of unemployed persons is AG.

---

15. If the dismissals follow a different pattern, then the welfare costs of the high-wage strategy are higher than shown above, since either the "wrong" workers are induced to migrate or migration is replaced with unemployment in the East. The criticism of the high-wage strategy would be even stronger. We are grateful to Ronnie Schöb for this comment.

The result is an additional reduction in efficiency in the form of a loss in the West German value added net of migration costs, shown by the area CFGA. Not only does the high-wage, high-tech strategy discourage employment in the East; since unemployment benefits are geared to wages, this strategy also means that stay-put premia are paid which limit the incentive to look for jobs in the West, and that a large part of the work force will not be employed anywhere.

The total loss of efficiency resulting from the fact that employment opportunities are denied to the East German work force both in the East and in the West is shown by the shaded areas ZXFGA. Germany's national product net of migration costs could have risen by this amount if the organic transformation strategy had been used instead of the high-wage strategy.

If (contrary to well-founded fears) the high-wage strategy does not deter capital investment and the demand curve shifts further to the right, the welfare loss will become smaller over time and will disappear completely when points Z and Y coincide. However, that process may take a long time, and before it is completed the economy will suffer year by year substantial disadvantages that could have been avoided if another strategy had been chosen.

The Misguided Wage Policy

The high-wage policy cannot have been introduced on efficiency grounds, because it induces massive efficiency losses. The arguments brought forward in its favor were obviously wrong. The reasons for its support must be sought elsewhere. We will argue that they stemmed from the interests of the unions and the employers, the parties involved in the wage negotiations.

In Germany wage agreements are reached by a process of collective bargaining between employers' associations and trade unions and apply to all members of these bodies. Firms and employees who are not represented in the bargaining round can negotiate their own agreements; however, when the government declares the collective agreements to be generally binding, individual agreements must not be less favorable to the employees than the collective ones. Collective wage agreements apply to all wage contracts within particular industry branches and regions (wage tariff areas). The right to take part in free collective wage bargaining is implicitly guaranteed by Article 9.3 of the German constitution.

In the past, the German system of collective wage bargaining proved to be very successful. The fact that it nevertheless failed to find wage levels for East Germany appropriate to market conditions can be traced back to the violation of one of its most important principles: that the weights of the parties to the negotiations should be balanced. An efficient, socially acceptable compromise can be reached only when the opponents at the bargaining table are equally strong. Such a compromise is impossible when only one side is represented.[16]

The side that was (and still is) inadequately represented during the negotiations was that of the employers. In West Germany, private owners of existing capital are the employers; they put up strong resistance to wage increases because these devalue their capital. The main employer in the East German negotiations was the Treuhand, a government agency. The Treuhand officials could have arranged for the firms' directors to represent the interests of existing capital, but no one can blame them for not doing so. It was not their own capital that was at stake, and anyway they would not have wanted to depart from the line taken by the government in its public statements.

The trade unions, on the other side, were very well organized. Long before unification, new industrial trade unions had been established in East Germany, coordinated by West German umbrella organizations. The East German workers joined these unions in droves. This development was reinforced by the First State Treaty, which set up the economic, monetary, and social union of July 1, 1990. In this treaty, freedom of association and free wage bargaining were formally introduced to the GDR.[17] The trade unions carried out the first wage negotiations with the directors of the East German firms, who theoretically took on the role of the employers but who, in fact, also represented the workers' interests. In effect, the same party was initially sitting on both sides of the table.[18]

The situation changed very little when the West German employers' associations joined the negotiations from the fall of 1990 so as to make the

---

16. The explanation given here is also given in a report on wage policy in East Germany to which one of us contributed (Wissenschaftlicher Beirat 1991b). See also the subsequent discussion by Franz (1992). We are grateful to Tyll Necker, the former president of the German Employers' Association, for useful information. Necker confirmed the above analysis including the description of the employers' negotiation strategy. For an analysis of East German wage bargaining in the light of existing labor market theories see Burda and Funke 1991.

17. The legal developments are set out in Clasen 1991.

18. This was even admitted by the Friedrich-Ebert-Stiftung (1990, p. 6 f.), a Social Democratic institute sympathetic to trade unions.

two sides formally independent. The employers' associations had no real interest in keeping wages low. High wages would certainly make planned investment projects in the East unprofitable, but this would not involve any reduction in the value of the existing capital in the West. Low wages in the East, and not high wages, were a threat to West German capital. Low wage rates in the East would have meant low-wage competition, and thus pressure on the Western firms' profits. There was plenty of lip service to the idea of low wages from the employers' side, but their willingness to fight for them was conspicuous by its absence. The incredible agreement for the metals industry of March 1, 1991, in which it was decided that wage levels in the East should reach those in the West by April 1, 1994, was vigorously defended by the chairman of Gesamtmetall, the Metal Trades Employers' Association, as an "acceptable compromise."[19] The union side concurred, expressly praising the cooperative spirit shown by the employers in the negotiations.[20] Neither side put up any kind of a fight during the bargaining process.

Of course, the Western trade unions that supported their Eastern comrades in the negotiations also had no interest in a low-wage policy for East Germany. Such a policy would have threatened the jobs of their own members, because cheap supplies of goods, teams of construction workers from the new states, and contract workers employed at Eastern-level wages in the West would have put pressure on West German markets. It was far better to avoid this danger from the start.

Unification meant that in Germany the supply of labor increased relative to the supply of capital. It has become impossible, at least in the medium term, for West German wage rates to rise as much as they would have if unification had not taken place.[21] The West German trade unions will obviously have to try to resist this development. The influence they were able to exercise in the wage negotiations was directed toward this purpose, and they were quite prepared to accept the East German unemployment that followed from the high-wage strategy. The president of the chemical industry trade union IG-Chemie, Hermann Rappe, had already guaranteed in November 1990 that dismissals of between 33 and 40 percent would not be resisted.[22]

In part, at least, the wage agreement was forged by proxy negotiators who themselves would not be affected by the compromises reached. The

19. Werner Stumpfe in an interview with *Die Zeit*, June 21, 1991.
20. See Arbeitgeberverband Gesamtmetall 1991, p. 131.
21. However, as mentioned above, the necessary wage cut is not very large. See Sinn 1990.
22. *Frankfurter Allgemeine Zeitung*, no. 268, November 16, 1990, p. 19.

only ones directly affected were the East German trade union representatives who formally led the negotiations on the workers' side. It could have been expected that they, at least, would argue for moderation in the interest of keeping their own jobs. But they were not experienced enough to realize how easily an aggressive wage policy could destroy jobs in a market economy, and they were justified in believing that the politicians would not stand idly by when large numbers of jobs were being destroyed. They were confident that ultimately the Treuhand or some other government body would pay their wages, and that anyone who found himself unemployed would at least be able to enter the German social security system on a high level. In this system the unemployment benefit a worker receives is calculated in relation to the wage he earned immediately before becoming unemployed,[23] so the higher the wage negotiated, the higher the unemployment benefit would be.

Thus, there was really no one willing to put up any resistance to high wages. The only ones who could have resisted were the West German taxpayers, who ultimately will have to foot the bill. But they took no part in the negotiations. They were the unrepresented "third party" to whom the burden of the wage bargain has been transferred.

Of course, West German taxpayers are to a large extent identical with West German employers and employees; thus, in a certain sense, they were present at the negotiating table. However, they were not present as an organized group, and therefore they could have no direct influence on the proceedings. Indirect representation, which resulted simply from the negotiators' being themselves taxpayers, could not save the negotiators from being caught in a rationality trap.

The trap existed because the negotiations were carried out separately on the basis of industry branches and regions. The high-wage strategy permitted the negotiators to dispose of unwelcome competition from the East within their own respective industry sectors. This was the advantage. The disadvantage was the resulting tax increase, which was necessary to finance the unemployment they themselves had created—but this disadvantage would be shared out among all the West German taxpayers and would thus primarily be borne by individuals who earned their incomes in other industry sectors. Ultimately, this behavior, which was characteristic of all the wage negotiations, produced a net disadvantage for the German unions and employers. But even if they had recognized this fact, the individual negotiators would not have been induced to choose a different

---

23. More precisely, it is related to the average wage of the previous three months.

strategy. If they had behaved reasonably in their own decision areas, other groups would have enjoyed lower taxes. They themselves, however, would still have had to share the tax burden imposed by the aggressive wage policy of these other groups, and they would also have had to fend off inconvenient competition in their own market sector. Settling for reasonable wages would have paid for all the groups taken together, but never for the single negotiators who had to determine their strategies independent of the others.

Escaping from the rationality trap would have been possible only if all the decision-makers had reached a collective agreement, as they had done on earlier occasions with the so-called concerted actions. This time, official economic policy had no provision for such actions, and it was assumed that free wage bargaining could be trusted to bring about the best results (although there was no way it could have done so before the East German economy had been privatized). This blind trust in free wage bargaining must be seen as the third major blunder associated with unification—along with the restitution rules and the Treuhand's sales policy. Fortunately, as the last section of this chapter will show, a resolute economic policy still has a chance to rectify this mistake.

Wage Subsidies

Some reputable economists[24] recommend massive wage subsidies as a remedy for the undesirable wage-rate developments. Subsidies would reduce the firms' wage costs and thus would modify the disastrous employment effects of the mistaken wage policy.

Some kinds of wage subsidies have, in fact, already been paid in East Germany.

• Many insolvent firms had filed their opening balance sheets very late, and until these could be assessed the firms were receiving support from the Treuhand. Since wages were the major costs of the firms, the support payments can be regarded partly as wage subsidies.

• Many firms have been receiving interest-bearing claims against the Treuhand following their balance-sheet assessment. Since these claims were to a very large extent made dependent on the number of employees, they also have the character of wage subsidies.

---

24. For example, Akerlof et al. 1991, Begg and Portes 1992, and Engels 1992.

• Purchasers of firms must give guarantees to the Treuhand that they will retain more jobs than are necessary from a management point of view. The Treuhand rewards them for these guarantees with price discounts.

The supporters of subsidies want far more extensive subsidies than these. The government is supposed to take over up to 75 percent of the East German firms' wage costs until the economy recovers.[25] In terms of total gross wages and salary payments in 1990, this would have required an expenditure of DM 107 billion[26]—almost as much as the annual transfer the government is already pumping into East Germany.[27]

The Council of Economic Experts (Sachverständigenrat 1990, pp. 234–236) opposed subsidies in the first annual report it made after unification. It stressed the role of the market in deciding which firms should close down: firms whose costs were not being covered by their revenues. Temporary injections of liquidity and government guarantees are, in the opinion of the Council, allowable during a short transition period, but then the normal German bankruptcy law should apply and should help carry out the death sentence of the market.

The Council's position is a reasonable one in a well-functioning market economy. A firm should continue to exist only when the social benefits it creates are greater than the social costs, and that is normally the case when a firm's private revenues are greater than its private costs. At present, however, East Germany is not a properly functioning market economy. When the report cited above was written, in the summer of 1990, the Council could not have anticipated the wage explosion. Today, East German wage rates far exceed the opportunity costs of labor, and in the future they will exceed them even more. The market therefore cannot even approximate the correct decisions. It closes down even a firm whose value added is greater than the potential value added, net of migration costs, that the redundant workers could produce in West Germany. The Council's model is essentially the organic transformation model, but unfortunately this model cannot be applied under the present circumstances. These circumstances differ so strongly from those assumed in the model, and the political situation is so explosive, that the suggestion that wage subsidies be introduced must be given serious consideration even if, in the end, it is rejected.

---

25. See Akerlof et al. 1991 and Begg and Portes 1992.
26. See DIW, *Volkswirtschaftliche Gesamtrechnung für Ostdeutschland*, June 21, 1991.
27. See table 2.2. As will be explained below, it is assumed that government subsidies will flow back through a variety of channels.

Efficiency Effects and Budgetary Effects

Figure 5.6 can be used in discussing the main arguments for wage subsidies. Suppose that the wage rate per worker agreed to in the negotiations is w^*, the level of unemployment benefits is w_F, and the wage rate appropriate for an organic system transformation is w_X. The ordinal magnitude pattern of the three variables is assumed, realistically, to be as shown. With union wages w^*, employment in East Germany is OA, and given the level of unemployment benefits w_F the number of commuters is GH. With a work force OH, this leaves AG unemployed. As was explained above, because the unemployed labor is not producing anything, there is an efficiency loss in the form of a reduction in the German national product net of migration costs. This loss is measured by the shaded area ZXFGA. The aim of the susidization strategy is to avoid this welfare loss either wholly or partly.

One obvious way to introduce subsidies is to pay East German firms an amount per job equal to the difference between the union wage rate w^* and the organic wage rate w_X. This would reduce the firms' wage costs to w_X and would have the effect of increasing employment in the East by AE. National product would be raised by the amount shown by the diagonally and vertically hatched area ZXEA (or an equivalent reduction in the national product induced by the high-wage strategy would be prevented).

This increase in national product is a genuine net gain for society, from which, at most, the utility of a certain amount of leisure that workers lose when they become reemployed must be subtracted.[28] The costs of financing the subsidies do not have to be subtracted; these simply represent a redistribution of the existing cake. What is most important is that the subsidies make the cake bigger and that therefore more is available to be shared out among the population as a whole. For the purpose of this analysis, the cake is the German national product minus any costs of migration that may be incurred.

The distributional effects of the measures are of course also important. The rectangle JKXN shows the aggregate amount of the subsidy when every person to be employed receives the same unit amount. If the whole amount had to be financed from the government budget there would certainly be a liquidity problem. However, those who advocate subsidies argue that most, if not all, of the funds spent by the government will return

---

28. In the opinion of some politicians this would mainly apply to women, who are said to be happy about the reduction in the rate of participation by women in the work force from 92% to the Western level of 60%. It is doubtful, however, that the unemployed in general gain very much in the way of utility from their enforced leisure.

to it in one way or another. This self-financing is the chief attraction of the subsidy strategy.

First, it is obvious that, when unemployment falls, the amount of unemployment benefits will also be reduced. In the figure, this reduction is shown by the rectangle LMEA. In addition, the government receives taxes and social security contributions from the wages of the holders of new or rescued jobs. If w^* represents the gross union wage rate, the revenue that the government loses when there is unemployment can be formally treated like direct unemployment benefits and can be included in w_F. Realistically, therefore, w_F must be very close to w^*. The government can recoup a large part of the wage cost subsidies when the workers are reemployed—perhaps even more than it paid out in subsidies.

Second, there is some hope that subsidies paid to firms will come back to the government in the form of higher Treuhand sales revenues.[29] With competitive bidding the increase in Treuhand revenue can be expected to equal the subsidies JKXN minus the gross loss ZKX which results from the employment of workers who would not have been hired without the subsidy. In the figure, the increase in the Treuhand sales revenue is measured by the area JZXN.

It is doubtful, however, that this second advantage can be realized, in view of the analysis of the determinants of the Treuhand's revenue presented in chapter 4. The return of subsidies by way of the Treuhand revenues assumes that the purchasers of the Treuhand properties face no credit constraints. The willingness to pay of buyers who are credit-constrained is determined by their own capital resources and by the minimum equity-asset ratio the bank requires them to have. Increases in the present value of revenues brought about by subsidies do not lead to higher bids from credit-constrained purchasers and therefore do not result in higher revenues for the Treuhand. The whole of the subsidies remains in the hands of the new owners; none flows back to the government. And, of course, the subsidies that are paid to firms privatized before the announcement of the subsidies cannot increase the Treuhand's revenue.

If no one faced credit constraints, if auctions were competitive, and if subsidies were introduced before privatization, then not only would the subsidization policy cost the government nothing; it would provide it with a net return. This is easy to see in figure 5.6. The cost of subsidies net of Treuhand revenue would be only as large as the decline in gross profits that results from increased employment—that is, ZKX. Unemployment

---

29. Akerlof et al. (1991), for example, argue this way.

benefits would fall by LMEA. On balance, there would thus be a budget surplus of LQXEA − ZKMQ.[30]

The calculation is no longer quite so favorable if the subsidies fail to return to the Treuhand (either because of credit constraints or because they are paid to firms that were already privatized). The subsidy costs (JKXN) must now be offset by the reduction in unemployment benefits (LMEA) alone. The net effect is no longer clear. What is certain, however, is that the net cost of the subsidies is still far smaller than what must be paid to the firms, and that the full amount of the increase in national product (ZXEA) would be realized anyway.

It would clearly be much better for the government if the subsidies could be limited to the marginal jobs that would be lost without them, with the intramarginal jobs that are in no danger left out. The employment effects would be the same, but the government's expenditure would be less. It would be ideal if the endangered jobs could be identified and the firms reimbursed only for the gross profit loss ZKX that arises from increased employment. The self-financing strategy would certainly work in this case and would produce a budget surplus for the government.

The Treuhand policy discussed above can be interpreted as an attempt to subsidize the marginal jobs. The Treuhand does not offer uniform price discounts for the jobs guaranteed by the buyers; rather, it compares in detail the offers made and negotiates with each buyer individually. In this way, it can reward the bidder whose employment guarantees are better than average and thus achieve large effects with relatively small discounts.

Subsidies for the reintegration of the unemployed can also be interpreted as marginal because they do not apply to the intramarginal workers already employed. For example, the government can pay part of the unemployment benefits saved to firms that provide jobs for the long-term unemployed. This measure is technically easy to carry out and is at present part of the legal repertoire.[31]

Bitter Pills

Even though from the point of view of a pragmatic labor-market policy it is not possible to disagree completely with the policy of marginal wage

---

30. To be precise, this statement will be valid only when the difference in the areas is positive. That this is likely to be the case is clear when it is considered that ZKML, the part of wages not covered by unemployment benefits, amounts to less than half of those benefits, while LQXEA is certainly more than half.

31. See section 49 of the Arbeitsförderungsgesetz of June 25, 1969 (BGBl I, p. 582).

subsidies, there are at least two arguments that can be leveled against it. Alas, these arguments are bitter pills to swallow, and they spoil the flavor of the subsidization policy.

The first is the moral-hazard problem. It was one of the reasons that the Advisory Council of the Economics Ministry (Wissenschaftlicher Beirat 1991b) rejected wage subsidies. When the wage negotiators know that the government will react to increased wages and growing unemployment with compensatory subsidies, there will be no restraints at all in the wage agreements. The Western delegates who sit on both sides of the table in East Germany will not give up their aim of keeping production costs in the East high so as to avoid competition from firms there, and the East German participants on the union side will observe that wage increases are no longer punished with job losses. All groups will therefore have an incentive to roll the subsidies completely over into wages.

Thinking up complicated incentive schemes in which subsidies fall automatically as wages rise is no help either.[32] Quite apart from the fact that formulas for a systematic reduction in subsidies lack credibility and cannot be put into effect unless they are embodied in the constitution, such incentive systems cannot solve the problem that some of the negotiators are West German proxies. Someone whose aim is to protect himself from low-wage competition and who has the power to achieve this aim is not going to be deterred by an incentive scheme that punishes someone else.

A second and even more important problem associated with wage subsidies is that, even if the moral-hazard problem did not exist, they would still not be able to achieve the economically efficient pattern of employment (that is, the pattern associated with the organic transformation strategy). Subsidies can help reduce the firms' costs, but they do not affect the wage-related unemployment benefits. They do nothing to reduce the incentive to stay in East Germany and be paid unemployment benefits instead of looking for temporary employment in the West; the stay-put premia are unaffected.

Figure 5.6 illustrates this problem, too. Wage subsidies eliminate the left part (ZXEA) of the shaded area that measures the welfare loss. The right part (XFGE), which represents the loss resulting from the fact that the unemployment benefit w_F is higher than the organic wage w_X, is not eliminated. The movement to the West is given by GH, but it would be more efficient if additional workers, EG, were to take jobs in the West

---

32. Akerlof et al. (1991) suggest a "self-eliminating flexible employment bonus" as an alternative to direct subsidies.

instead of staying in the East and waiting for an economic miracle. After the costs of migration were subtracted, these people could produce value added in the West equal to XFGE.

The best policy from an efficiency point of view would be to reduce unemployment benefits in step with the subsidization of wage costs at least to the organic wage w_X, but this policy is ruled out for a variety of reasons. The alternative would be to increase employment in the East by EG, by reducing wage costs not just from w^* to w_X but even to w_R. Since it would be optimal to provide this employment in the West, this can only be a second-best solution, though. Compared with subsidies at the organic level of wages, it increases the East German value added by the amount XRGE, but this increase is smaller than the increase in West German value added, net of migration costs, that could have been created by an equal increase in employment in the West (XFGE). Even an extreme subsidization policy that got rid of all unemployment would not be able to eliminate the welfare loss that is shown in the figure by the dotted area XFR. The policy would retain too many jobs in the East and induce too little migration to the West.

Workshops for Robots

The alternative to wage subsidies is capital subsidies. In principle, these can also bring firms from the brink of bankruptcy back into the profitable range and offset the effects of excessive wages. Capital subsidies are much favored by industry and have come to be accepted by some economists, too. Typically, though, these economists do not have subsidies for existing capital in mind. They think almost entirely in terms of support for new capital investment.[33]

East Germany is already receiving extensive support of this kind. The most important of these support schemes are an "investment premium," an "investment credit," and "accelerated depreciation allowances." The investment premium amounts to 12 percent of the expenditure on plant and equipment and is tax-exempt. The investment credit is between 15 and 23 percent of the value of investment and is given for the establishment of new plants and the expansion and modernization of existing ones. It reduces the taxable depreciation base, and to this extent it is partly taxed. The accelerated depreciation allowances permit 50 percent of the investment to be deducted from the tax base in the year of acquisition; they

---

33. See Wissenschaftlicher Beirat 1991b, especially the minority view put forward in a footnote.

are given for investment in plant and equipment and in buildings. In addition, various loan programs are available to investors which are, in effect, capital subsidies. These include loans from the European Recovery Program totaling DM 6 billion, with interest-rate reductions of between 1.5 and 2 percentage points, and low-interest-rate loans from various government banking institutions (e.g., the Kreditanstalt für Wiederaufbau and the Ausgleichsbank). Apart from these, there are various equity capital subsidies offered by the federal government, and various liquidity and reconstruction loans given by the Treuhand. Although there have been widespread calls for tax relief for East German firms, they receive direct tax benefits only in the form of exemption from the wealth tax and the "company capital tax" (Gewerbekapitalsteuer). It is estimated that, taken together, these measures may reduce the capital costs in East Germany by up to half.[34]

The main argument given for preferring capital subsidies to wage subsidies is that, at present, modern capital and know-how are scarce, but labor is not, so that building up an efficient capital stock must have priority. Other arguments focus on the need to overcome the investors' risk aversion and on the long-term nature of the effects of promoting investment.

These arguments are not convincing. Wage subsidies that promote the establishment of new jobs would work by way of investment and would also have long-term effects. Risks cannot be reduced by providing fixed grants—and even if this were possible, wage subsidies would be no less suitable than capital subsidies.[35] The main point, however, is that it does not follow that all kinds of capital should be subsidized in East Germany simply because capital is scarce there. Setting up workshops to employ robots would not help solve East Germany's problems.

The danger that capital subsidies would have just this kind of effect cannot simply be dismissed out of hand. They could easily result in the use of overly capital-intensive methods in the new plants and firms. The aggressive wage policy has already raised the labor-capital cost ratio far above the appropriate organic level and has thus provided an artificial stimulus to the installation of excessively labor-saving, capital-intensive

---

34. See Institut der deutschen Wirtschaft, *IWD* no. 9, February 28, 1991, and Wissenschaftlicher Beirat 1991b.

35. To eliminate risks, large subsidies would be paid when things were going badly for a firm, and small ones when things were going well. However, this brings moral hazard into the picture. A better way of dealing with risks is to spread and diversify them by having shares taken into the portfolios of shareholders or investment funds. The proposal made in the last section of this chapter makes use of this idea.

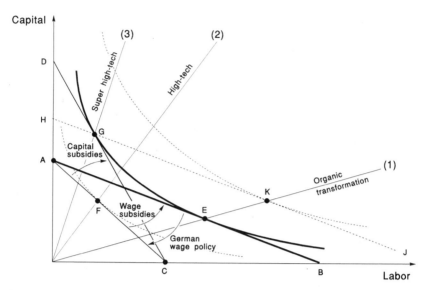

Figure 5.7
The effects of capital subsidies.

production processes. If the labor-capital cost ratio is increased still further by capital subsidies, the harmful effects of the wage policy can only be reinforced. It would be not just high technology that was being promoted, but superhigh technology. This cannot be the correct strategy for a capital-poor, labor-abundant country such as East Germany. Promoting superhigh technology might solve the employment problems of Japan's industrial robots, but it certainly cannot solve those of Saxony's workers.

Figure 5.7 permits a somewhat less impressionistic critique of capital subsidies. It shows the decisions open to a cost-minimizing investor who has the choice of various technical possibilities and production processes. The production processes that are both possible and efficient are shown by the convex curves (the production isoquants). Each point on an isoquant represents some particular well-defined production process that embodies known technology. Points on different isoquants but on the same ray from the origin represent different levels of output with the same production process or type of plant. Moving outward along a ray involves more units of the given plant type, more units of both factors, and more output. The straight lines sloping downward to the right (the isocost lines) show the different combinations of the factors that incur the same cost outlay. The isocosts slope to the right because, for a given total cost, less labor must be used when more capital is employed, and vice versa. The lower the labor-capital cost ratio, the flatter the isocost lines. The point of tangency between an isoquant and an isocost shows the production process that produces the largest possible output for a given cost outlay (or incurs the lowest cost with a given output).

Assume that the relatively flat isocost AB represents the labor-capital cost ratio corresponding to the organic transformation conditions. It incorporates the true social cost ratio of the two factors of production, and it results in a choice of the relatively labor-intensive plant type (1) at point E. The number of plant units needed and the level of costs that can be financed cannot be derived in this diagram. Without limiting the generality of the anlaysis, it is assumed that the total factor costs represented by the line AB are exogenously given. The firm's aim is to undertake the investment that will maximize its output and thus its revenue.

The German high-wage policy causes the isocost to pivot around A from AB to AC.[36] If nothing but capital had been used in producing the output, the firm would not be affected by this policy; however, to the extent that the firm used labor, it has to reduce its factor inputs and its scale of production. The unilateral increase in the cost of labor makes it wise, though, not to reduce both factors proportionately but to economize more on labor and to choose the more capital-intensive process (2)— assuming, of course, that the investment is still worth making at all. Point F shows the best possible investment decision that can now be made for the given cost outlay. It corresponds to the high-wage, high-tech strategy described above.

Because point F is on a lower isoquant than point E, it may be possible that the best investment project will no longer be able to generate enough revenue to cover the costs. Subsidies may therefore be considered as a means of solving this problem. If the subsidies reduce the firm's labor costs, the isocost will pivot back toward its old position, AB, and point E may again become attainable. Wage subsidies promote investment because they make it possible to produce more for a given outlay of costs and because they can obviously remove the distortion caused by the aggressive wage policy.

However, profitability could also be restored by using capital subsidies instead. These subsidies would pivot the isocost line at point C from AC

---

36. It may be objected from the perspective of Austrian capital theory that a rise in wages also raises the price of capital, so that the isocost line will not necessarily pivot when wages increase. This objection may well be valid for a closed economy which produces its own capital goods, but it is not relevant in the present connection. The price of capital goods in East Germany is determined on the world market and will not be affected by changes in East German wage rates.

to DC, and with the appropriate amount of subsidy they can shift the optimal point from F to G. Point G represents the same output as E, and the firm's cost outlay net of the subsidy is the same as at F or E. However, the process chosen will be (3) which is a superhigh-tech strategy choice. It is not only more capital-intensive than (1); it is even more capital-intensive than the high-wage, high-tech strategy choice (2).

The investor is indifferent between points E and G because the private costs and the revenues are the same in each case. Wage subsidies are equivalent to capital subsidies from his private accounting point of view. The two alternatives are, however, not equivalent from an economic point of view. From the latter perspective there are obvious disadvantages in choosing capital subsidies and the resulting superhigh-tech strategy.

The main disadvantage is that the superhigh-tech strategy involves much higher economic costs than the organic strategy at E. This can easily be seen if a parallel to AB is drawn through point G. Since this parallel, HJ, has the same slope as AB, it too must reflect the true economic cost ratio. However, it is located further from the origin than AB, and thus it represents a higher sum of economic costs. Given that at G no more output is produced than at E, it is obvious that G is inferior. Alternatively, more could be produced without using more resources than at G by choosing the organic capital intensity—that is, by producing at point K, which is on a higher isoquant than, but on the same economic isocost as, point G.

Another disadvantage of subsidizing capital rather than labor is that the economic absorption problems associated with building up the capital stock in East Germany are made very much worse because a much larger capital stock will be needed if the whole of the work force is to be employed. As a rule of thumb, a 1 percent reduction in capital costs, which is offset by a cost-neutral rise in wage costs, increases the capital-labor ratio by approximately 1 percent.[37] As already mentioned, it is estimated that the investment promotion programs already available for East Germany add up to almost half of the capital costs. If these programs are sufficient to offset the wage increases, they will obviously induce a doubling of capital intensity. Every second unemployed worker who with a given amount of capital investment could have been usefully employed when capital inten-

---

37. Under the usual neoclassical assumptions, the interest elasticity of the demand for capital with a given quantity of labor is given by σ/α, where σ is the elasticity of substitution between labor and capital and α is the share of wages in the private-sector value added. The quotient is approximately 1 because both the numerator and the denominator are in the region of 0.6. See appendix A, where the estimate of α is shown to be 0.62. Arrow et al. (1961) estimated σ at 0.57; Berndt and Wood (1981) gave a value of 0.63.

sity was at the organic level will remain unemployed, and twice as much investment will be needed to employ a given number of workers in the new production plants.

In view of these facts, special capital subsidies should be firmly rejected. They result in completely false investment decisions that waste economic resources and create far too few jobs.

It is not possible to defend capital subsidies by alluding to the moral-hazard effect of wage subsidies. To the extent that the capital subsidies can actually create jobs, they also encourage trade unions in their aggressive wage policy and this again nullifies the effect of the subsidies. When the double disadvantage in the form of wasted resources and the moral hazards is considered, it becomes quite obvious that capital subsidies are no solution to East Germany's problems.

Value-Added-Tax Preferences for East Germany?

In view of the drawbacks of both capital and wage subsidies, an alternative method of providing subsidies could be value-added-tax preferences. Various recommendations for reducing the VAT in East Germany have in fact been made, including one by the former Economics Minister Karl Schiller.[38]

To ensure that a reduction in the VAT would not simply lead to a transfer of sales offices to East Germany, the VAT arrangements would have to be patterned on the subtraction method—that is, instead of the taxes on inputs being subtracted from the gross turnover tax payable (invoice method), the tax base would have to be determined by subtracting the cost of purchased materials and services from the sales revenues.

From an administrative point of view, setting up such a VAT preference scheme is relatively uncomplicated and could certainly be done. However, there is no advantage in doing this rather than introducing wage subsidies. The reason for this becomes obvious when it is realized that a VAT is the equivalent of a tax on wages plus a tax on the real economic cash flow— that is, on the difference between the return on capital and net investment.[39] Because of this, any advantages of VAT preferences over wage subsidies would have to come entirely from the cash-flow component.

If investment projects are risk-free, cash-flow taxes are investment-neutral, because they do not change the sign of the present value of an

---

38. The recommendation was first brought to our attention by Thomas Seifert, a management consultant in Hamburg.
39. See Sinn 1987, chapter 5.

investment project's cash flow. Because the cost of an investment can be deducted from the tax base, the government implicitly has a share in the investment cost in proportion to its future share in the returns. It is, in effect, a sleeping partner, sharing the investment costs and returns but having no say in the decision-making process.

With risky investments, the cash-flow tax is no longer neutral. Interestingly enough, such a tax now encourages investment because some part of the investor's risk is removed. The subsidy effect, which occurs in the phase in which the investment takes place, is certain, but the later tax burden varies with the volume of returns—the tax is payable only if, and to the extent that, there are returns. This circumstance favors riskier though more profitable projects that without the tax might not have been carried out.

Reducing the VAT promotes investment by way of its wage component, and to this extent it has the same effect as a wage subsidy. However, through the cash-flow component, it discriminates against risky investments. Because this effect is an unfavorable one, and because in other respects a reduction in the VAT is no better than a wage subsidy, a VAT preference for East Germany must be ruled out as a suitable alternative.

The Role of the Government

Although government subsidies cannot be justified as a means of solving the unemployment problem, this does not imply that government has no useful role in the rebuilding of the East German economy. Laissez-faire is by no means the right policy. Quite the contrary. Beyond the reasons mentioned so far in connection with the organic transformation model, there are a great many reasons why government intervention on a large scale is needed to get the economy in the new states moving.

Rules and Referees

Some people may have believed that once communism was removed the free play of market forces would create a miracle in the East. It is now patently obvious that this belief was completely mistaken. Even a dyed-in-the-wool critic of government activity must realize that a market economy does not mean anarchy and a complete absence of rules. On the contrary, such an economy is defined by a complex set of laws and rules embodied in institutions created in a lengthy evolutionary process. In most of the Eastern European countries, the main problem of the transformation process is to find an efficient institutional framework for economic activity and to set it up quickly. These countries will have to spend the next decade carrying out this task, and the market economy will only be able to develop properly there after this task is completed.

East Germany is in the happy position of being able to take on West Germany's institutional framework. The legal system, the organizations, and the trading practices and customs that the new states need are all, in principle, defined and available for use. This is the great advantage acquired by carrying out unification according to article 23 of the West German constitution—that is, by the GDR's simply being gobbled up by the FRG.

The play of market forces can only bring about efficient results when the rules of the game are defined and when there is a referee to ensure that these rules are obeyed. The rules of the game have been established for East Germany; all that is missing now is the referee.

The East German administrators, judges, and lawyers do not yet know what they have to do. The civil service is still in the process of being built up. The old municipal administrative structure of the GDR is not appropriate for today's conditions, and because there were no states (Länder) there was no state civil service at all. The size of this problem can best be recognized by pointing to the fact that in the old FRG the Länder and municipalities were responsible for by far the largest part of government activities. The municipalities of West Germany employ almost four times as many people as the federal government, and the Länder employ six times as many.

In the first few months after unification, the fact that there was no effective civil service constituted a major obstacle to investment. Neither land records offices nor land survey offices existed, and this proved to be a particularly serious problem. It was not possible to assign property rights when these offices did not exist, and without property rights the risks involved in investment were prohibitive. It will take years before complete land records are available and all the land in the new states has been surveyed.

The limited capacity of the civil service has also reduced the effectiveness of the extensive transfers which the federal government has set aside for the new states. A large proportion of the grants planned for 1990 (see table 2.2) could not be used because of administrative difficulties.

It is obvious that strong measures are necessary to build up an efficient civil service. Financial incentives, training possibilities, and above all the transfer of administrative experts from West Germany are urgently needed. West German municipalities could be assigned partners in the East and be made responsible for providing them with help. Also, because the circumstances are exceptional, the government should not hesitate to use its right to transfer officials from one location to another. When millions are being forced to move because they have lost their jobs, it is not unreasonable to demand some degree of flexibility from West German civil servants too.

Priority for the Infrastructure

In a poll of East German investors conducted by the Ifo Institute in December 1990, improving telecommunications and transport facilities topped the list of the most urgently needed infrastructure measures, ahead of improvements in the civil service. Eighty-one percent of respondents put telecommunications in first or second place, and 50 percent did the same for transport facilities, while one-third nominated public administration for first place.[40]

By the summer of 1991, telecommunications had been greatly improved. The big East German cities had all been connected to the West by means of digital networks. In 1992 the biggest problems in this area have all been overcome.

Improving transportation will be a much longer process. The productive capacity needed to build up the whole transport system quickly is just not available, and there are major bureaucratic hurdles that have to be overcome before building plans can be realized. Even in the West it takes years for a major new highway to be completed.

To circumvent the normal complicated planning procedures, the federal government has considered decreeing the construction of new roads and highways for East Germany by law. The importance for overall economic development of improving the transport infrastructure makes this a useful policy option despite the considerable legal problems it would involve. East Germany's transport system is at present in serious difficulties. It is clogged up by the enormous increase in traffic volume immediately following unification. Emergency measures must be authorized regardless of the legal difficulties. The financial burden of modernizing the transport system is not all that large relative to its importance. The Federal Transport Ministry has estimated that the total amount needed to finance the modernization of the East German transport system over several years is DM 130 billion.[41] This includes DM 28 billion for the construction of federal highways and roads, DM 30 billion for local roads, DM 48 billion for

---

40. *Ifo-Schnelldienst* 6/44, February 22, 1991.
41. See Institut der Deutschen Wirtschaft, *IWD* no. 4, April 11, 1991.

modernizing the railways, and DM 12 billion for short-distance passenger transport. This is a small amount in comparison with the social transfer payments, which were at least DM 45 billion in 1991 alone. These transfers are used mainly for consumption purposes and are dissipated very quickly. Diverting some of this money into building up the transport system would help set the upswing in motion and make a permanent increase in consumption possible.

The Network Problem

Improving the transport system is especially important because it would also help solve a major coordination problem that currently puts serious obstacles in the way of setting up new industries in East Germany. Every industrial firm needs a large number of complementary suppliers and customers with whom it can trade at low transportation costs. It is not normally enough for an individual firm to establish itself in the East; at the same time a whole network of interconnected firms must be set up so that agglomeration economies can be realized. A single firm may not be able to survive alone, but many firms together can operate profitably when each is part of a network or agglomeration. This complementary relationship creates problems of coordination. Very large firms such as Volkswagen or Siemens may be able to overcome these problems because they are themselves networks, but medium-size firms cannot.

If perfect forward markets existed, the invisible hand could be expected to ensure that such networks are set up. The firms involved could agree on forward contracts and all set up at once if they decided this was worthwhile. However, such far-reaching trading possibilities are rarely (if ever) available. Typically, the individual firm must make its own location decision and hope that others will also decide to set up there, but this cannot be guaranteed.

One of the implications of the lack of such forward markets is that an inferior market equilibrium may emerge. In such an equilibrium, the joint profit opportunities of firms that are potentially parts of the network may not be taken up even though these firms' individual economic plans are rational, are based on correct expectations, and are compatible with one another. If an individual firm expects the other firms to set up in the new location, it will set up there too. However, if it is pessimistic and expects that other firms will not set up there, then it will not do so either. An equilibrium is possible where all expectations are correct, and all actions are individually rational, but nevertheless the firms do not set up in the East.

Government action on a large scale is necessary to bring about the correct equilibrium. It can certainly do no harm for politicians to make optimistic speeches. Moral suasion is cheap. Firm promises of government investment in the infrastructure, however, would be far more credible than speeches. The public infrastructure is an important component of the network of complementary economic activities that makes it worthwhile for a firm to move to East Germany. If the government gives clear signals with regard to the part of the network that is under its own control, it can influence expectations in the desired direction and induce industry to go east. Sometimes the invisible hand needs the help of a highly visible government hand before it can achieve its beneficial effects.

In principle, all infrastructure investment that creates public goods for private firms has the effect just described. Improving the transport links between East and West Germany, however, brings about a second network coordination effect, and this effect may be even more important than the government's role as part of the network. Well-functioning networks of firms already exist in West Germany, but under present conditions a firm can take advantage of such networks only if it is located in the West. The situation would be very different if there were well-developed transport links between East and West Germany. To the extent that transport costs can be reduced between the two parts of the country, an individual firm can dare to set up in the East by itself even if its trading partners do not follow. It can be linked to the West German trading network without having to be located in the West. Obviously, development of the East-West transport linkages makes the coordination problem less severe and lowers the threshold for profitable agglomerations of firms. Even small agglomerations could be established, which could then gradually grow into units comparable to those in the West.

The fact that poor transport connections have induced some West German companies to set up branches near their markets in East Germany is not a convincing counterargument. Many of these companies are working with fairly immobile inputs or outputs, such as building materials with high transport costs or perishable agricultural goods. However, competitive industries with mobile goods that contribute significantly to the wealth of highly developed economies require sites with optimal traffic connections. East Germany's greatest need is for competitive industries that will be able to supply the world market in order to earn the funds that are currently granted by West Germany.

Private Accounting Profitability for Public Goods?

Various suggestions have been made for handing over the German govern-ment's infrastructure responsibilities to private firms.[42] There has been serious discussion of a proposal to allow consortia of private firms to construct highways in East Germany at their own expense and recoup these expenses by means of tolls.[43] Such solutions may appear efficient from an accounting point of view but are rather dubious from an economic one. No charge should be made for public goods whose provision incurs costs but whose utilization does not. From the viewpoint of economic efficiency, there is no reason for excluding road users whose willingness to pay for using the road is less than the toll but whose use of the road imposes no costs. The argument that letting a private firm operate the road would cost the government nothing does not go deep enough. Private operation would involve a loss of utility to road users without reducing the costs of providing the road. Nothing could be more wrong than mak-ing the integration of East German firms into existing West German net-works more difficult by artificially creating transport costs that, from a truly economic perspective, do not exist.[44]

One argument in favor of using road tolls relates to congestion. If the roads to be built become congested at peak times, tolls should be levied so that scarce space can be allocated efficiently among the users. Tolls restrict less important usage and reserve the space available for those who have no other alternatives to using the road at these times.

---

42. This section takes up arguments exchanged by Möllemann (1991), Roth (1991), and Sinn (1991c). See also Oberhauser 1992.

43. For example, a private American company has offered to build a stretch of the highway between Berlin and Prague and to finance it with the income from a road toll.

44. A similar objection can be raised against the decision to reorganize the East German railway network, which despite the lower population density is more closely knit than the Western one. (In 1984 there were 124 kilometers of rail per 1000 square kilometers in West Germany and 131 kilometers per 1000 square kilometers in East Germany. See Bundes-ministerium für innerdeutsche Beziehungen 1987, p. 461.) It would be wrong to cut the East German net down to the West German level simply because it is making accounting losses. Prices that induce the efficient use of the railways cannot cover the total costs, because user costs are low relative to capital costs. Given the type of cost structure a railway has, private accounting losses are a necessary condition for efficiency, and accounting profits are a sure sign of inefficiency. There is no point in repeating the mistakes of the West by adapting the East German railway system to the incorrect West German model. This warning becomes even more necessary when it is considered that the current low prices of oil are due to an oversupply brought about by insufficiently guaranteed property rights in the producing countries. The era of cheap energy from petroleum will be over in a few decades. The future belongs to the railway, not to the automobile.

Nevertheless, the rationing function of tolls cannot be used to justify the private operation of the roads, because, although rationing may well be necessary at peak times, it is unnecessary at other times when the roads are used less heavily. A private firm, which has to maximize its profits, would charge a toll at all times, even when rationing is not necessary.

Moreover, a private firm would not be able to make an optimal decision about building a road. The revenue it would be able to earn is not obviously related to the total economic benefits of the road, and indeed there would be a tendency for the firm's revenue to grossly underestimate these benefits. When a price discrimination between users is not possible, it may well be the case that the value of the total benefit exceeds the maximum present value of the toll revenues by 100 percent.[45] Even though it is possible to levy a road toll, a private decision concerning the supply of roads carries the risk that investment projects that are highly profitable in economic terms may not be carried out.

A sensible way to use private economic activity in building up the infrastructure would be to direct it toward the construction of roads rather than toward their use. In general, the public bodies that normally would be given the tasks of planning roads and organizing the work involved do not exist yet in East Germany; where they do, they have little experience with standard business practices. It would therefore make sense to employ West German road-construction firms as prime contractors to supervise the construction up to the stage where the roads were "ready for occupancy," just as prime contractors involved in housing construction take over the planning and coordination of subcontracting for private owners. The roads could be handed over to the government at an agreed-upon price; the government could then allow the public to use them free of charge.

A model similar to this is currently being considered by the federal government. However, in this model, the prime contractors would also be responsible for financing the construction, and the government would then lease the roads from them. The idea behind this proposal is undoubtedly the wish to circumvent or (to put it more correctly) disguise the debt the government would have to take on if it financed the construction itself. Taking on an obligation to pay leasing charges, of course, also involves government debt. From the viewpoint of the politicians who want to

---

45. This is, for example, the case when the demand curve is linear, the operating firm charges profit-maximizing tolls, and the roads are not congested. If there are times when the roads are congested, the difference between the money equivalent of the economic advantages and the revenue from the tolls is smaller, but even in this case there is still a difference unless complete price discrimination is possible.

present themselves as responsible, sound financial managers, leasing has the great advantage that it is not officially counted as public debt. From the viewpoint of the people, however, this aspect is a major disadvantage of the leasing model. The citizens who have voted the government into office have a right to know what their future tax burdens will be and should have exact information about the true economic size of the government's debt.

This is all the more important because it is very unlikely that the leasing contract will be favorable for the taxpayers. A private owner of public roads will certainly have to borrow the funds needed to construct them on less favorable terms than the government could have obtained, and this will make the leasing method expensive for the taxpayers. There is a sensible role for private operators in the building of roads, but it is not in the selling of road usage or in the financing of road construction. The actual building of the roads is the part of the process where private participation could be used to a far greater extent than has been the case in the past.

Protecting the Environment

Obviously, measures to protect the environment are also among the infrastructure activities that the government must undertake in East Germany. The most flagrant violation of basic economic-efficiency requirements under the old regime was the neglect of environmental protection. Socialist planning had focused even more on optimizing production in a private accounting sense than the strictly regulated firms in the capitalist market economy, and had taken no account of the real costs to the environment. Something must be done very quickly to reduce water and air pollution and thus make the industrial regions in East Germany attractive places for firms and people.

Nevertheless (and we say this without wanting to detract in any way from the importance of environmental goals), many commentators on environmental problems exaggerate the problems and engage in too much scaremongering. Not all the astronomical figures bandied about can be taken at face value.[46] Some of the damage cannot be made good no matter how much is spent. Any amount of money, plucked at random out of the air, could be suggested, but spending it would not restore nature to a pristine condition. Calculations of the cost of cleaning up the environment

---

46. According to Angelika Zahrnt of the Association for the Protection of Nature and the Environment, in a statement made at the 91st meeting of the Parliamentary Budget Committee, cleaning up the East German environment will cost DM 400 billion.

are always arbitrary. In the medium term the government must concentrate its efforts on bringing emission levels down to those of the West, removing all the environmental damage of the last forty years cannot have priority in an economy struggling for survival.

First priority must be given to getting the upswing started as soon as possible, and the government must therefore focus on providing the public goods that promote the productive activities of private firms. If it takes the lead here it can do far more to improve the living conditions in the East than it could by trying to repair the ravages of the past.

Promoting Occupational Training

"Coals to Newcastle" would be an apt description of any attempt to raise the general level of occupational training in East Germany. By any measure, occupational training is better developed there than in West Germany. Whatever its faults, the communist state did give high priority to investing in human capital. A drive in the 1970s to raise the skills and qualifications of the population was particularly successful. Table 5.1 gives an overview of occupational training in the two parts of Germany. It is worth noting that, while 23 percent of those employed in West Germany had not completed any formal professional training, the corresponding figure for East Germany was only 21 percent. The difference is even greater when the population of persons of age 20 and over is chosen as the base instead of the number of persons employed. In 1982, 29 percent of people 20 and over in East Germany had not completed any formal professional training and 40 percent in West Germany had not.[47] These numbers neglect

Table 5.1
Percentages of employed persons who had completed training program.

	FRG (1987)	GDR (1988)
Apprenticeship	58.0	55.0
Foreman's certificate	2.6	3.7
Technical school	5.2	12.7
University[a]	11.0	7.3
No professional training completed	23.2	20.9

a. In the FRG this includes technical universities and colleges.
Source: Weiss 1991.

47. See Bundesministerium für innerdeutsche Beziehungen 1987, p. 283.

the fact that many East Germans have multiple qualifications; for example, many East German workers have completed more than one apprenticeship. In this respect unification gave an enormous boost to Germany's stock of human capital.

Nevertheless, this does not mean that it is unnecessary to provide the East German workers with additional training. Much retraining will be needed and many new skills will have to be acquired if these workers are to be assimilated into the new system and a competitive economy is to be established. The following aspects are particularly important.

To reach the technical standards required in the West in particular occupations, a great deal of new knowledge must be acquired. The knowledge gaps are particularly large in computing and data processing.

The structural changes described in chapter 2 will affect the whole of the East German economy, and this will mean that many people in the work force will have to change their occupations. Many of those now employed in agriculture, textiles, and heavy industry will no longer be able to keep their jobs, and many will have to find employment in trade and in the modern service sectors. Only a part of the restructuring will be brought about through the natural process of generational change.

Finally, people must become familiar with the new legal arrangements and with the way things are done in a market economy. The East German employees cannot know much about the millions of kinds of contracts and trading procedures that have become integrated into the market system, yet these are the foundations of the West German economy. If recovery in the East is to be permanent, the same foundations must be established there.

Private initiative by itself will not be sufficient to ensure that all the necessary skills and qualifications are acquired with the appropriate amount of intensity. Although it may not be immediately obvious, here the state also has a very important role. Private incentives for supplying and acquiring further education and training certainly exist. A person whose qualifications are improved can expect to earn a higher income and therefore has an incentive to pay for his own further education. For this reason, a private market in which new skills and qualifications can be acquired is sure to emerge even if the government does nothing. Nevertheless, strong justification for large-scale government intervention in this area is provided by the large positive external effects of the production and dissemination of knowledge. A positive external effect is an economic activity for which no payment is received and whose advantages partly accrue to others. The absence of payments implies the absence of an appropriate incentive to carry out this activity, and it is the government's role to provide one.

The dissemination of successful economic activities by a process of imitation is one very important external effect. Once it is available, the knowledge of new technology, new processes, new organizational forms, new markets, and much else spreads like wildfire among competitors and within local communities, firms, and circles of friends. In view of the utility to be gained for society when the dissemination of knowledge is costless, subsidizing the production of knowledge can be classified as efficiency-enhancing government intervention.

Another external effect, also very important for the East German labor market, is that a worker who improves his skills in effect advertises the skills of his fellow workers. The more workers there are who improve their skills, the more attractive East Germany becomes as a place in which to produce. The more investors are attracted, the higher the wages that free riders who have not themselves upgraded their skills can obtain. This external effect would not appear if an individual worker's skill level could be determined just by inspection, for the firm would then be able either to employ only workers who had the skill wanted or to offer the less skilled workers inferior pay and conditions. The incentive for a person to invest in improving his own skills would then be very strong. This, however, is not what the world is like. Despite certificates and other objective evidence of a person's skills, there remains a great deal of uncertainty with regard to the individual worker's ability and motivation to do the job. Employment decisions can therefore normally be made only on the basis of estimates of average skill levels. The result is underinvestment by individuals in acquiring skills. The government should compensate for this by introducing special measures to promote training and the acquisition of skills.

Training and Employment Schemes

The Job-Promotion Law (Arbeitsförderungsgesetz) of June 25, 1969 provides the legal framework for the government to promote retraining and education schemes in Germany as a whole. Although the law was originally intended to be applied on an individual basis, many training groups have been set up in West Germany by firms undergoing restructuring and reorganization. One such firm is Grundig, which made use of the possibilities offered by the law when it was going through a necessary contraction. Another example is Neue Arbeit Saar, which organized extensive employment and training programs for redundant steelworkers and received grants from the government for that purpose. The introduction of group schemes like these is increasingly being discussed for East Germany; they are called "Qualification Associations" (Qualifizierungsgesellschaften), and indeed some have already been set up. One of the first associations to concentrate formally on the provision of training is the Qualification Association for Energy and the Environment (Qualifizierungsgesellschaft Energie und Umwelt) in East Berlin, which is to provide retraining for former employees of the electricity combine.

Training schemes, whether in the form of associations established especially to provide them, in the form of subsidiary activities of existing firms, or in the form of individual training programs, are usually subsidized by the Bundesanstalt für Arbeit (Federal Labor Office) to the level of 65 percent of a standardized net wage income. In East Germany, this percentage proved to be too low because a very large part of the work force consisted of "short-time" workers (Kurzarbeiter), who received 68 percent of their previous net income from the Labor Office. Short-time workers were therefore allowed to participate in the training schemes without changing their formal occupational status and reducing their incomes. Often firms even added a small wage to the short-time work benefits to stimulate participation in the qualification and training programs. This additional wage increased the overall income in many cases to about 90 percent of the ordinary wage income. The 90 percent compensation certainly made retraining schemes an attractive alternative to both working part-time and being unemployed. (The unemployment benefits were also 68 percent of ordinary net wage income.) However, it also overrode the incentive to look for ordinary jobs. There have been reports of vacancies in East German firms that could not be filled because the qualification and training benefits had been made so attractive.

The "job-creation measures" (Arbeitsbeschaffungsmassnahmen) included in section 91 ff. of the Job-Promotion Law (Arbeitsförderungsgesetz) are closely related to the training measures. Unlike the latter, the job-creation measures were intended from the beginning as group schemes to be provided by institutions. Municipalities, states, nonprofit organizations, churches, and ordinary firms are all eligible to set up such schemes. An institution established especially for this purpose is spoken of as an Employment Association (Beschäftigungsgesellschaft).

Measures that improve the infrastructure, such as the repair and restoration of public buildings, garbage depots, local and regional roads, forest trails, or municipal housing, can be subsidized. So too can social programs that provide help for the aged, child care, and similar services. These kinds of schemes are supported more generously than the training programs. In East Germany they pay full union-level wages and provide interest-free loans for materials. The main criteria for government support are the prevention of unemployment and the usefulness and supplementary nature of the schemes. Programs are considered to be supplementary when, without the subsidy, they would not be carried out at all or would be carried out at a later date. The West German rule that workers must have been unemployed for at least six months before the subsidy can be paid does not apply to East Germany.

In principle, the employment and training schemes may include many very efficient government activities, and it would certainly be wrong to condemn all of them as ineffective.

Employment Associations can help carry out the urgently needed infrastructure investment in a phase during which state and municipal administration are not yet functioning properly. They are a kind of decentralized solution to the problem of an adequate provision of public goods. Anyone can put up a proposal for a project, and the government authority only has to decide whether to accept or to reject it. The administrators and the legislators do not have to take part in the cumbersome project-development stage.

The provision of training programs under the Job-Promotion Law is an important way of overcoming the externalities associated with the acquisition of vocational knowledge discussed above. Ideally it reduces the private costs by the amount of the social benefits and thus leads to an efficient level of training activity.

These abstract virtues of public training programs do not, however, mean that certain concrete proposals now being taken up in East Germany should not be looked at carefully and critically.

It is quite obvious that some proponents of Qualification Associations see them essentially as measures for keeping the unemployed off the streets rather than for providing them with the training they need to go into new occupations. It is difficult to see how old and outdated firms which have trouble coping with high wages, but which nevertheless want to save their workers from becoming unemployed, could turn themselves into effective modern training centers. Where would the instructors come from, and what kind of knowledge would they impart in the old working environment? The danger that the Qualification Associations will only prolong unemployment and postpone the search for new jobs cannot be disregarded. If this happens, structural change will be delayed, rather than promoted.

There is a similar problem with the Employment Associations. Who can be sure that the activities being carried out are really useful? Is it sensible for workers to be used to tidy up East Germany's forest trails if they could have been more profitably employed elsewhere at lower wages? The criterion of supplementarity, especially, must be looked at from this perspective, because this criterion can lead to the selection of projects that do not have very high priority. Might it not be better, as Engels (1991) ironically suggests, to replace the Employment Associations with "Production Associations"? Like Employment Associations, Production Associations are supposed to be subsidized by the labor offices, but they would be normal firms that produce marketable goods, and the focus would be on doing something useful rather than merely providing employment opportunities. Production Associations are simply meant to be private firms that receive employment subsidies from the government.

The justification for the Employment Associations must derive from the usefulness of the functions they perform. If their only function is to bypass unemployment, then they cannot be justified. Quite apart from the fact that letting them absorb millions of unemployed workers would be like setting up communism in another guise, these associations would simply have the effect of raising unemployment benefits to the level of wages. The loss of efficiency caused by stopping the migration of workers to the West, discussed above in connection with wage subsidies, would become even greater. In figure 5.6, point F on the supply curve would be pushed up to the same level as point Z, with the result that the disadvantage resulting from artificially preventing workers from moving to the West (shown in the diagram by XFGE) would become even larger. The German national product net of migration costs would be reduced by the Employment Associations.

Under the present circumstances, with an acute shortage of skilled workers in West Germany, the usefulness of the Employment and Qualification Associations appears doubtful. West Germany is full of firms that would make ideal Employment and Qualification Associations. These West German firms have a much greater intake capacity than any associations that can be artificially set up in East Germany, produce useful things, and can show the workers how a market economy actually works.

The validity of this fact cannot be denied by the argument that movement of East German workers to the West would put pressure on wages there and would therefore be detrimental to West German workers. Publicly supported idleness in the East does not benefit West German wage earners either; the social transfers that pay for this inactivity ultimately come out of the pockets of the West German workers, since they are financed from taxes and social security contributions.

A Social Compact for the Upswing

The winter of 1991–92 was, one hopes, the lowest point in East Germany's economic development, the trough of the worst depression ever. After the trough comes the upswing, and after the upswing prosperity. East and West Germany will have the same standard of living—some day.

The fact that these events follow one another as night follows day, does not justify economists sitting back and passively watching the march of time. They must be commentators and not mere spectators. Given the time span involved, the nature of the transformation process and the speed with which the upswing proceeds are far from irrelevant. Developments in the East could go like the wind (in another German economic miracle) or could be difficult and drawn out (a mezzogiorno nonmiracle). What will happen is not only in the lap of the gods, nor does it depend entirely on the diligence of the population. It also depends on the political and economic decisions that were taken after unification and those that will be taken in the future. Inherently, the economist's task is to comment on these decisions and discuss the alternatives.

There can, unfortunately, be no guarantee that a rapid upswing will be the consequence of the decisions taken so far. Three major mistakes in economic policy have been identified in this book:

• the attempt to restore old property rights (natural restitution),

• the attempt to sell off two-thirds of the East German economy in the marketplace, and

• the attempt to push East German wages up to world peak levels in a very short span of time and induce the upswing by means of a high-tech strategy.

The general public recognized quite early that natural restitution was a mistake, and the policy-makers reacted quickly by introducing the Obstacle-Removal Law. In theory this law partly suspended the restitution principle for two years, but in practical terms it did not make much difference. The other mistakes have as yet received very little attention, either because they are not recognized as mistakes (since their effects have not yet shown up) or because they are regarded as unavoidable (since no better alternative can be imagined). In pointing out these mistakes, we are concerned not with placing the blame but with showing that there are better alternatives that can and should be taken up.

Of all the problems discussed in this book, the most serious is certainly the problem of wages, because it effectively imposes an employment ban on the new states. Figure 5.4 makes it clear how very utopian the present German wage policy is. Wage negotiations with proxy negotiators have abused the constitutional right to free collective wage bargaining and have turned it into a farce.

The attempt to correct the mistakes of the wage policy by means of massive subsidies cannot be supported. Such subsidies are too expensive, they encourage further wage increases, and they can do nothing to offset the discouragement of westward migration that results from unemployment benefits and other social transfers. Subsidization of capital must be rejected even more strongly than subsidization of labor. Job-creation schemes and Qualification Associations simply cover up unemployment and are therefore also not solutions. They make the ban on productive employment easier for those affected to swallow, but at the same time they clamp down the ban even more tightly.

In our opinion, the key to the whole East German problem is to be found in the shift of the distribution problem from factor endowments to factor prices. In a market economy, the initial distribution of factor endowments can be chosen quite arbitrarily without affecting the efficient operation of the economy. By contrast, a redistribution that distorts the price structure must lead to a loss of efficiency. The most important price in a market economy is the wage. It is one of the main indicators of scarcity, and it has important allocation functions. It is hardly surprising that problems arise when this price is manipulated as in the present East German case.

We shall now outline a social compact that takes account of this basic economic wisdom, moderates the wage distortions, and provides for a better distribution of the endowments. In concrete terms, the pact combines a temporary ban on further rises in union wages with the privatization model developed in chapter 4, in which the Treuhand retains a fractional ownership in the assets privatized and hands it over to the East German population.[48] Although it would put limits on the growth of union wages, it would nevertheless clearly be in the interests of the East

---

48. Discussions of our social compact can be found in Michaelis and Spermann 1991, Berthold 1992, and Sinn and Sinn 1992. Other versions of a social compact are described in Erber and Pirschner 1992.

German wage earners because it avoids two of the three mistakes mentioned above. The next two subsections outline the social compact, the third explains how it differs from the investment wage models, and the fourth summarizes the advantages it has over the present policy.

The Wage-Moratorium Accord

The increase in East German wages, either planned or agreed to, will be postponed for four years (retroactive to April 1991). Wage increases granted since April 1991 will not have to be paid back, but these increases will be rescinded for the future. In principle, the standard wages in place at that date will remain in force for the four-year period. However, to combat a loss of real wages from inflation, and to keep wages from falling relative to those in the West, the same percentage wage increases and reductions in working hours agreed to in West German wage settlements will be carried over to the corresponding industrial branches in East Germany.

This program fixes the gross average monthly industrial wage per employee at about 47 percent of the West German level,[49] just below the Irish level. Since the progressive income-tax rates fall disproportionately on West German wages, the ratio of East and West German net wages will be somewhat higher—certainly more than 50 percent.[50] Another positive aspect of the relative position of the East German workers shows up when the relatively low prices for nontraded local goods (for example, housing or personal services), whose prices are directly determined by the level of wages, are taken into account. The West German price level in the spring of 1991, measured in terms of the East German basket of goods, was about 28 percent above the East German level[51]; thus, the ratio of net real wages in East and West Germany then was clearly above 60 percent.[52]

The wage moratorium just described relates to union wages, not to effective wages. In line with the expediency principle, privatized firms and their employees are free to agree individually on higher wages if they wish to do so. The use of this principle excludes the possibility that too-low

---

49. Cf. press release of Statistisches Bundesamt, August 19, 1991.

50. Calculations based on Genser 1990.

51. This result was calculated from the data in table 3.1 and from data in the DIW *Volkswirtschaftliche Gesamtrechnung*, June 21, 1991, p. 25.

52. Other things equal, this percentage is likely to fall somewhat, because the freeing of rents will increase the cost of living more quickly in the East than in the West. (In chapter 3 we calculated an inflation rate of 24% for the year 1991.) However, the price levels cannot become exactly the same as long as the nominal wage in East Germany remains below the West German level.

wages will cause undesirable migration of workers to the West. A shortage of supply in the labor market caused by too much migration would quickly be eliminated by wage increases, and this would make it possible to find the right balance between those leaving and those staying. This argument would be particularly relevant to regions near the former border, including East Berlin. The union wage moratorium would not prevent wages in these regions from quickly adjusting to Western levels.

To prevent a self-service effect, firms not yet privatized should normally not be allowed by the Finance Ministry to pay wages above the union level. However, in individual cases, departures from this rule could be permitted at the discretion of the Finance Ministry if competitive conditions warranted it.

Article 9, section 3 of the constitution gives the partners in wage bargaining the right to make collective agreements if they want to, so a relative wage halt could not be established by introducing a simple law for this purpose. Instead it must take the form of an agreement between the parties. The government cannot force them to make such an agreement, but it could encourage them to do so by means of a concerted action—a round-table conference in which all parties participate. If this did not work, the government could introduce monetary incentives like those it uses to influence other private contracts. An appropriate incentive in the present circumstances would be to make the initial distribution of shares associated with the participation model dependent on the agreement to the wage moratorium described above.

This suggestion may be seen as a severe encroachment on the right to free collective bargaining, but this right is already being severely abused in Germany. Since so much is at stake, the abuse must be curbed; thus, the government ought to be allowed to influence the negotiations by introducing appropriate economic incentives. Bending the intention of the constitution in order to further the interests of some particular group at the expense of most of the people in East and West Germany should not be permitted.

The Deregulation Commission (Deregulierungskommission) set up by the federal government has recently been investigating the problems associated with free wage bargaining and has criticized abuses that have occurred (including, in general terms, the aggressive wage policies of West German trade unions). The commission takes the view that the price of labor must not be set so high that the "individual is unable to exercise his capacity to work" (Deregulierungskommission 1991, p. 319), and has called the neglect of the interests of the unemployed reflected in the setting of high union wages an "infringement of the right to work" (p. 322). These general statements fit the union wage agreements in East Germany exactly.

The Deregulation Commission has recommended a variety of measures designed to make employment contracts more flexible and to strengthen individual bargaining rights. Among these are the possibility of (where necessary) reaching an agreement at the firm level to set aside the industry-wide employment contract temporarily and the possibility of hiring the long-term unemployed at below-union wages.

Whether the measures recommended by the Deregulation Commission would be sufficient to bring to a halt the collective irrationality now threatening East Germany is open to doubt. Only the firms that have already been privatized are likely to make use of the opportunity to conclude below-union-wage agreements. The Treuhand firms will not do so, because they can expect the union wages to be subsidized if necessary. It follows that the privatized firms would be unable to compete with the Treuhand firms in the labor market, because they would be offering lower wages. Only the subsidized Treuhand firms would have good survival chances—a clear perversion of the privatization task given to the Treuhandanstalt in the Unification Treaty.

One of the advantages of fixing union wages at a low level while allowing privately paid effective wages to rise in response to market conditions is that it creates an incentive for rapid privatization and thus helps the Treuhand to carry out the task assigned to it. Privatized firms will tend to pay wages higher than the Treuhand firms, the Treuhand firms will find it difficult to attract labor, and the interest of employees in having their firms privatized—which at present is not very strong—will increase considerably.

The Participation Model as a Bargaining Ploy

Basic aspects of the way the Treuhand incorporates private investors have already been described in chapter 4. In the case of firms that are required to file balance sheets, the Treuhand retains a minority shareholding which reflects the value of the existing capital, and the investor takes over a majority shareholding in return for his investment of capital and know-how. For other types of property, the Treuhand contents itself with interest-bearing claims against the purchaser. As with the cash-sales method, a competitive bidding process determines the conditions of the privatization contract. In the current legal situation, this method of placing the properties could be introduced immediately; however, the details of the transfer to the

East German population of the shares retained would have to be specified in a new law to be passed by the Bundestag.

The following method is suggested as a basis for discussion. The shares initially retained by the Treuhand are divided into three parts. One third is shared out among the workers employed by the firm at the time of privatization. The other two thirds are transferred to regional investment funds, which hold well-diversified portfolios of shares in all the privatized firms. The shares in the funds are distributed to East German savers and to the population as a whole, the former receiving at most half of the funds' shares. In accordance with Article 25 of the Unification Treaty, the savers are reimbursed for their savings deposits converted to deutschmarks at the rate of $2:1$. The general population's shares in the funds can be distributed according to the pattern used for the $1:1$ conversion of the money holdings—$3:2:1$, for people over 59, between 15 and 59, and under 15 respectively.

The funds' shares and the employees' shares of the Treuhand properties are to be allotted cumulatively. A worker who was also a saver at the time of monetary union receives an employee's share by virtue of his being an employee, a share in the fund by virtue of his status as a saver, and a further share in the fund as a member of the general public. The employees of firms that have already been privatized, for which there are no employees' shares, can be given extra shares in the funds so that they are under no disadvantage.

During the time when wages are fixed, shares in the firms or the funds cannot be sold except for the purpose of financing real investment projects. As was explained in chapter 4, this limitation may be desirable for the transition period, because the East German people have no experience in capital-market transactions.

Although the participation model described has important merits in its own right, its special advantage is that it can serve as a bargaining ploy in the implementation of the wage moratorium. At first sight it may seem that a share in the Treuhand properties has less value than the forgone wage increases and that the social compact cannot be attractive for the East German population. The truth, however, is the reverse. The participation model is likely to overcompensate the comparative decline in wage incomes by capital incomes which accrue to the shareholders. The main reason for this is the competitive bidding procedure that characterizes the participation model. Knowing that the wage moratorium has been enacted, investors will place much higher values on the Treuhand properties and will therefore be willing to cede a higher fractional ownership to the Treuhand than they otherwise would. Ideally, the bidding process will channel all the additional profits resulting from the wage moratorium to the owners of the shares retained, and these are larger than the wage cuts.

If the number of jobs available under the current high-wage strategy were fixed, the additional profits would just be equal to the comparative wage cuts resulting from the moratorium. The East German population could therefore be indifferent to the size of the wage cuts. Wage cuts would simply reallocate funds from one pocket to the other. However, the number of jobs is not fixed. Employment certainly increases when a more moderate wage policy is chosen. The employment effect of the wage cut increases labor incomes, and it also raises profit incomes. Since the additional profit income, too, can be reclaimed by the East Germans via the Treuhand shares if a competitive bidding process is chosen, the value of the Treuhand shares will rise by more than the present value of the wage cuts. Surely the overall factor income which East Germans can earn in their country will increase considerably when the social compact is realized.

In addition to these advantages from the social compact, the East Germans would also gain from the accrual of those capital incomes that could be earned despite a high-wage strategy. The high-wage strategy destroys much Treuhand value, but not all of it. Under the present cash-sales program there is no chance for the Treuhand to seize these incomes, but the participation model would make it possible to collect them for the East German population. The participation model would be of great help to the East Germans even if it were not connected with a wage cut. After all, the land values of the Treuhand properties alone are between DM 250 and DM 300 billion.

The various redistributive effects mentioned can be illustrated by once again referring to figure 5.6. If the high-wage strategy w^* is chosen, the value of the Treuhand properties is given by the present value of the profits that are represented by the area under the demand curve D^*D^* above the line JZ. A switch to the low-wage strategy w_X would reduce the wages by the area JZUN and increase the profits carried by Treuhand shares by this same amount if employment were constant. However, employment is not constant but increases from OA to OE. Thus, there is a positive effect on the wage incomes (equal to UXEA) and a further increase in Treuhand share profits (equal to ZXU). The sum of the East Germans' factor incomes earned in East Germany increases from JZAO to the total area under the labor demand curve to the left of line XE when the social compact is introduced.

There are further relevant income effects when social transfers are taken into account. Some social transfers are closely related to the wage level and will therefore automatically be reduced when there is a comparative wage cut. Unemployment benefits are the most important example. The reduction in transfers in itself is a disadvantage for the East Germans, one that can only partly be mitigated by the outmigration it will induce. Thus, undoubtedly, the overall advantage of the social compact for the East Germans will be somewhat lower than derived above.

The endogenous cut in social transfers should not be overestimated, though. Unemployment benefits are paid in Germany for two years at most, and the social benefits that replace them after this period are rather low. Moreover, the legal rules would certainly be changed if persisting mass unemployment in East Germany were to create substantial budget problems for the Bundesanstalt für Arbeit, the central labor office for Germany. It would be naive to believe that West Germany will be willing to finance indefinitely the large social transfers that are currently being pumped into the East German economy. To the extent that the wage moratorium cannot be expected to carry with it effective cuts in social transfers which otherwise would not have occurred, the huge distributional gain which the East German population can expect from the social compact can be maintained. Substantial reductions in this gain will, however, result from a continued privatization through cash sales. Of course it is impossible to apply the participation model to firms that have already been privatized. Time works against the social compact. At some point, the opportunity it offers will be lost.[53]

Investment Wage versus Social Compact

At first sight, the social compact we are suggesting may be reminiscent of the investment-wage or profit-sharing models discussed extensively in Germany in the 1960s and the 1970s[54] and now receiving much attention

53. In the *ex ante* situation when the first edition of this book was published, the income increase of the East Germans could have been realized to its full extent. As of the spring of 1992, up to one-half of the Treuhand firms may have already been privatized. The remainder should still provide a basis for the social compact, but it may soon be too late for that. See the epilogue.

54. See for example Krelle et al. 1968; Mückl 1972; Folkers 1973−74; Sachverständigenrat 1975, items 370−374; Tomann 1975; Oberhauser 1978, 1982; Weitzman 1984; and the papers edited by Sauermann and Richter (1977) in a special issue of the *Zeitschrift für die gesamte Staatswissenschaft.*

from American economists. Despite certain similarities, however, the social compact is basically very different from these models.

Investment-wage models, like the social compact, involve giving up wage increases in return for shares in the firm; however, in the case of the former, compensation is continuous: not only present employees but future employees too get shares. It is as if employees were receiving a money wage which they were then required to use to buy shares in the firm. Since the investment-wage bill increases with the number of people employed, investment wages enter into the marginal-cost calculations of the firm and reduce the profit-maximizing level of employment. This is the opposite of what the East German economy needs.

By way of contrast, the participation model in itself provides no incentive to reduce the number of employees, and it allows the employment-increasing effect of the wage moratorium to be felt to the full. The equities, issued only once (at the time the firm is privatized), are in no sense costs, because they are neither increased when new workers are taken on nor reduced when workers leave. Later changes in the fractional ownership can only be carried out on a voluntary basis in the context of new equity injections. This is precisely what distinguishes a redistribution of income by means of allocating endowments from a redistribution via the manipulation of factor prices.

In contrast to investment-wage models, profit-sharing models involve charges that resemble profit taxes whose revenue is used to buy newly issued shares which are to be distributed to the firm's employees. Because the base for calculating the share distributions includes the normal return to capital, profit-sharing arrangements typically also have the character of costs.[55] The charges increase with the amount of the shareholders' equity capital and thus encourage a reduction in the amount of this capital used.

The participation model, which is part of the social compact, does not raise the cost of equity capital, because the shares distributed are treated in exactly the same way as other equities and cannot be increased without the firm's receiving something in return. If the majority shareholders decide to build up the equity capital by retaining profits, the value of the equities held by the employees and the funds will increase, but the latter will have contributed to this increase in value because some of the profits retained belonged to them. If the majority shareholder puts in more of his own equity capital than the amount agreed to at the time of privatization, then

---

55. An exception is the scheme proposed by Atkinson (1972).

his compensation takes the form of an increase in the proportion of shares owned by him.

It is true that a cost-neutral profit-sharing model could be constructed by means of an unexpected one-time transfer of equities, but from the point of view of the existing shareholders this would amount to expropriation. Our model cannot be said to have such a confiscatory element. If the term is applicable at all, expropriation of the East German employees is what results from the sales the Treuhand is making at giveaway prices. The social compact gives back to the East German people what they have paid for by forgoing wages[56] without taking anything from private owners. This is restitution, not expropriation.

Help for the Jumpstart

The social compact provides a firm basis for the transformation of East Germany into a fully functioning market economy. With its help, the economy's stalled engine can be started up again and the new states can soon be on their way to a more prosperous future. Much of the harm inflicted by the present inadequate attempt to get things moving will be avoided. A summary of the numerous advantages of the social compact follows; it provides a fitting conclusion to the book.

• Lower wages create more employment in East Germany. There is no longer the danger that all the old production plants will be dismantled at once. Some of·them will continue to be used efficiently during a transition phase. Lower wages also provide a stimulus to investment, which in turn quickly creates new jobs. East Germany has a better chance to compete with the other former Comecon countries.

• The shares in the firms which the social compact directly or indirectly distributes to workers reduce the incentive to reintroduce aggressive policies once the moratorium has run out. The advantages stemming from low wages will be retained over the long term.

• The wage strategy now being planned drives up the payments for idleness, and the payments reduce the incentive to look for productive employment. The social compact avoids this. In particular, it enables the mobile part of the East German population to take up productive employment in the West during the transition period and, by so doing, to acquire

---

56. As was mentioned in chapter 4, the East German share of wages was significantly below that in West Germany.

the knowledge and skills necessary to make East Germany into a modern market economy.

• The increase in employment in East and West means a reduction in the level of transfer payments financed by the West German taxpayer.

• The social compact increases the East Germans' factor incomes.

• Under the current policy there is no chance of realizing the goal set out in Article 25 of the Unification Treaty—that is, to give the East German savers a share in the formerly state-owned property. The social compact enables this goal to be achieved.

• The whole stock-flow problem disappears, because the Treuhand receives no cash revenue. There will be less pressure on the capital market, interest rates will be lower, and more resources will be available for private investment. The Treuhand has less incentive to slow down privatization in order to avoid spoiling the market, and it is able to sell on better terms.

• For similar reasons, the microeconomic credit constraints are loosened. All the capital an investor can raise can be used for reorganization investment. The investor is prepared to offer the owners of the shares retained a higher present value of payments than when he had to buy the firm against cash.

• Risks are lower for the investors than with the cash-sales procedure, and a more substantial engagement can be dared. The reduction in risk also makes the investors willing to "pay" more than in the case when the firms are sold against cash.

• The monetary union left the East German people with almost no financial claims over and above what they needed for transactions purposes, so they cannot take part in the bidding for the Treuhand properties. The social compact solves this problem: shares in the existing properties are distributed free of charge to the population, and East German managers do not need finance to be able to buy a firm. East Germans thus have a far better chance of taking over the role of entrepreneurs.

So far, East German capitalism has appeared to fit the communist caricature. Many old cadres must be rubbing their hands with glee as they observe how fierce the struggle over distribution has become. It is very dangerous for economic policy-makers to stand on the sidelines and make no attempt to find a peaceful solution to this struggle. Euphoria disappointed can easily turn into hatred, and the evil genie who was supposed to be shut away in the bottle has a chance of getting free. Establishing

West Germany's "Social Market Economy" in the East means giving everybody a fair chance of achieving prosperity in his own way. The present separation of Germany into two nations—West German capitalists and East German workers—is eliminating this chance. Our object in writing this book was to show that other policy options are available and should indeed be taken up.

6   Epilogue

The social compact described above offers, as we see it, a last-minute chance for Germany's unification policy to escape the trap into which it has fallen. It exemplifies the fundamental economic wisdom that distributional goals should be reached by changing factor endowments, not by distorting factor prices.

Unfortunately, there is little hope that the escape route we have pointed to will be followed. The German leaders are committed to their mistaken economic decisions and are unable to turn around. Restitution will go on, the Treuhand will continue its Sisyphean task of selling an economy, and East German wages will indeed be catapulted beyond the Japanese and American levels before 1995. The German economy is strong enough to survive these mistakes, but at the risk of social unrest and extremism. Living standards cannot become equal in East and West Germany within "three or four or five" years after unification, as Chancellor Kohl has kept predicting. Instead, high levels of unemployment in East Germany will destabilize the East Germans, and the West Germans will grow tired of transferring large amounts of money to the East.

Economic policy can only change under pressure from the population when the problems are clearly seen and felt, but then it will be too late for the social compact. Massive wage cuts will not be enforceable and the privatizations carried out by the Treuhand cannot be undone.

The public-choice theorist should not be surprised by this policy failure. He knows that public policy does not, in general, satisfy the axioms of collective rationality. Public choice is simply an equilibrium between pressure groups that balances conflicting interests and may or may not satisfy economic efficiency requirements.

As predicted by the theory of public choice, the few are more powerful than the many in affecting the nature of the equilibrium, because, with a given stake, their per-capita gain from a successful political action is higher. The 1.5 million who claimed restitution rights are fewer than the 16 million who will suffer as a result. The few thousand West German firms that bought Treuhand assets also are fewer than the "people" whose property is being sold. The members of trade unions and employers' organizations who settle wage contracts are fewer than the taxpayers who have to foot the bill. It is more than obvious why the unification policy has run into trouble.

Why do economists write books like this one if they know about the nature of the political equilibrium? There are two and a half reasons.

The first is a matter of principle. The economists' job is to give policy advice. In doing so they take the preferences of the people and the technological constraints of the economy into account, but they disregard political constraints. Respecting political constraints would mean that feasible policy measures are just those that are actually carried out. Policy advice would be useless under these circumstances; economists would be apologists, not social scientists. The essence of giving political advice is to change the political constraints to satisfy the people, not to respect these constraints to satisfy the politicians.

The second reason is simply analysis and cognition. The main difficulty in writing this book lay in understanding what was actually going on in a unique and unprecedented historic event. We hope that those readers who do not share our policy recommendations will nevertheless be able to learn from the analysis we have offered.

The half reason is that we hope that our judgment on the nature of the political equilibrium is wrong and that there are some wise men and women in influential political positions who will, in fact, listen to the arguments we present. There are self-fulfilling and self-denying prophecies. We very much hope that ours are among the latter.

Appendix A   Statistical Comparison of GDR and FRG (1989)

Unless otherwise stated, the data are from the following sources: Statistisches Bundesamt, *DDR 1990, Zahlen und Fakten* (Wiesbaden, 1990); Statistisches Bundesamt, *Statistisches Jahrbuch 1990 für die Bundesrepublik Deutschland* (Wiesbaden, 1990); *Monatsberichte der deutschen Bundesbank 42*, No. 5, May 1990; *Statistisches Jahrbuch 1990 der Deutschen Demokratischen Republik 34* (Berlin, 1990); *Jahresbericht 1989 der Staatsbank der DDR*.

Work-Force Potential	GDR	FRG
Population	16.4 million	62.3 million
	(GDR/FRG ratio = 26%)	
Work force	8.9 million	29.7 million
Employed	8.9 million	27.7 million
Participation rate	54%	48%
Female participation rate	50%	37%
Unemployment rate	0%	7.1%

Productivity and Income	GDR (Mark)	FRG (DM)
National material income (excluding services)	260.4 billion	—
per person employed in productive sector	38,759	—
Gross value added (excluding service firms)	—	1,449 billion
per person employed	—	67,400
Gross domestic product at market prices	353.4 billion[1]	2,237 billion
	(GDR/FRG ratio = 15.8%)	
per person employed	39,700	80,750
	(GDR/FRG ratio = 49.2%)	

per person in work force	39,700	75,300
	(GDR/FRG ratio = 52.7%)	
per head of population	21,500	36,300
	(GDR/FRG ratio = 59.2%)	
Private value added (excluding indirect taxes)	—	1,505.1 billion
Gross income from wages (including employers' social security contributions)	141.2 billion	1,171.5 billion
Gross income from wage in private sector	—	948.8 billion
Share of wages in private-sector value added (partial production elasticity of labor under competitive conditions)	—	63.0%
Return on investment in private sector: (Value added − Wages)/ (Net fixed assets + Real estate values). (See Assets and Liabilities)	—	7.0%

Gross average monthly wages (including employers' social security contributions

economy as a whole	1,322	3,966
	(GDR/FRG ratio = 33%)	
industry or processing sector	1,324	3,657
building and construction	1,310	2,958
agriculture and forestry	1,242	2,597
trade	1,168	2,893
transport and communications	1,436	3,311
Net money income (GDR): Y_{GDR} per year	167.5 billion	
Personal disposable income (FRG): Y_{FRG} per year		1,403.8 billion
	(GDR/FRG ratio = 12%)	

Net money income or personal disposable income per head

per year	10,200	22,500
per month	850	1,900
	(GDR/FRG ratio = 45%)	

Government Income and Expenditures

	GDR (Mark)	FRG (DM)
Income from taxes	269.7 billion (1988)[2]	535.5 billion
value-added taxes	—	131.5 billion
income taxes	10.0 billion (1988)	278.6 billion
taxes on enterprise	—	34.2 billion
consumption taxes	43.1 billion (1988)[3]	53.6 billion
other	—	97.6 billion
social security contributions	18.8 billion (1988)	413.5 billion
Subsides (to firms, excluding price subsidies)	106.8 billion (1988)	75.6 billion
Transfers (to households)	36.3 billion (1988)	61.8 billion
Price subsidies for essential commodities	49.8 billion[3] (1988) (1971: 8.5 billion)	
of which:		
food	31.9 billion	
industrial goods	11.9 billion	
transport services	5.0 billion	
Rent subsidies[4]	16.0 billion (1988)	
Pensions	17.2 billion (1988)	173.9 billion (1988)
Average monthly pension	427	1,108
Taxes/GNP	—	23.9%
Social security contributions/GNP	5.3%	18.5%
Government budget deficit	−0.2 billion	26.3 billion
Government budget deficit/ GNP	—	1.2%
	(1990: 2.7%[5]–3.7%[6]) (1991: 3.2%–5%[5]) (USA 1989: 2.6%)	
Government value added in NNP	—	222.7 billion
Government expenditure/ GNP	76.3%	31.2%
Government consumption/ GDP	—	18.5%

Money Supply	GDR (Mark)	FRG (DM)
Currency in circulation (households and non-banks)		
(a) Total	17.0 billion	146.9 billion
Per capita	1,036	2,350
(b) Demand deposits (GDR: savings deposits)	159.7 billion	303.7 billion
(c) Demand deposits of firm with Staatsbank	60.6 billion[7]	0
(d) Time deposits and funds of less than 4 years held by domestic households and firms	0	325.8 billion
(e) Savings deposits (in FRG with legal withdrawal notice)	—[8]	479.1 billion
M1 (a + b + c)	237.3 billion	450.6 billion
M2 (a + b + c + d)	237.3 billion	776.4 billion
M3 (a + b + c + d + e)	237.3 billion	1,255.5 billion
Financial assets of private households[9]		
total	191.4 billion	2,515 billion (1988)
per capita	11,670	40,400

Percentages of net money income (Y_{GDR}) or personal disposable income (Y_{FRG})

	GDR	FRG
Cash	10.1%	10.5%
Demand deposits (GDR: savings deposits and demand deposits of firms)	131.5%	21.2%
M1	141.7%	32.1%
M2	141.7%	55.3%
M3	141.7%	89.4%
Financial assets	114.3%	187.2% (1988)

Money overhang with 1:1 exchange rate, using West German aggregate ratios:

Lower estimate (M3 overhang in DM)

1989: 237.3 billion − 89.4% · 167.5 billion = 87.5 billion

Middle estimate (M2 overhang)

1989: 237.3 billion − 55.3% · 167.5 billion = 144.7 billion

Upper estimate (M1 overhang)

1989: 237.3 billion − 32.1% · 167.5 billion = 183.5 billion

Explanation: Money overhang $\equiv M_{GDR} - k_{FRG} \cdot Y_{GDR}$, where $M_{GDR} \equiv$ Currency in circulation + Savings deposits + Demand deposits of non-banks with GDR central bank, $k_{FRG} \equiv$ Cash balances coefficient in FRG (relative to personal disposable income in FRG), and $Y_{GDR} \equiv$ Net money income of private households in GDR.

Because savings could be withdrawn without advance notice in the GDR, these were as fungible as demand deposits in the FRG. On the other hand, there were almost no longer-term financial assets (with the exception of savings-like personal insurance, ≈ 14.7 billion). The size of the money overhang depends on the money-supply definition used (M1, M2, or M3). The Bundesbank based its calculations on the M3 overhang only.

Given the GDR price level, according to the estimates made above, the values of the necessary money supply components were:

M1 (Cash + Demand deposits)	= 167.5 billion · 32.1%	= 53.8 billion
M2 − M1 (fixed-term assets of less than 4 years)	= 167.5 billion · (55.3% − 32.1%)	= 38.9 billion
M3 − M2 (savings deposits with legal withdrawal notice)	= 167.5 billion · (89.4% − 55.3%)	= 57.1 billion
		149.8 billion

The GDR currency was converted on July 1, 1990 in accordance with the following rules, which were set down in the unification treaty. All amounts were converted into DM equivalents and could be withdrawn as cash at any time. Many advisors had recommended that some funds be frozen, but none were.

Exchange rate 1:1

Persons up to 14 years	2,000
Persons between 15 and 59	4,000
Persons over 59	6,000

Given the structure of the GDR population, this meant an increse in M3 of 65.5 billion.

Exchange rate 1:2

In principle the surplus of M3 above 65.5 billion (that is, 237.3 billion − 65.5 billion = 171.8 billion) could be exchanged at this rate. The increase in M3 was 85.9 billion.

Exchange rate 1:3
A small part of the surplus of M3 above 65.5 billion DM was owned by
persons resident outside the GDR. Here the exchange rate of 1:3 was used
for the amounts held in accounts established in 1990 in GDR banks. The
exact amounts that come into this category are not known to the authors.

Total: DM — M3 in accordance with the Unification
Treaty   151.4 billion

M3 money overhang exchanged in accordance with the unification treaty
and assuming West German ratios: 151.4 billion − 32.1% · 167.5 billion =
97.6 billion.

Prices	GDR	FRG
Cost of living index (1970 = 100)	99.5	197.7

Purchasing-power parity: see table 3.1.

Assets and Liabilities	GDR (Mark)	FRG (DM)
Gross fixed assets[10]	—	10,032.7 billion
Net fixed assets[11]	575.8 billion[12]	6,512.6 billion
(total)	up to 1,745.0 billion	
in productive sector	462.5[12]−1,250.0 billion	—
Net fixed assets of private sector	—	5,850.5 billion
Value of private real estate	—	2,049.8 billion[13]
Value of private and privatizable real estate (GDR)	420.9−524 billion[14]	—
Capital coefficient[15]		
total	—	3.3
in productive sector	4.8	—
Net foreign debt	21.2 billion	− 426.8 billion
Firms' debt (GDR: gross debt with central bank)	260.4 billion	1,196.6 billion
Housing loans	108.5 billion	729.4 billion
Internal government debt	—	923.5 billion

Investment and Saving	GDR (Mark)	FRG (DM)
Gross investment	77.1 billion	435.6 billion
Depreciation	33.4 billion	276.7 billion

Net investment	43.7 billion	199.6 billion
Saving	—	267.9 billion
Savings rate[16] (relative to personal disposable income or net money income)	6.3%	13.6%

Foreign Trade	GDR (Mark)	FRG (DM)
Exports[17]	141.1 billion	641.0 billion
Imports[17]	144.7 billion	506.5 billion
Trade balance	−3.6 billion	134.5 billion
Current-account balance[18]	—	104.2 billion
Capital-account balance	—	−136.2 billion

Consumption as Percentage of Disposable Income[19]	GDR	FRG
Food, beverages	41.5%	23.2%
Industrial goods	45.3%	40.0%
Services (including housing) of which:	13.2%	36.8%
rents	2.7%	20.1%
other costs included in rent (electricity, gas, oil)	1.9%	5.7%

Households Equipped with Consumer Durables[20]	GDR	FRG
Car	54%	96%
Television set	96%	99%
of which: color	57%	95%
Telephone	17%	99%
Refrigerator (without freezer)	99%	81%
Freezer (with or without refrigerator)	43%	75%
Washing machine	99%	97%

Housing		
Units	7 million	26.6 million[21]
persons per unit	2.3	2.3
Square meters per person	27.6	35.5
Postwar housing as percentage of total	35%	70%
Percentage of housing units with bath	82%	96%

Notes to Appendix A

1. An alternative estimate from the DIW (*Wochenbericht* 57, No. 17/90, April 26, 1990, p. 223) gives 346.1 billion ostmarks.

2. Total government income.

3. Most price subsidies and consumption taxes were removed at the time of unification (October 3, 1990). All prices, with the exception of rents, were freed.

4. According to Cornelsen 1991.

5. Arbeitsgemeinschaft deutscher wirtschaftswissenschaftlicher Forschungsinstitute, "Die Lage der Weltwirtschaft und der deutschen Wirtschaft im Herbst 1990," in *DIW Wochenbericht* 57, No. 43, October 25, 1990.

6. Estimate by Deutsche Bundesbank (see *Frankfurter Allgemeine Zeitung*, No. 260, November 7, 1990, p. 17).

7. *Jahresbericht 1989 der Staatsbank der DDR.*

8. Savings deposits in the GDR could be withdrawn daily and thus were equivalent to demand deposits.

9. Financial assets in the GDR include cash, savings deposits, and 15 billion ostmarks in savings-like personal insurance. Financial assets in the FRG also include securities.

10. At replacement prices.

11. Excluding land. (In GDR statistics "Grundmittelbestand.")

12. Estimate of Institut für Angewandte Wirtschaftsforschung (*Die ostdeutsche Wirtschaft 1990/1991*, October 22, 1990).

13. Our estimate; see appendix B.

14. Our estimate; see appendix B.

15. FRG: net fixed assets to net national product at market prices. GDR: stock of land in productive sector to national material income.

16. The savings rate of the representative four-person household in the GDR was, however, 12.7%. See Gemeinsames Statistisches Amt, *Monatszahlen*, December 1990, p. 58 f.

17. Gemeinsames Statistisches Amt, *Monatszahlen*, December 1990, p. 60, and Sachverständigenrat, Jahresgutachten 1990/91, p. 410 f.

18. Statistisches Bundesamt, *Volkswirtschaftliche Gesamtrechnungen*, Fachserie 18.

19. GDR: all households. FRG: four-person households with gross incomes from wages and salaries between DM 2900 and DM 4400.

20. GDR: percentage of households with the consumer durables listed. FRG: four-person households with incomes from employment of between DM 3000 and DM 4500. (*Statistisches Jahrbuch für die Bundesrepublik 1990*, Wiesbaden, 1990.)

21. 1987: Statistisches Bundesamt, *Wirtschaft und Statistik* No. 8, August 1989, p. 494.

Appendix B

Land Values in East and West Germany (1989) (in collaboration with Ronnie Schöb)

Values of West German Land

The sizes of private land areas in the old FRG recorded in table B.1 are taken from the *Statistisches Jahrbuch 1990* and the *Statistischer Monatsbericht* of the Federal Ministry of Finance. The prices are also taken from the *Statistisches Jahrbuch 1990* and from information given to the authors by the Federal Forestry Office in Stockdorf. The price of building land is the average price of land sold in 1989. The value given is an underestimation because most of the land sold was in areas on the outskirts of towns and cities, where land prices are lower than in inner-city areas. As land used for roads, railways, and airports is not included in the table, it was not possible to estimate how much land has public buildings on it. It can be assumed that this makes up only a small proportion of the total land value.

Values of East German Land

The estimation of values which correspond to those in table B.1 for East Germany is difficult because there were no market prices for land in the GDR and the amount of land that could be privatized is unknown. This section provides two different estimates based on alternative assumptions: (i) that Western prices apply immediately; (ii) that they apply only after an adjustment period that lasts until the year 2000, and that during this period the land produces no rents.

(i) The structural pattern of the total East German land area is taken from the *Statistisches Jahrbuch 1990*, but the amount that could be privatized is not reported there. The sizes in table B.2 were calculated from the available data, and it was assumed that all agricultural land would be privatized, that the forest area privatized would be in the same proportion as in West

Table B.1
Actual values of private land areas in the old FRG (1989).

Land category	Size (million hectares)	Price per hectare (DM)	Value (DM billion)
Agricultural land (excl. forests)	13.488	30,924	417.1
Forests	2.832	12,500	35.4
Building land	1.685	947,700	1,597.3
Total,	18.006	—	2,049.8
average	—	113,839	—

Sources: Statistisches Bundesamt, *Statistisches Jahrbuch 1990 für die Bundesrepublik Deutschland* (Wiesbaden, 1990), tables 8.13, 8.18, 23.10; Bundesministerium der Finanzen, *Statistischer Monatsbericht* 6/1990, p. 401; information from the Bundesforstamt, Stockdorf; authors' own estimates.

Table B.2
Value of private and privatizable land areas in East Germany.

Land category	Size (million hectares)	Immediate adjustment		Adjustment by the year 2000	
		Price per hectare (DM)	Value (DM billion)	Price per hectare (DM)	Value (DM billion)
Agricultural land (excl. forests)	6.171	30,924	190.8	24,817	153.1
Forests	1.133	12,500	14.2	10,031	11.4
Building land	0.337	947,700	319.5	760,547	256.4
Total,	7.641	—	524.5	—	420.9
average	—	68,642	—	55,080	—

Sources: Statistisches Bundesamt, *Statistisches Jahrbuch 1990 für die Bundesrepublik Deutschland*, (Wiesbaden 1990), appendix 1, table 5.1; authors' own estimates.

Germany (38%), and that the ratio of East German to West German building land is in the same proportion as the present housing areas (20%). The "immediate adjustment" values were obtained by multiplying the land areas by the West German land prices current in 1989. On the basis of 1989 West German prices, the total value of private and privatizable land in East Germany is DM 524.5 billion. This must be seen as the upper limit, because it implies that East and West German land rents became the same as soon as unification occurred. The method used underestimates the residential and factory land areas because they are presumably larger relative to the population than in West Germany. We do not know the exact size of this error.

(ii) The alternative to assuming that the prices become equal at once is that up to the year 2000 East German land produces no rents at all and that after that date it produces the same rents as in West Germany. The estimates based on this assumption are set out in the two rightmost columns in table B.2.

With a perfect capital market, the market rate of interest equals the expected growth rate of land prices plus the land rent per unit of land value. If the West German land prices are calculated for the year 2000 and discounted at the market rate of interest, the resulting present values are equivalent to land prices current in 1989 discounted at the rate of return on land over the adjustment period. The net average rate of return on agricultural land in the FRG was approximately 1.1% between 1975 and 1987.[1] If all land prices grow at the same rate, this rate of return can be used for all land categories. A conservative estimate is reached by calculating the implicit East German land prices at a rate of return of 2%. These prices are given in the second column from the right in table B.2. The corresponding values of the different land categories are given in the last column. A conservative estimate of the present value of all the East German land that will end up in private hands is DM 420.9 billion.

---

1. Source: Statistisches Bundesamt, *Statistisches Jahrbuch 1990 für die Bundesrepublik Deutschland* (Wiesbaden, 1990), tables 8.8 and 8.13.

Appendix C

Profit Maximization and the Putty-Clay Hypothesis

This appendix explains the adjustment problems of an East German firm faced with the West German factor-price and goods-price ratios after the opening of the borders.

The discussion of the factor-price problem is based on figure C.1, which compares the minimum-cost factor combination at the old and new prices.

In the figure, the case where there are two factors of production, X and Y, is examined. Under autarchy, the firm's minimum-cost combination of the factors is at point A, assuming that the price of Y in terms of X is relatively high. At this point the firm's isoquant (which represents the technologically feasible factor combinations that would produce a given level of output) is tangent to the lowest possible isocost line of a group of parallel isocosts (shown by the broken lines), and the marginal rate of factor substitution is equal to the factor-price ratio. After the opening of the border there is a new factor-price ratio, shown by the flatter isocost lines. With this new ratio it is optimal to substitute X for Y, which has become relatively less expensive, and thus to use the minimum-cost factor combination represented at point B. This, however, cannot be done unless there is a fundamental reorganization of the production process and replacement investment is undertaken. If, because of the adjustment problems, the factor combination at point A continues to be used, additional costs will be incurred, the amount of these being given by the distance between the two flatter parallel lines passing through A and B. Compared to the Western firm, which has the same know-how and is already producing with the techniques of point B, the Eastern firm is under a competitive disadvantage even if it operated in a perfectly efficient manner under the old factor-price ratio. It has to bear extra costs which threaten its survival.

If the West German firm were forced to produce with the East German factor-price ratio without being able to reorganize its production, it would be on the broken line passing through B and its costs would be higher than

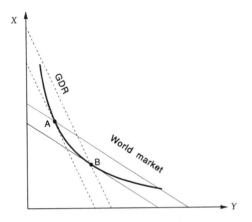

Figure C.1
New factor prices. The isocost lines show the different combinations of the factors of production X and Y whose total cost would be the same. Higher isocosts represent higher total costs. Mathematically, the isocosts are given by $K = P_X \cdot X + P_Y \cdot Y =$ constant, or, in terms of X, by $X = (K/P_X) - (P_Y/P_X)Y$, where K is the production cost and P_X and P_Y are the factor prices. The convex curve is one of the firm's isoquants. It represents the known and technologically possible production processes that are efficient for the different price ratios and produce the same level of output. A point on the isoquant represents a fully determined production process. Before the process is in place, the point at which to produce can be freely chosen; afterwards, a change is possible only when high refitting and reorganization costs are undertaken. The cost-minimizing production decision is shown by the point where the isoquant is tangent to the lowest possible isocost line. With GDR prices, this is point A; with world market prices, it is point B.

those represented by the broken line passing through point A (which shows the factor combination used by the Eastern firm). In this case, it is the Western firm that would be faced with bankruptcy unless it could restructure.

While the figure shows the nature of the pressure to adjust that the East German firm is under, it does exaggerate the magnitude of this pressure in that it does not take into account the fact that factor immobility between the regions can keep factor prices from adjusting to Western levels immediately. This applies to labor because, even with large wage differentials, only a small part of the East German work force will move to the West, and thus the natural adjustment pressure is limited in the case of wages. (This is a major aspect of the real transformation problem. If labor were completely mobile, wages would adjust immediately, but then it would also be efficient to completely depopulate East Germany until the new economic structures were in place.) Some capital is, of course, also immobile; old plant and equipment cannot be moved elsewhere. Even if its return fell to zero, there would be no danger of its moving. To the extent that the factors of production do not migrate across regions, the tendency of equalizing the factor prices is mitigated, and the survival chances of the East German industry are higher.

This, of course, does not mean that the problem disappears. Not all factors are immobile, and some prices do adjust quickly to world price levels. This is the case particularly with intermediate factor inputs, such as energy, raw materials, and semi-finished goods, that can now be bought on world markets. East German firms have to accept the world market prices. They cannot react by adjusting their factor demands, because the quantities needed are fixed by the production processes previously chosen. And intermediate factor inputs make up a considerable part of the costs of production of the typical East German industrial firm.

The problem of the new goods prices is illustrated by figure C.2, where a combine that produces two goods X' and Y' with given factor endowments is considered. The concave transformation curve shows the feasible output patterns with the given endowments. The combine can produce more of one good without increasing total costs if it produces less of the other. It does so by transferring some factors of production to the good whose output increases. The profit-maximizing combination is at point A', because here the transformation curve is tangent to the highest isorevenue

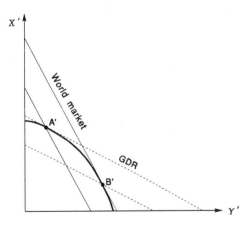

Figure C.2
New goods prices. The combine's isorevenue lines show alternative output combinations of the goods that would produce the same amount of revenue. Higher isorevenue lines represent higher levels of revenue. Mathematically, the isorevenue lines are given by $R = P_X' \cdot X' + P_Y' Y' = \text{constant}$, or by $X' = (R/P_X') - (P_Y'/P_X') Y'$ (with R representing the revenue, and P_X' and P_Y' the prices of X' and Y'). The concave curve is the combine's transformation curve. It shows the technologically possible combinations of goods X' and Y' that the combine can produce with given quantities of the factors and thus with given production costs.

line. An isorevenue line shows alternative output combinations that would bring about the same amount of revenue if they could be realized. The slope of the isorevenue lines measures the goods-price ratio. The lower the price of good Y' relative to that of good X', the flatter the isorevenue curves: a large amount of Y' is needed to compensate for the loss of revenue from producing less of X'. In the figure it is assumed that under the GDR conditions good Y' had a rather low price, and that the price ratio was that shown by the broken isorevenue lines. It was efficient for the combine to produce a small amount of good Y' and a large amount of good X'—that is, to choose a point like A'.

If the world market price ratio is represented by the steeper isorevenue lines, the price of Y' has risen relative to that of X' and the profit-maximizing combination of goods is at B' instead of at A'. It therefore becomes efficient to produce more of Y' and less of X'.

To reach B', a fundamental reorganization of production is, again, necessary. If this adjustment does not take place, there is a loss in revenue shown by the distance between the two steeper isorevenue lines through A' and B'. If the combine is competing with a Western firm already producing at point B', the former will have a revenue disadvantage which will endanger its survival. The situation would be no different for a Western firm faced with the Eastern price ratio if it were not able to make the necessary adjustments. Its revenue disadvantage would be measured by the distance between the two broken isorevenue lines that pass through A' and B'.

The problem illustrated in figure C.2 can be interpreted from the viewpoint of the East German economy as a whole rather than from that of a single combine. The economy uses the available quantities of the factors labor and capital to produce the combination of goods X' and Y' that maximizes its national product. With the price ratio associated with Comecon trade, it may have been optimal to produce at point A' (that is, a large amount of X' and a small amount of Y') and then sell X' and buy Y' to provide the population with the bundle of goods it wanted. With the new world market prices, this strategy is no longer optimal. Because the price of Y' rises relative to the price of X', the combination of goods that maximizes the national product is no longer given by A'; it is now given by B'. More Y' and less X' are produced than with Comecon prices, and it is likely that the foreign trade pattern is reversed. If the structural adjustment necessary with the new prices cannot be made immediately, a smaller amount of national product is produced than would have been possible under ideal conditions with the same factor quantities and the same technological knowledge as represented by the shape of the transformation curve.

Bibliography

Articles and Books

Abelshauser, W. 1983. *Wirtschaftsgeschichte der Bundesrepublik Deutschland (1945–1989)*. Frankfurt/Main: Suhrkamp.

Adler, U., R.-U. Sprenger, and J. Wackerbauer. 1991. "Umweltschutz in den neuen Bundesländern—Anpassungserfordernisse, Investitionsbedarf, Förderungsmöglichkeiten." *Ifo-Schnelldienst*, no. 11, Munich.

Akerlof, G. A., A. K. Rose, J. L. Yellen, and H. Hessenius. 1991. "East Germany in from the Cold: The Economic Aftermath of Currency Union." *Brookings Papers on Economic Activity* 1991, pp. 1–87.

Albach, H. 1991. "Upswing with Brakes." Manuscript of speech delivered to the Metra Board of Directors, Wissenschaftliche Hochschule für Unternehmensführung, Koblenz.

Arbeitgeberverband Gesamtmetall. 1991. *Geschäftsbericht 1989–1991*. Cologne.

Arbeitsgemeinschaft deutscher wirtschaftswissenschaftlicher Forschungsinstitute. 1990. "Die Lage der Weltwirtschaft und der deutschen Wirtschaft im Herbst 1990." *DIW Wochenbericht*, no. 43–44, October 25, Berlin.

Arbeitsgemeinschaft deutscher wirtschaftswissenschaftlicher Forschungsinstitute. 1991. *Die Lage der Weltwirtschaft und der deutschen Wirtschaft im Herbst 1991*. Berlin, Hamburg, Munich, Kiel, and Essen.

Arrow, K. J., M. B. Chenery, B. S. Minhas, and R. Solow. 1961. "Capital-Labor Substitution and Economic Efficiency." *Review of Economics and Statistics* 43, pp. 225–250.

Atkinson, A. B. 1972. "Capital Growth Sharing Schemes and the Behaviour of the Firm." *Economica* 39, pp. 237–249.

Balassa, B. 1964. "The Purchasing-Power Doctrine: A Reappraisal." *Journal of Political Economy* 72, pp. 584–596.

Baltensperger, E., and T. M. Devinney. 1985. "Credit Rationing Theory: A Survey and Synthesis." *Zeitschrift für die gesamte Staatswissenschaft* 141, pp. 475–502.

Barro, R. J. 1974. "Are Government Bonds Net Wealth?" *Journal of Political Economy* 82, pp. 1095–1117.

Begg, D. 1991. "Economic Reform in Czechoslovakia: Should We Believe in Santa Klaus?" *Economic Policy* 6, pp. 243–286.

Begg, D., and R. Portes. 1992. "Eastern Germany since Unification: Wage Subsidies Remain a Better Way." Centre for Economic Policy Research Discussion Paper 730, London.

Berndt, E. R., and D. O. Wood. 1981. "The Speculation and Measurement of Technical Change in U.S. Manufacturing." MIT Energy Laboratory Working Paper 46.

Bernholz, P. 1992. "Property, Markets, and Money: Guidelines for Reform." *Cato Journal* 11, pp. 409–424.

Berthold, N. 1992. "Arbeitslosigkeit in Deutschland—Auf der Suche nach einer effizienten Arbeitsmarktpolitik." Wirtschaftswissenschaftliche Beiträge des Volkswirtschaftlichen Instituts, Universität Würzburg.

Biedenkopf, K. 1992. "Zwischen Wiedervereinigung, europäischem Binnenmarkt und der Zusammenarbeit mit Osteuropa. Was kann Deutschland leisten?" Manuscript of speech delivered to Forum für Deutschland, Palasthotel Berlin, March 18.

Blanchard, O., R. Dornbusch, P. Krugman, R. Layard, and L. Summers. 1991. *Reform in Eastern Europe.* MIT Press.

Bofinger, P. 1991. "Geld- und Kreditpolitik nach Bildung der deutschen Währungsunion." Presented at meeting of Wirtschaftspolitischer Ausschuss des Vereins für Socialpolitik, March 12–14, Marburg.

Bolton, P., and G. Roland. 1992. "Privatization in Central and Eastern Europe." *Economic Policy* 15, pp. 274–309.

Bös, D. 1991a. *Privatization: A Theoretical Treatment.* Oxford: Clarendon.

Bös, D. 1991b. "Privatization and the Transition from Planned to Market Economies: Some Thoughts About Germany 1991." *Annals of Public and Cooperative Economics* 62, pp. 183–194.

Bröcker, J. 1992. "Faktorbewegungen im vereinten Deutschland—Ein Simulationsmodell mit überlappenden Generationen." Inaugural lecture, University of Kiel Department of Economics, February 15.

Bundesministerium für innerdeutsche Beziehungen. 1987. *Materialen zum Bericht zur Lage der Nation im geteilten Deutschland.* Bonner Universitäts-Buchdruckerei.

Bundesministerium für Wirtschaft. 1991. *Jahreswirtschaftsbericht 1991.* Bonn.

Bundeszentrale für politische Bildung. 1989. "Aussiedler." *Informationen zur politischen Bildung* 222. Munich: Franzis.

Burda, M. 1990. "The Consequences of German Economic and Monetary Union." Centre for Economic Policy Research Discussion Paper 449, London.

Burda, M., and M. Funke. 1991. "German Trade Unions After Unification—Third

Degree Wage Discriminating Monopolists?" Unpublished paper, INSEAD, Fontainebleau, and Freie Universität, Berlin.

Burda, M., and S. Gerlach. 1990. "Exchange Rate Dynamics and Currency Unification: The Ostmark-DM Rate." INSEAD Working Paper 90/78/EP, Fontainebleau.

Burda, M., and C. Wyplosz. 1991. "German Unification and European Integration." Paper presented to workshop, Centre for Economic Policy Research, Bonn, November 23.

Claassen, E.-M. 1990. "Radical Transformation: The Case of the German Monetary Union." Prepared for Second International Conference on Stabilization and Exchange Rate Policies of Less Developed Markets and Socialist Economies, May 10–12, Freie Universität and Landeszentralbank, Berlin.

Clasen, L. 1991. "Erstmals gesamtdeutsch." *Bundesarbeitsblatt* No. 3/1991, Bundesministerium für Arbeit und Sozialordnung. Stuttgart: Kohlhammer.

Coase, R. 1960. "The Problem of Social Cost." *Journal of Law and Economics* 3, pp. 1–44.

Collier, J. L. J. 1986. "Effective Purchasing Power in a Quantity Constrained Economy: An Estimate for the German Democratic Republic." *Review of Economics and Statistics* 68, pp. 24–32.

Cornelsen, D. 1991. "Privatization—The Example of East Germany." Paper presented at International Economic Outlook Conference on Eastern Europe and the Soviet Union, April 22–26, Berlin.

Demougin, D., and H.-W. Sinn. 1992. "Risk-Taking, Privatization and the Communist Firm." CES Working Paper 16, University of Munich.

Deregulierungskommission. 1991. *Marktöffnung und Wettbewerb*, second report.

Deutsche Bank. 1990. *Die neuen Bundesländer*. Frankfurt/Main.

Dietl, R., and S. Rammert. 1990. "DM-Eröffnungsbilanzen in der DDR." *Börsenzeitung*, Frankfurt/Main, August 10.

Donges, J. B. 1991. "Arbeitsmarkt und Lohnpolitik in Ostdeutschland." Paper presented at meeting of Arbeitsgemeinschaft wirtschaftswissenschaftlicher Forschungsinstitute, May 14–15, Bonn.

Dornbusch, R. 1990. "Comment on Sinn (1990)." In P. J. J. Welfens, ed., *Economic Aspects of German Unification*, proceedings of a conference held at the American Institute for Contemporary German Studies, Johns Hopkins University, November 13, 1990. Heidelberg: Springer, 1992.

Edwards, J. S. S., and K. Fischer. 1992. *Banks, Finance and Investment in Germany*.

Engels, W. 1991. "Produktionsgesellschaften statt Beschäftigungsgesellschaften." Unpublished paper, University of Frankfurt.

Erber, G., and R. Pirschner. 1992. "Wir brauchen einen Sozialpakt. Welchen Sinn machen Modellrechnungen zur Anpassung der Arbeitsproduktivität in Ost- und Westdeutschland?" DIW Diskussionspapier 45, Berlin.

Filip-Köhn, R., and U. Ludwig. 1990. "Dimensionen eines Ausgleichs des Wirtschaftsgefälles zur DDR." DIW Diskussionspapier 3, Berlin.

Fleischer, H., and H. Proebsting. 1989. "Aussiedler und Übersiedler—Zahlenmäßige Entwicklung und Struktur." *Wirtschaft und Statistik*, no. 9, pp. 582–589 and 608*.

Folkers, C. 1973–74. "Die Wirkungen einer verstärkten Beteiligung der Arbeitnehmer am Vermögenszuwachs auf die Verteilung des Vermögensbestandes." *Finanzarchiv* N.F. 32, pp. 194–217.

Franz, W. 1992. "Im Jahr danach—Bestandsaufnahme und Analyse der Arbeitsmarktentwicklung im vereinigten Deutschland." In B. Gahlen, H. Hesse, and J. Ramser, eds., *Von der Plan- zur Marktwirtschaft. Eine Zwischenbilanz.* Tübingen: J.C.B. Mohr (Paul Siebeck).

Friedrich-Ebert-Stiftung. 1990. "Grundlinien künftiger Tarifpolitik in den neuen Bundesländern." *Wirtschaftspolitische Diskurse*, no. 8, Bonn.

Gandenberger, O. 1972. "Zur Rationalität der öffentlichen Kreditnahme." *Finanzarchiv* N.F. 30, pp. 369–391.

Genser, B. 1990. "Tax Policy Options for a United Germany." IMF Working Paper 89, Washington.

Grabitz, E. 1983. *Kommentar zum EWG Vertrag.* Munich: Beck.

Gros, D. 1991. "The Effects of Unification on Germany's External Accounts." Unpublished paper, CEPS, Brussels.

Haendcke-Hoppe, M. 1990. "Aussenhandel." *Deutschland Archiv* 23, pp. 651–652.

Hampe, P. 1989. *Währungsreform und Soziale Marktwirtschaft.* Munich: Günter Olzog Verlag.

Hare, P., and T. Révész. 1992. "Hungary's Transition to a Market Economy. The Case against a 'Big-Bang'." *Economic Policy* 14, pp. 227–264.

Hegel, G. W. F. 1821. *Grundlinien der Philosophie des Rechts.* Berlin: Nicolaischer Buchhandel.

Heilemann, U. 1991. "Christmas in July? The Economics of German Unification Reconsidered." RWI-Papiere no. 27, RWI Essen.

Heldrich, A., and H. Eidenmüller. 1991. "Die rechtlichen Auswirkungen der Wiedervereinigung Deutschlands aus der Sicht von Drittstaaten." *Juristische Blätter* 113, pp. 273–283.

Hoffmann, L. 1990. "Integrating the East German States into the German Economy: Opportunities, Burdens and Options." In P. J. J. Welfens, ed., *Economic Aspects of German Unification*, proceedings of a conference held at the American Institute for Contemporary German Studies, Johns Hopkins University, November 13, 1990. Heidelberg: Springer, 1992.

Hoffmann, W. G., et al. 1965. *Das Wachstum der Deutschen Wirtschaft seit der Mitte des 19. Jahrhunderts.* Berlin: Springer.

International Monetary Fund. 1990. "Federal Republic of Germany—Economic Developments and Issues." Unpublished paper.

Jens, U., ed. 1991. *Der Umbau. Von der Kommandowirtschaft zur öko-sozialen Marktwirtschaft.* Baden-Baden: Nomos-Verlagsgesellschaft.

Kantzenbach, E. 1990. "Ökonomische Probleme der deutschen Vereinigung— Anmerkungen zur jüngsten Wirtschaftsgeschichte." *Hamburger Jahrbuch für Wirtschafts- und Gesellschaftspolitik 35*, pp. 307–326.

Kaser, M. C., and E. A. Radice, eds. 1985. *The Economic History of Eastern Europe 1919–1975*, vol. I, Economic Structure and Performance between the Two Wars. Oxford: Clarendon.

Kloten, N. 1990. "Vereinigtes deutsch-deutsches Währungsgebiet: Chancen und Risiken." Unpublished paper, Landeszentralbank von Baden-Württemberg.

Kloten, N. 1991. "Eingliederung des östlichen Deutschland und Europäische Währungsunion: Zwei Paar Stiefel." *Stuttgarter Zeitung*, March 30 and April 5.

Krelle, W., J. Schunck, and J. Siebke. 1968. *Überbetriebliche Ertragsbeteiligung der Arbeitnehmer mit einer Untersuchung über die Vermögensstruktur der Bundesrepublik Deutschland*, vols. I and II. Tübingen: J. C. B. Mohr (Paul Siebeck).

Kroeschell, K. 1991. "Die ländliche Eigentumsordnung in der DDR." In M. Löwisch, C. Schmidt-Leithoff, and B. Schmiedel, eds., *Beiträge zum Handels- und Wirtschaftsrecht*. Munich: Beck.

Kronberger Kreis. 1991. *Wirtschaftspolitik für das geeinte Deutschland*. Frankfurter Institut für wirtschaftspolitische Forschung, Frankfurt/Main.

Kruse, J. von, ed. 1988. *Weissbuch über die "Demokratische Bodenreform" in der Sowjetischen Besatzungszone Deutschlands*. Munich: Vögel.

Läufer, N. K. A. 1990. "Vier Papiere zur Deutschen Währungsunion." Sonderforschungsbereich 178 Diskussionsbeiträge, no. 105, Universität Konstanz.

Lehmann-Grube, H. 1991. "Zeitbombe im Grundbuch." *Die Zeit*, no. 50, December 6, pp. 36–37.

Lipschitz, L., and D. McDonald, eds. 1990. *German Unification: Economic Issues*. Occasional Paper 75, International Monetary Fund, Washington.

Leipold, H., ed. 1992. *Privatisierungskonzepte im Systemwandel*. Marburg: Forschungsstelle zum Vergleich wirtschaftlicher Lenkungssysteme.

Luders, R. J. 1990. "Privatization in Chile—Lessons from a Massive Divestiture Program in a Developing Country." Unpublished paper, UCLA and Catholic University of Chile.

Luxemburg, R. 1921. *Die Akkumulation des Kapitals oder was die Epigonen aus der Marxschen Theorie gemacht haben. Eine Antikritik*. Leipzig: Vereinigung internationaler Verlagsanstalten.

Luxemburg, R. 1906. *Massenstreik, Partei und Gewerkschaften*, Ausgewählte Reden und Schriften, Band 1. Hamburg: Dubber. Reprinted by Dietz, Berlin, 1951.

Marx, K. 1859. *Zur Kritik der Politischen Oekonomie*. Quoted from: K. Marx und F. Engels Werke, vol. 13 (Berlin: Dietz, 1964).

Marx, K. 1873. *Das Kapital. Kritik der politischen Ökonomie*, vol. 1, book 1: Der Produktionsprozess des Kapitals. Quoted from K. Marx and F. Engels Werke, vol. 23 (Berlin: Dietz, 1962).

Melitz, J. 1991. "German Reunification and Exchange Rate Policy in the EMS." Discussion Paper 520, Centre for Economic Policy Research, London.

Michaelis, J., and A. Spermann. 1991. "Investivlohn. Sozialpakt für den Aufschwung, Gewinnbeteiligung—Lösungen für Ostdeutschland?" *Wirtschaftsdienst* 12/71, pp. 614–622.

Mieth, W. No date. "Die zweigeteilte Konjunktur im vereinigten Deutschland und das ostdeutsche Lohnniveau." Manuscript, Department of Economics, University of Regensburg.

Möllemann, J. 1991. "Über neue Finanzierungswege sollte nachgedacht werden." *Wirtschaftsdienst* 10/71, pp. 491–494.

Möller, H. 1988. "Die westdeutsche Währungsreform von 1948." *WiSt*, no. 6, pp. 277–284.

Möller, H. 1989. "Die Währungsreform von 1948 und die Wiederherstellung marktwirtschaftlicher Verhältnisse." In P. Hampe, ed., *Währungsreform und Soziale Marktwirtschaft*. Munich: Günter Olzog Verlag.

Möller, H. 1990. "Ordnungspolitische Aspekte der westdeutschen Währungs- und Wirtschaftsreform von 1948 mit vergleichenden Hinweisen auf die Währungsstabilisierung von 1923 in der Weimarer Republik und auf die Einführung der DM in der DDR am 1. Juli 1990." Unpublished paper, University of Munich.

Möschel, W. 1991. "Treuhandanstalt und Neuordnung der früheren DDR-Wirtschaft." *Zeitschrift für Unternehmens- und Gesellschaftsrecht* 20, pp. 175–188.

Mückl, W. J. 1972. *Langfristige Probleme der Lohnpolitik, des Investivlohnes und der Kapitalbeteiligung in Arbeitnehmerhand*. Dissertation, University of Tübingen.

Nachtkamp, H., and H.-W. Sinn. 1981. "Die konjunkturellen Wirkungen der Schuldenstrukturpolitik." *Finanzarchiv* 39, pp. 279–305.

Nattland, K.-H. 1972. *Der Aussenhandel in der Wirtschaftsreform der DDR*. Berlin: Duncker & Humblot.

Neumann, M. J. M. 1991. "German Unification: Economic Problems and Consequences." Presented at Carnegie-Rochester conference on Public Policy, April 19–20.

Oberhauser, A. 1978. "Investivlohn und investive Gewinnbeteiligung in verteilungs- und stabilitätspolitischer Sicht." *WiSt*, no. 2, pp. 60–65.

Oberhauser, A. 1982. "Förderung unternehmensinterner Kapitalbildung. Ein Modell zur Mitarbeiterbeteiligung." In W. Ehrlicher and D. B. Simmert, eds., *Geld- und*

Währungspolitik in der Bundesrepublik Deutschland, Beihefte zu *Kredit und Kapital,* no. 7, pp. 337–447.

Oberhauser, A. 1992. "Probleme des Aufbaus der Infrastruktur in der Bundesrepublik Deutschland." Diskussionsbeiträge des Instituts für Finanzwissenschaft der Universität Freiburg no. 16.

Palinkas, P. 1990. "Energy and Environment in the Former GDR: Problems and Prospects (A Short Comment)." In P. J. J. Welfens, ed., *Economic Aspects of German Unification,* proceedings of a conference held at the American Institute for Contemporary German Studies, Johns Hopkins University, November 13, 1990. Heidelberg: Springer, 1992.

Panther, S. 1991. "Die ehemalige DDR, Osteuropa und die 'Neue Wachstumstheorie'." In J. Backhaus, ed., *Systemwandel und Reform in östlichen Wirtschaften.* Marburg: Metropolis.

Penig, L. 1991. "Die Klärung offener Vermögensfragen unter besonderer Berücksichtigung des Grundstückerwerbs zur Durchführung gewerblicher Investitionen in den neuen Bundesländern." Presented at Arbeitskreis Wirtschaft und Recht, Munich, January 25 and 26.

Preusse, H. G. 1991. "Der Beitrag des ausländischen Risikokapitals zur wirtschaftlichen Transformation in den neuen Bundesländern." *Zeitschrift für Wirt-* 40, pp. 219–237.

Ricardo, D. 1817. "On the Principles of Political Economy and Taxation." In P. Sraffa, ed., *The Works and Correspondence of David Ricardo.* Cambridge University Press, 1951.

Richter, R. 1990. "Die Währungsunion mit der DDR—Wird sie den Übersiedlerstrom nachhaltig stoppen?" Unpublished paper, Universität des Saarlandes, Saarbrücken.

Ritschl, A. 1989. "Was ist ökonomische Umgestaltung des Sozialismus? Kann es für die DDR einen Dritten Weg geben?" Manuscript, Department of Economics, University of Munich.

Roth, W. 1991. "Eine private Finanzierung entlastet die öffentlichen Haushalte nur scheinbar." *Wirtschaftsdienst* 10/91, pp. 494–497.

Sachverständigenrat zur Begutachtung der gesamtwirtschaftlichen Entwicklung. 1975. *Vor dem Aufschwung,* Jahresgutachten 1975/76. Stuttgart: Kohlhammer.

Sachverständigenrat zur Begutachtung der gesamtwirtschaftlichen Entwicklung. 1990. *Auf dem Wege zur wirtschaftlichen Einheit Deutschlands,* Jahresgutachten 1990/91. Stuttgart: Metzler-Poeschel.

Sachverständigenrat zur Begutachtung der gesamtwirtschaftlichen Entwicklung. 1991a. *Marktwirtschaftlichen Kurs halten—Zur Wirtschaftspolitik für die neuen Bundesländer,* Sondergutachten, April 13.

Sachverständigenrat zur Begutachtung der gesamtwirtschaftlichen Entwicklung. 1991b. *Die wirtschaftliche Integration in Deutschland: Perspektiven—Wege—Risiken,* Jahresgutachten 1991/92. Stuttgart: Metzler-Poeschel.

Salowsky, H. 1991. "Industrielle Arbeitskosten im internationalen Vergleich 1970–1990." In *IW-Trends*, Institut der Deutschen Wirtschaft, Cologne.

Sauermann, H., and R. Richter, eds. 1977. *Profit-Sharing*. Special issue, *Zeitschrift für die gesamte Staatswissenschaft*.

Say, J.-B. 1803. *Traité d'Economie Politique*. Paris: Deterville.

Schlesinger, H. 1990. "Die Wirtschaft der Bundesrepublik Deutschland: Vor wichtigen Weichenstellungen." *Deutsche Bundesbank—Auszüge aus Presseartikeln*, no. 29, April 6, Frankfurt/Main.

Schmähl, W. 1991. "Alterssicherung in der DDR und ihre Umgestaltung im Zuge des deutschen Einigungsprozesses." In Schriften des Vereins für Socialpolitik, new series, vol. 208/I: *Sozialpolitik im vereinten Deutschland I*. Berlin: Duncker & Humblot.

Schmieding, H. 1990. "Währungsunion und Wettbewerbsfähigkeit der DDR-Industrie." Kieler Arbeitspapiere, no. 413, Institut für Weltwirtschaft, Kiel.

Schöb, R. 1992. "Kreditrationierung und Privatisierung des Treuhandvermögens." Manuscript, Department of Economics, University of Munich.

Schrettl, W. 1991. "Transition with Insurance: German Unification Reconsidered." Osteuropa-Institut Working Paper 149, Munich.

Schulte-Döinghaus, U., and R. Stimpel. 1990. "Auf wackligem Grund." *Wirtschaftswoche*, no. 30, pp. 32–43.

Siebert, H. 1990. "The Economic Integration of Germany." Kieler Diskussionsbeiträge, no. 160, Institut für Weltwirtschaft, Kiel.

Siebert, H. 1991a. "The Transformation of Eastern Europe." Kieler Diskussionsbeiträge, no. 163, Institut für Weltwirtschaft, Kiel.

Siebert, H. 1991b. "German Unification." *Economic Policy*, October, pp. 289–340.

Sinn, G., and H.-W. Sinn. 1991. "Sozialpakt für den Aufschwung. Kommentar zum Beitrag von Michaelis und Spermann." *Wirtschaftsdienst* 12/71, pp. 622–623.

Sinn, H.-W. 1975. "Das Marxsche Gesetz des tendenziellen Falls der Profitrate." *Zeitschrift für die gesamte Staatswissenschaft* 131, pp. 646–696.

Sinn, H.-W. 1984. "Die Bedeutung des Accelerated Cost Recovery Systems für den internationalen Kapitalverkehr." *Kyklos* 37, pp. 542–576.

Sinn, H.-W. 1986. "Risiko als Produktionsfaktor." *Jahrbücher für Nationalökonomie und Statistik* 201, pp. 557–571.

Sinn, H.-W. 1987. *Capital Income Taxation and Resource Allocation*. New York: North-Holland.

Sinn, H.-W. 1988. "U.S. Tax Reform 1981 and 1986: Impact on International Capital Markets and Capital Flows." *National Tax Journal* 16, pp. 327–342.

Sinn, H.-W. 1989. "Die amerikanische Wirtschaftspolitik und die Weltschuldenkrise." In G. Bombach, B. Gahlen, and A. E. Ott, eds., *Die nationale und internationale Schuldenproblematik*. Tübingen: J. C. B. Mohr (Paul Siebeck).

Sinn, H.-W. 1990. "Macroeconomic Aspects of German Unification." In P. J. J. Welfens, ed., *Economic Aspects of German Unification*, proceedings of a conference held at the American Institute for Contemporary German Studies, Johns Hopkins University, November 13, 1990. Heidelberg: Springer, 1992.

Sinn, H.-W. 1991a. "Verteilen statt verkaufen." *Wirtschaftswoche*, no. 5, pp. 78–81.

Sinn, H.-W. 1991b. "Privatization in East Germany." Forthcoming in P. Pestieau, ed., *Public Finance in a Changing Environment*, proceedings of the 47th meeting of the Institute of Public Finance, planned to be held August 26–29, 1991, in Leningrad, but cancelled because of the coup d'etat.

Sinn, H.-W. 1991c. "Privatisierung am falschen Ende." *Wirtschaftsdienst* 10/91, pp. 497–499.

Smyser, W. R. 1990. "United Germany: A New Economic Miracle?" *Washington Quarterly* 13, pp. 159–176.

Streibel, G. 1990. "Environmental Protection: Problems and Prospects in East and West Germany." In P. J. J. Welfens, ed., *Economic Aspects of German Unification*, proceedings of a conference held at the American Institute for Contemporary German Studies, Johns Hopkins University, November 13, 1990. Heidelberg: Springer, 1992.

Sweezy, P. M. 1959. *Theorie der kapitalistischen Entwicklung*. Cologne: Bund.

Tiebout, C. M. 1956. "A Pure Theory of Local Expenditures." *Journal of Political Economy* 64, pp. 416–424.

Tietzel, M., M. Weber, and O. F. Bode. 1991. *Die Logik der sanften Revolution—Eine ökonomische Analyse*. Tübingen: J.C.B. Mohr (Paul Siebeck).

Tocqueville, A. de. 1856. *L'Ancien Régime et la Révolution*. Oeuvres Complètes, tome II. Gallimard, 1952.

Tomann, H. 1975. *Risikoübertragung als Mittel der Vermögenspolitik*. Cologne and Berlin: Carl Heymanns.

Treuhand. 1991a. *Erfolgreich im Dienst aller Bürger—Neun Monate Arbeit der Treuhandanstalt*. Press release, April 12, Berlin.

Treuhand. 1991b. *Privatisierung*. Report, October 31, Berlin.

Tugan-Baranowsky, M. 1905. *Theoretische Grundlagen des Marxismus*. Leipzig: Duncker & Humblot.

Van Suntum, U. 1990. "Kaufkrafteffekte der Währungsunion in der DDR." *Wirtschaftsdienst* 8, pp. 398–401.

Venohr, W. 1989. *Die roten Preussen—Vom wundersamen Aufstieg der DDR in Deutschland*. Erlangen: Straube.

Vogel. 1991. "Lösungsansätze zur Beseitigung von vermögensrechtlichen Hemmnissen." Manuscript of lecture given at the conference Eigentumsfragen als Investitionshemmnis, Evangelische Akademie, Tutzing.

Wagner, H. M. 1991. "Einige Theorien des Systemwandels im Vergleich—und ihre Anwendbarkeit für die Erklärung des gegenwärtigen Reformprozesses in Osteuropa." In J. Backhaus, ed., *Systemwandel und Reform in östlichen Wirtschaften.* Marburg: Metropolis.

Walters, A. 1990. "How Fast Can Market Economies be Introduced?" Presented at European Business Forum, November 26 and 27, Rome.

Watrin, C. 1990. "Der schwierige Weg von der sozialistischen Planwirtschaft zur marktwirtschaftlichen Ordnung." In J. M. Graf von der Schulenburg and H.-W. Sinn, eds., *Theorie der Wirtschaftspolitik.* Tübingen: J.C.B. Mohr (Paul Siebeck).

Weber, H. 1982. *DDR—Grundriss der Geschichte 1945–1981,* third edition. Hannover: Fackelträger.

Weiss, R. 1991. "Innovations- und Integrationsfaktor berufliche Bildung." In *Bildungssituation und Bildungsaufgaben in den neuen Bundesländern,* Berichte zur Bildungspolitik 1991/92, Institut der deutschen Wirtschaft, Cologne.

Weitzman, M. L. 1984. *The Share Economy.* Harvard University Press.

Welfens, P. J. J. 1990. "Economic Reforms in Eastern Europe: Options and Opportunities." In P. J. J. Welfens, ed., *Economic Aspects of German Unification,* proceedings of a conference held at the American Institute for Contemporary German Studies, Johns Hopkins University, November 13, 1990. Heidelberg: Springer, 1992.

Wenzel, H.-D. 1991. "Wirtschaftsentwicklung und Staatshaushalt ein Jahr nach der deutschen Einheit." Volkswirtschaftliche Diskussionsbeiträge, no. 49, University of Bamberg.

Wissenschaftlicher Beirat beim Bundesministerium für Wirtschaft. 1989. "Wirtschaftspolitische Herausforderungen der Bundesrepublik Deutschland im Verhältnis zur DDR." BMWi Studienreihe 67, Bundesministerium für Wirtschaft, Bonn.

Wissenschaftlicher Beirat beim Bundesministerium für Wirtschaft. 1990. "Schaffung eines gemeinsamen Wirtschafts- und Währungsgebietes in Deutschland." In *Gutachten vom Juni 1987 bis März 1990.* Göttingen: Otto Schwartz.

Wissenschaftlicher Beirat beim Bundesministerium für Wirtschaft. 1991a. "Probleme der Privatisierung in den neuen Bundesländern." BMWi Studienreihe 73, Bundesministerium für Wirtschaft, Bonn.

Wissenschaftlicher Beirat beim Bundesministerium für Wirtschaft. 1991b. "Lohn- und Arbeitsmarktprobleme in den neuen Bundesländern." BMWi Studienreihe 75, Bundesministerium für Wirtschaft, Bonn.

Wyplosz, C. 1991. "On the Real Exchange Rate Effects of German Unification." *Weltwirtschaftliches Archiv* 127, pp. 1–17.

Statistical Sources

(Detailed refererences in text)

Bundesanstalt für Arbeit: *Amtliche Nachrichten der Bundesanstalt für Arbeit (ANBA)*, Nuremberg.

Bundesausgleichsamt: *Statistischer Bericht*, Bad Homburg von der Höhe.

Bundesministerium der Finanzen: *Finanzbericht 1991*, Bonn.

Bundesministerium der Finanzen: *Finanznachrichten*, Bonn.

Bundesministerium der Finanzen: *Statistischer Monatsbericht*, Bonn.

Deutsche Bundesbank: *Monatsberichte der Deutschen Bundesbank*, Frankfurt/Main.

Deutsche Bundesbank: Statistische Beihefte zu den Monatsberichten der Deutschen Bundesbank, Reihe 3, *Zahlungsbilanzstatistik*, Frankfurt/Main.

Deutsches Institut für Wirtschaftsforschung: *DIW Wochenberichte*, Berlin.

Deutsches Institut für Wirtschaftsforschung (DIW): *DDR-Wirtschaft im Umbruch*. Manuscript, Berlin, 1990.

Deutsches Institut für Wirtschaftsforschung (DIW): *Volkswirtschaftliche Gesamtrechnung für Ostdeutschland*. Manuscript, Berlin, 1991.

Gemeinsames Statistisches Amt der Länder Brandenburg, Mecklenburg-Vorpommern, Sachsen, Sachsen-Anhalt, Thüringen: *Monatszahlen*, Berlin.

Handbook of World Stock and Commodity Exchanges 1991. Cambridge, Mass.: Basil Blackwell.

Infratest: *Arbeitsmarktmonitor für die neuen Bundesländer*, Munich.

HWWA-Institut für Wirtschaftsforschung: *Strukturbericht 1987*, Hamburg.

Ifo Institut: *Ifo-Schnelldienst*, Munich.

Ifo Institut: *Wirtschaftskonjunktur*, Monatsberichte des Ifo-Instituts, Munich.

Institut für angewandte Wirtschaftsforschung (IAW): *Die ostdeutsche Wirtschaft 1990/1991*, October 22, 1990.

Institut der Deutschen Wirtschaft: *IDW-Informationsdienst*, Cologne.

Institut der Deutschen Wirtschaft: *IW-Trends*, Cologne.

Institut für Arbeitsmarkt- und Berufsforschung: *Werkstattbericht*, Nuremberg.

Institut für Konjunkturforschung: *Konjunkturstatistisches Handbuch 1933*. Berlin: Hobbing.

OECD: *International Financial Statistics*, Paris.

OECD: *Main Economic Indicators*, Paris.

OECD: *Short-Term Economic Statistics Central and Eastern Europe*, Paris.

Principal Statistical Office in Warsaw (Glowny Urzad Statystyczny, Warszawa): *Biuletyn statystyczny.*

Staatsbank der DDR: *Jahresbericht,* East Berlin.

Statistisches Amt der DDR: *Statistisches Jahrbuch für die DDR,* East Berlin.

Statistisches Bundesamt: *Bevölkerung und Erwerbstätigkeit,* Fachserie 1, Wiesbaden.

Statistisches Bundesamt: DDR 1990, Zahlen und Fakten, Wiesbaden.

Statistisches Bundesamt: *Mikrozensuserhebung,* 1987, Wiesbaden.

Statistisches Bundesamt: *Statistisches Jahrbuch für das Ausland,* Wiesbaden.

Statistisches Bundesamt: *Statistisches Jahrbuch für die Bundesrepublik Deutschland,* Wiesbaden.

Statistisches Bundesamt: *Unternehmen und Arbeitsstätten,* Fachserie 2, Wiesbaden.

Statistisches Bundesamt: *Volkswirtschaftliche Gesamtrechnungen,* Fachserie 18, Wiesbaden.

Statistisches Bundesamt: *Wirtschaft und Statistik,* Wiesbaden.

Statistisches Bundesamt: *Zahlen, Fakten, Trends: Extra* , Wiesbaden.

U.S. Department of Commerce—Bureau of the Census 1975. *Historical Statistics of the United States, Colonial Times to 1970,* Part I, Bicentennial Edition, Washington.

Vienna Institute for Comparative Economic Studies 1990. *Comecon Data 1989.* London: Macmillan.

News Media

(Detailed references in text)

Bildzeitung

Bundesministerium der Finanzen, Finanznachrichten

Deutschlandfunk

Economist

Frankfurter Allgemeine Zeitung

Handelsblatt

News agency *ADN*

News agency *AP*

Neue Zürcher Zeitung

New York Times

Süddeutsche Zeitung

Washington Post

Die Zeit

Laws and Treaties

Germany Treaty: Vertrag über die Beziehungen zwischen der Bundesrepublik Deutschland und den Drei Mächten (Deutschland-Vertrag), May 26, 1952, Bundesgesetzblatt, Teil II, March 29, 1954, pp. 61–77.

Declarations of the Governments of U.S.A., U.K., and France: Erklärungen der Regierungen der Vereinigten Staaten von Amerika, des Vereinigten Königreichs und Frankreichs, October 3, 1954 (NATO Beitrittserklärung der Westmächte). In I. von Münch, ed., *Dokumente des geteilten Deutschland*, vol. 1, second edition, 1976. Stuttgart: Körner.

Germany Treaty (amended): Vertrag über die Beziehungen zwischen der Bundesrepublik Deutschland und den Drei Mächten (in der gemäss Liste I zu dem am 23. Oktober 1954 in Paris unterzeichneten Protokoll über die Beendigung des Besatzungsregimes in der Bundesrepublik Deutschland geänderten Fassung). *Bundesgesetzblatt*, part II, no. 8, March 31, 1955, pp. 305–320.

Treaty of Rome: Vertrag zur Gründung der Europäischen Wirtschaftsgemeinschaft (Römische Verträge), March 25, 1957, *Bundesgesetzblatt*, Teil II, no. 23, August 19, 1957, pp. 766–984.

Internal German Trade—Proceedings: Protokoll über den innerdeutschen Handel und die damit zusammenhängenden Fragen (Zusatzprotokoll zum innerdeutschen Handel), March 25, 1957, *Bundesgesetzblatt*, Teil II, no. 23, August 19, 1957, p. 984.

Job-Promotion Law: Arbeitsförderungsgesetz (AFG), June 25, 1969. *Bundesgesetzblatt*, part I, p. 582.

Ten-Point Plan: Zehn-Punkte-Plan, *Bulletin der Bundesregierung*, no. 134, pp. 1141 f., November 29, 1989.

Foreign Participation in GDR Firms—Ordinance: Verordnung über die Gründung und Tätigkeit von Unternehmen mit ausländischer Beteiligung in der Deutschen Demokratischen Republik, January 25, 1990. *Gesetzblatt der Deutschen Demokratischen Republik*, part I, no. 4, January 30, 1990, pp. 16–19.

Private Firms Law: Gesetz über die Gründung und Tätigkeit privater Unternehmen und über Unternehmensbeteiligungen, March 7, 1990. *Gesetzblatt der Deutschen Demokratischen Republik*, part I, no. 17, March 16, 1990, pp. 141–144.

Ordinance for the Conversion of Combines etc. into Companies: Verordnung zur Umwandlung von volkseigenen Kombinaten, Betrieben und Einrichtungen in Kapitalgesellschaften, March 1, 1990. *Gesetzblatt der Deutschen Demokratischen Republik*, part I, no. 14, March 8, 1990, pp. 107–108.

First Trusteeship Law: Beschluss zur Gründung der Anstalt zur treuhänderischen Verwaltung des Volkseigentums (Treuhandanstalt), March 1, 1990. *Gesetzblatt der Deutschen Demokratischen Republik*, part I, no. 14, March 8, 1990, p. 107.

Economic, Monetary and Social Union Agreement (first State Treaty): Vertrag über die Schaffung einer Währungs-, Wirtschafts- und Sozialunion zwischen der Bundesrepublik Deutschland und der Deutschen Demokratischen Republik, May 18, 1990. *Bundesgesetzblatt*, part II, no. 20, June 29, 1990, pp. 537–567.

Second Trusteeship Law: Gesetz zur Privatisierung und Reorganisation des volkseigenen Vermögens (Treuhandgesetz), June 17, 1990. *Gesetzblatt der Deutschen Demokratischen Republik*, part I, no. 33, June 22, 1990, pp. 300–303.

Municipal Property Law: Gesetz über das Vermögen der Gemeinden, Städte und Landkreise (Kommunalvermögensgesetz—KVG), July 6, 1990. *Gesetzblatt der Deutschen Demokratischen Republik*, Part I, no. 42, July 20, 1990, pp. 660–661.

Unification Treaty (second State Treaty): Vertrag zwischen der Bundesrepublik Deutschland und der Deutschen Demokratischen Republik über die Herstellung der Einheit Deutschlands (Einigungsvertrag), August 31, 1990. *Bulletin der Bundesregierung*, no. 104, September 6, 1990, pp. 877–1120.

Municipal Property Law (amended): Gesetz zur Änderung und Ergänzung des Gesetzes über das Vermögen der Gemeinden, Städte und Landkreise vom 6. Juli 1990 (Kommunalvermögensgesetz—KVG), September 13, 1990. *Gesetzblatt der Deutschen Demokratischen Republik*, part I, no. 61, September 19, 1990, p. 1537.

"2 + 4" Treaty Ratification: Gesetz zu dem Vertrag vom 12. September 1990 über die abschliessende Regelung in bezug auf Deutschland "2 + 4"-Vertrag. *Bundesgesetzblatt*, part II, no. 38, October 13, 1990, pp. 1317–1329.

Obstacle-Removal Law: Gesetz zur Beseitigung von Hemmnissen bei der Privatisierung von Unternehmen und zur Förderung von Investitionen, March 22, 1991. *Bundesgesetzblatt*, part I, no. 20, March 28, 1991, pp. 766–789.

Judgment of the Federal Constitutional Court: Urteil des Bundesverfassungsgerichtes, April 23, 1991, file 1EVR1170/90.

Property Law: Gesetz zur Regelung offener Vermögensfragen (Vermögensgesetz —VermG), April 18, 1991. *Bundesgesetzblatt*, part I, no. 26, April 26, 1991, pp. 957–970.

Investment Law: Gesetz über besondere Investitionen in dem in Artikel 3 des Einigungsvertrages genannten Gebiet (Investitionsgesetz—BInvG), April 22, 1991. *Bundesgesetzblatt*, part I, no. 26, April 26, 1991, pp. 995–998.

Index